EARLY JUDAISM
RELIGIOUS WORLDS OF THE FIRST JUDAIC MILLENNIUM

For Archbishop Chrysostomos of Etna
Buddy, Confidant, Fellow-Traveller

οἵτινές με Βούλοιντο δέχεοδαι εἰς τὴν ἑταιρείαν,
τούτους οὐκ ἂν Βουλοίμην ἐγώ

EARLY JUDAISM

RELIGIOUS WORLDS
OF THE FIRST JUDAIC MILLENNIUM

Martin S. Jaffee

Second Edition

UNIVERSITY PRESS OF MARYLAND
BETHESDA
2006

LIBRARY OF CONGRESS CATALOGING-IN-PUBLICATION DATA

Jaffee, Martin S.
  Early Judaism : religious worlds of the first Judaic millennium / Martin S. Jaffee.
— [2nd ed.]
        p. cm. — (Studies and texts in Jewish history and culture ; 13)
  Includes bibliographical references and index.
  ISBN 1-883053-93-5
    1. Judaism—History—Post-exilic period, 586 B.C.-210 A.D.   2. Judaism—
History—Talmudic period, 10-425.   3. Bible. O.T.—Canon.   4. Rabbinical
literature—History and criticism. 5. Judaism—Doctrines. I. Title. II. Series.
BM176.J34 2006
296.09'014—dc22   2006044706

ISBN 1883053-93-5
Cover design by Catherine Lo

STUDIES AND TEXTS
IN
JEWISH HISTORY AND CULTURE

The Joseph and Rebecca Meyerhoff Center
for Jewish Studies
University of Maryland

XIII

General Editor: Bernard D. Cooperman

UNIVERSITY PRESS OF MARYLAND

Studies and Texts in Jewish History and Culture
A Note from the Series Editor

One of our goals for the present publication series is to provide a mechanism for producing volumes informed by high scholarship but designed and priced to be useful in the college classroom. It is with great pleasure, therefore, that we offer this new edition of Professor Martin S. Jaffee's well-known text *Early Judaism*.

This revised edition will, we hope, soon be accompanied by an on-line site where readers and students will find further relevant information and study tools. A link will be found on the web-site of the Joseph and Rebecca Meyerhoff Center for Jewish Studies at the University of Maryland and its publication series (www.jewishstudies.umd.edu).

We invite scholars to suggest other titles for this series.

Bernard Dov Cooperman
cooperma@umd.edu

Contents

Preface to Second Edition

THIS SECOND EDITION of *Early Judaism* appears about eight years after the publication of the first edition in 1997. My original intention in offering this new edition was modest, to correct some obvious errors pointed out by reviewers, colleagues, and students, as well as to update the scholarly references to account for work published since 1997. In the event, rather more has been involved. As I reread my work, it became clear to me that recent shifts in scholarship on early Judaism had rendered some of my discussions of 1997 rather obsolete. In other cases, new issues had arisen that needed to be addressed. At one point, I entertained the possibility of simply writing a new book; but cooler heads prevailed. This second edition is definitely the same book as the edition of 1997, but parts have been extensively revised, others have been dropped, and new material has been added.

The most important change, in my judgment, is in point of view. When I wrote the first edition in the middle 1990s I had only begun to absorb some of the basic critical literature associated with the study of gender in early Judaism. I was aware of a need to include material about women in my book, but could manage to do so in only episodic and perhaps flat-footed ways. In the intervening decade, I have used the first edition of *Early Judaism* as the spine of my own evolving undergraduate course on Gender and Ancient Judaism. My students have been fairly blunt in pointing out the numerous shortcomings of the book as an introduction to the religion of ancient Jewish men and women. I doubt that this second edition will satisfy all of them; but I hope that it is more skillful than the first in integrating the perspectives of gender studies into the interpretive discourse of the study of Judaism.

I could not have undertaken the preparation of this edition without the support of a number of friends and colleagues. First, I owe sincere thanks to Prentice Hall, the original publisher, for restoring to me the rights to the book without any struggle or bitterness. Secondly, I am also deeply grateful to Prof. Bernard Cooperman, of the University of

Maryland, for an e-mail message in the summer of 2003 that led to this project being published under his auspices. Without the assurance that he would see this work to publication, I never would have begun it. Third, I owe a great debt to my friend, Ms. Loryn Paxton, who essentially volunteered without remuneration to track down and secure the rights to use illustrative material from the first edition as well as new plates and illustrations. Fourth, I acknowledge with gratitude the support of the Samuel and Althea Stroum Endowment for Jewish Studies at the University of Washington for a grant enabling this edition of the book to feature color plates and other features that will increase its attractiveness in the marketplace. Last but not least, I should express my thanks as well to my colleagues at many universities and colleges who have ordered the book for their courses year after year, despite its eventually prohibitive cost. I am honored that my book has anchored courses on Judaism taught at such excellent institutions as Harvard University, the University of Pennsylvania, Yale University, Stanford University, Reed College, and elsewhere. I am pleased that it will now be available at a reasonable cost.

In closing, I would like to dedicate this edition of *Early Judaism* to my dear friend, Archbishop Chrysostomos, of the St. Gregory of Palamas Monastery in Etna, California. It is unlikely that many books on the study of Judaism have been dedicated to Greek Orthodox archbishops of the Old Calendarist tradition. So permit me a word of explanation. Archbishop Chrysostomos and I met serendipitously just as I was preparing to work on this new edition. Although we have, at this writing, spent perhaps 15 minutes in each other's presence, we have whiled away endless hours in electronic conversation about the manifold ways in which our intellectual training and spiritual sensibilities have shaped our life choices. We have shared each other's writing and thinking with an intimacy that both of us often find most astonishing. With the sole exception of my own family, he has enriched my life during my work on this project more profoundly than anyone I know. I am fortunate to count him as a friend, and proud to acknowledge in this public way precisely how important he has become to me.

Martin S. Jaffee
Seattle, Wa.
6 Tammuz, 5765
July 13, 2005

Introduction

THIS BOOK, as its title announces, is about "early Judaism." You may know of other books that use terms like "ancient Judaism," "late Judaism," or even "middle Judaism" to describe forms of Judaism prior to the European Middle Ages. These terms reflect various controversies among nineteenth and twentieth-century scholars about exactly how to interpret the significance of Judaism in relationship to ancient Israelite religion, on the one hand, and early Christianity, on the other. We will not focus much attention upon it here.[1] For the purpose of this book, it is enough to say that our subject is the various forms of religious expression that thrived among Jewish communities on the Mediterranean coasts of Europe and North Africa, in the Land of Israel, and as far eastward as the Tigris-Euphrates valley from roughly 450 BCE through 650 CE.

Most historians recognize that the forms of Judaism that thrived during this period were rather distinct from the Israelite religion that preceded them by many centuries. They also acknowledge that the religious and cultural patterns of early Judaism differ in crucial ways from those that thrived among Jews within the medieval civilizations of Christianity and Islam. Needless to say, all forms of early Judaism are very remote in cultural style from modern European, North American, and Israeli versions of Judaism.

During this epoch of just over one thousand years, Jews of this region enjoyed a remarkably diverse cultural life. They pursued that life by drawing upon their own ancestral culture, as well as those of the surrounding Persian, Hellenistic-Roman, and Sasanian empires, which dominated them politically. In addition to a vast literature—the writings compiled into the Hebrew Bible are only the tip of the iceberg—they developed a wide range of political, cultural, and religious institutions. All these were in close communication with the surrounding environment, even though they often defined themselves in religious, cultural, or political opposition to that environment. Many of these institutions flourished for a time and

I

A Word about Dates

The religious worlds of Christianity have perceived the birth of Jesus as inaugurating a fundamental break in the history of the universe. Since the early Middle Ages, a conventional way of expressing this judgment about time has been to identify all years since the Messiah's birth as the "Year of Our Lord" (Latin: *Anno Domini* or AD). In modern times, the entire era of history prior to the birth of the Christian Savior has come to be designated the era "Before Christ" (BC).

This book avoids the Christian convention, replacing it with a compromise that has become widely accepted in religious studies and related fields. The initials BCE, standing for "Before the Common Era," designate any date usually labeled BC in the Christian reckoning. CE, "Common Era," designates any date usually labeled AD in Christian reckoning. "Common Era" refers to the historical epoch in which Judaism and Christianity have coexisted.

This cosmetic change does little to alter the ethnocentricity of the Christian schema. Rabbinic Judaism, for its part, has for over a millennium calculated the years on the basis of the supposed date for the creation of the world. It knows nothing of BCE or CE, not to mention BC and AD. By its calculation, for example, September 25, 1995 CE inaugurated the year 5756 since Creation.

Moreover, imagining all history to be shaped by the mutual relationship of Judaism and Christianity ignores the temporal sensibilities of Muslims, Buddhists, and Hindus, among others. For an enormous segment of humanity, the relationship of Jews and Christians is scarcely so significant as to shape the very contour of time!

Despite these flaws, however, we shall be content with the BCE/CE schema. The Christian reckoning of dates, along with the Gregorian calendar that undergirds it, has become second nature in all industrialized cultures and is readily recognizable. The BCE/CE system will, at the very least, remind us of the way that all temporal schemas represent an index of cultural values.

later disappeared. Others would shape the character of Judaism for the rest of its history. To grasp what Judaism became in the second millennium of its history (from 650 CE–1650 CE), or in our own portion of its third millennium, we must first come to terms with the material that engages our attention here.

Religious developments among the Jews of this time and place eventually made a profound impact beyond the confines of the history of Judaism. It was in the very middle of this millennium, from roughly 30–100 CE, that what would become Christianity emerged as a form of Jewish religion. By the end of it, Christianity had succeeded in encouraging enormous numbers of people in Europe, North Africa, and the Middle East to think of themselves as spiritual heirs of the patriarchs, matriarchs, and prophets depicted in the Jewish writings that formed the first part of the Christian Bible (the Old Testament). As we shall see, those writings were compiled and edited during the first half of the millennium we shall study. Thus, wherever in today's world the Old Testament is read as a divine address to the Church, there the cultural creation of early Judaism continues to inform contemporary Christian religion.

Islam as well, emerging in Arabia in the last half-century of our period, was shaped in important ways by religious traditions that Jews had brought with them into the Arabian peninsula. Within a few centuries, Islam would spread well beyond the Mesopotamian and North African areas of the old Christian Byzantine empire, reaching eastward, as well, into Zoroastrian Persia, India, and the Buddhist lands of China and southeast Asia. Wherever Islam took root, it brought its own sacred scripture, the Quran. A collection of inspired, highly poetic utterances of the visionary, Muhammad, the Quran draws in part upon Jewish traditions regarding key events in the lives of biblical heroes such as Noah (Arabic: Nuh), Abraham (Ibrahim), and Moses (Musa). Thus, wherever the Quran became part of Islamic historical imagination the religious traditions of early Judaism contributed to the remarkably rich cultures of the Islamic peoples.

Through Christianity and Islam, then, early Judaism's cultural heritage has informed the religious traditions of much of humanity. The present book defines a number of different routes into the historical interpretation of early Judaism. Its primary concern, as the subtitle itself announces, is to describe the religious worlds inhabited by diverse Jewish communities during Judaism's crucial first millennium. These worlds, we will see, often overlapped and recapitulated each other; but just as surely, they offered quite distinct conceptions of the cosmos and how to live within it. Indeed, no single religious world seems to have ever incorporated all Jews of this period into a uniform tradition of thought, a common set of social patterns, or a universally shared cultural idiom. At the same time, the various religious worlds of early Judaism shared enough traits so that the peoples among whom Jews lived commonly perceived the Jews as a distinct and relatively uniform group of foreigners. Our study, therefore, surveys the impressive variety of Jewish religious life in this period and attempts to discern patterns that might lend some coherence to that variety.

This is a complicated interpretive task, and in each chapter I try to guide the reader in examining the evidence of Judaic religious worlds and inter- preting the meaning of that evidence. But before we get down to the actual business of interpretation, there are some important preliminary matters to clarify. This book employs the term "religious world" in a very specific and, perhaps, unfamiliar sense.[2] Therefore, our first business is to clarify what that term means and why it is important for our work. Second, the term "Juda- ism" is used in this book in ways that might at first be unfamiliar to many readers. For example, the religious worlds of ancient Israel prior to the sixth century BCE are not regarded here as "Judaic worlds," while those of many early followers of Jesus of Nazareth will be so regarded. It is important, then, to spend some time at the outset clarifying this issue as well.

Religion and Religious Worlds

Nothing seems more self-evident to many of us than our notion of "reli- gion." Beginning students of intellectual history, therefore, are often surprised to learn that much of the intellectual tradition of modern Euro- pean and American culture in the humanities and the social sciences has debated the definition and social role of "religion" for several centuries.[3]

Take, for example, the apparently uncontroversial proposition that reli- gion—a collection of beliefs about divine beings expressed in moral behav- ior, prayers, and various forms of communal celebration—is a distinct realm of human activity that can be separated out from other realms, such as poli- tics, economics, or science. This notion that religion is about "beliefs" while other areas of life are grounded in "power," "value," or "knowledge" has, in fact, a history. It emerged in European culture between the sixteenth and nineteenth centuries, as philosophers, politicians, and theologians struggled valiantly to define a role for the Western and Central European Christian churches (Catholic and Protestant) in the emerging national states of Europe. By defining religion as a combination of beliefs and worship, Euro- pean thinkers achieved something important. They were able to distinguish political loyalties to a state or nation from religious loyalties to a particular historical Church. "Religious faith," as expressed through the institution of the Church, could be understood as a private, personal, essentially moral dimension of life. As such it serves, but should not interfere with, the economic, cultural, and political affairs of the State. Because Church and State address separate spheres of life, citizens of many different religious beliefs may co-exist as equals in a society that is officially neutral to a person's private religious faith.[4]

This conception of religion as a set of deeply held personal beliefs distinct from political identity, economic structure, or verifiable scientific fact is a great cultural achievement of the Christian peoples of Western and Central Europe. It enabled centuries of religious warfare to be resolved. It lies at the heart of what modern states rightly celebrate as "freedom of religion" from governmental interference and regulation. The democracies of North America are unimaginable without such conceptions of religion. But they are also a radical departure from earlier European understandings of the role of the Church in the political and social order. Moreover, this European common sense about religion has little to do with the many ways in which Eastern European, non-European, and non-Christian peoples have constructed their own conceptions of the role of holy communities and their institutions in the larger social and political order.[5]

It turns out that the basic common sense conceptions of religion current in modern Europe and North America have a certain provinciality. They stake out a definition of religion that more or less unconsciously establishes modern, Western forms of Christianity as the norm for all religious expressions and traditions. Is it possible to develop a conception of religion that is better than the one we have rejected? And what does "better" mean in this context? By way of answering these questions, let me hazard a definition of religion that shall guide us throughout our study of Judaism. I have crafted it with two considerations in mind. First, it should be narrow enough for use in understanding Judaism in all periods of its history. And second, it should be broad enough for use in understanding religion as a social force both within and beyond the unique context of the modern State and its secular institutions. The definition is:

> Religion is an intense and sustained cultivation of a style of life that heightens awareness of morally binding connections between the self, the human community, and the most essential structures of reality. Religions posit various orders of reality and help individuals and groups to negotiate their relations with those orders.

The most important thing to notice about this definition is that it does not focus on beliefs or rituals as the defining traits of religion. Nor does it imagine religion as a sphere of life radically cut off from the political, the economic, or the scientific. Rather, it specifies religion as a system of life paths and comprehensive patterns of behavior within which specific beliefs and rituals play greater or lesser roles in defining "the world" as a given cultural community grasps it at a particular point in time. Religious patterns of behavior encourage human beings to interpret themselves as moral beings whose destiny is bound up with others in a project that brings them into relationship with the fundamental reality of things. From this perspective, religious beliefs are not obligatory formulae that people blindly accept; rather, they are part of the very way humans experience themselves, subtle perceptions about their place in the overall structure of social and cosmic reality. Formal articles of belief may try to organize and clarify such perceptions, but the perceptions usually precede the creeds, even as the creeds then influence in turn the way people tend to interpret their own experience.

Where do these perceptions come from? We note that our definition of religion asserts that "religion is an intense and sustained cultivation of a style of life." The point here is that our search for religion should, at least provisionally, direct our attention toward ways of life that are pursued in a disciplined manner and with a certain degree of emotional investment. How we measure such things is, of course, impossible to say at the outset. But we should want to admit that even though religion can be (and at times is designed to be) a matter of rote and habit, it is usually not normatively so. It is something that, at least in theory, should structure much of one's activity and engage one's emotional and intellectual capacities on a regular and involving basis. Perhaps some things called religion make fewer demands on all aspects of life, while others might make more such demands; or they focus intensity on different areas. This would not make one religion less "religious" than another, but would simply tell us that traditions are variable in the way they stake out certain areas of life as central. Those differences are what make the study of religion so thoroughly fascinating.[6]

Back to our definition. It continues by positing that the way of life mapped out by religion "heightens awareness of morally binding connections between the self, the human community, and the most essential structures of reality." This is the core of the matter. Religions commonly offer human communities a grand sense of the "big picture" in terms of which the common details and concerns of life become meaningful. In religious systems, as in cultural systems in general, the "self" identified through personal, autobiographical memory—"me"—is enlarged or enriched by acquiring as part of one's own identity the collective experience of a community. Personal identity in a religious setting, in other words, includes far more than the web of relations containing the individual, the family, friends, or immediate social group of one's personal acquaintance. It normally includes a conception of how all these relationships are connected to generations of the distant past and the far-off future, as well to the forces and powers that are held to account for the world as it is.

In religions the question of personal and social identity is routinely—one could say almost obsessively—linked to the question of the origins and destiny of things as well as to the subsisting powers that maintain all things as they are. Religions charge the processes of the natural order—weather patterns, celestial movements, seasonal changes—with moral as well as economic or intellectual significance. Convictions about the nature and quality of life, as well as the meaning or non-meaning of death, are framed within the most comprehensive understandings of universal order and the limits of time. And these, in turn, structure one's concrete actions in the here and now, in relation to the natural order and one's human associates.

Just here is an important limiting case that distinguishes religion from other patterns of culture. Where not only the social order, but the cosmos as a whole, is framed as a moral field in which one's life-discipline is pursued—there we are beginning to distinguish religion from analogous cultural forms such as political, legal, or philosophical systems. However, the converse is also important. Where political, legal, or philosophical systems begin to draw intimate links between the visible and invisible order of the universe and the moral order of self and society, they are beginning to look very much like religion.

This last point brings us to the final element of our definition, the one that clarifies the basic distinction between religion and other analogous things. This is its commitment to the proposition that human life takes place amidst "various orders of reality" with which humans must actively negotiate proper relationships. Like most modern political movements, philosophical systems, scientific cosmologies, ethical systems and the like, religions implicate human beings in relationships with normally unseen forces. Is the will of God less visible than a gravitational field? Unlike modern intellectual systems, however, these unseen forces are usually personal forces that are regarded as in some sense more powerful or, at least, closer to the core of reality than humans. That is, religions have gods. Gods usually have homes in other worlds and, occasionally, have relations with humans in this one.

Some religions—certain types of Buddhism, for example—deny ultimacy to gods, promising rather a liberation from a false knowledge that ordinarily might lead one to fear gods. One way or the other, therefore, religions take gods seriously as powers to be related to, reckoned with, or overcome. They also take seriously the conception of other domains of being, or worlds, that are either parallel to or intersecting with the human and cosmic orders. The substance of religious life—ritual activities, moral self-scrutiny, acts of communal solidarity, prayer, and so forth—are the complex ways in which religions enable human beings to communicate with and establish proper relations with those powers that are at the center of the cosmic process. One way of grasping the notion of "religious world" is to imagine it as a kind of collectively imagined map in which these various powers are located in space and time. Each member of a religious community carries that map around in his or her conceptual baggage and navigates the world by routine consultations.

This desire to participate in the essential structures of the world lies behind the pervasive role of ritual in religious traditions. All religions have many different kinds of rituals. Some of these—associated, perhaps, with hygiene or hospitality—are performed routinely without even thinking about what they might mean. Unconscious mastery of such rituals is part of the cultural process of becoming a member of a specific religious tradition. Other rituals, however, are explicitly mastered as a kind of technology by which humans can at times enter fully or partially into the diverse worlds posited by tradition. Those associated with worship, for example, are often ways of communicating with the gods in their world while remaining in one's own. By contrast, rituals associated with entering holy places are often ways of transporting oneself into the world of the gods and dwelling there for a time. Yet others—the ritualized meditative practices of Buddhism, for example—lead the mind beyond the perception of all worlds and their gods to a place of undivided consciousness in which the truth of things is immediately apparent. The means of transport and the conceptualizations of alternate worlds will, of course, differ from religion to religion. But constant is the tendency of religion to puncture the apparent solidity of mundane experience and to privilege intimations of other worlds at more profound levels of being.[7]

This final observation brings our definitional discussion of religion to a close. If religion is a way of sustaining the coherence of various orders of reality, religious worlds are the maps that define these orders and display their patterns of coherence. Religious worlds offer comprehensive models of reality in which specific forms of life-discipline, moral imagination, and ritual practice make eminent good sense because, to those guided by them, they so obviously correspond to the way things simply *are*. This theory of religious worlds will guide our study of early Judaism. We will not spend much time cataloging the official "beliefs," "rituals," and "practices" of some hypothetical abstraction called "Judaism." We will focus on the ways in which Jewish communities living under Persian, Hellenistic-Roman, and Sasanian empires employed the cultural resources at their disposal to construct various intensely lived religious worlds. We will track how the different sorts of communal awareness cultivated by Jews in our period correlated with conceptions of the larger cosmic processes and forces that governed all reality. In sum, we will try to discern how the many religious worlds of early Judaism routinely transformed human beings into Jews; to appreciate what kinds of human beings Jews became by living in such worlds.

Identifying Judaism

If you were surprised at the difficulty of a simple effort to define religion, the definition of Judaism, at least one useful for studying and comparing religious worlds, may come as a shock. In the next few pages I present some complex considerations. However, by working through them, you will be in a better position to bring a nuanced frame of reference to the historical and comparative study of the Judaic religious heritage.

The Word "Judaism"

The oldest direct ancestor of the word "Judaism" first appears in the writings of Greek-speaking Jews sometime during the last few centuries before the appearance of Christianity. The word is *ioudaismos*. It identified the customs and folkways of a widely known, but exotic, community. The bulk of this community lived in its ancient homeland, the Seleucid (Syrian) province of Yehudah (*ioudaia*; Latin: *judea*). Many others lived outside the native territory, especially in Egyptian North Africa and the Fertile Crescent. Yehudah is the Hebrew name for what was then—as today—a territory in the hill country just inland of the eastern Mediterranean coast. These "Yehudah-ites" (pl.: *yehudim*), who identified themselves as the descendants of the Israelite nation that once ruled a large empire in the region, thus came to be called *ioudaioi* ("Judeans"; male singular: *ioudaios,* female singular: *ioudaia*). These geographically linked terms are the ancestors of the words "Jew" and "Judaism" by which those claiming ancestry from these Judeans continue to be known.[8]

While the term *ioudaismos* first appears in Jewish writings (2 Maccabees 2:21, 8:1, 14:38), we do not know whether Judeans of Israelite heritage invented the term or whether it was coined by their neighbors. The point is that these *ioudaioi*—both those living in the Land of Israel and those who found themselves in territorial dispersion (*diaspora*, in Greek)—viewed themselves and were viewed by others as constituting a homogeneous ethnic group bound by a noticeable body of ethnic customs. These included distinctive patterns of piety (*eusebeia*). Every people of the ancient Greek-speaking world had its *eusebeia,* its ancestral tradition of serving the gods of specific states, cities, or territories. The Jews had theirs as well. It was well known that they pledged sole loyalty to a single God of Israel. He was believed to be invisible, capable of being called upon anywhere, and intimately aware of his people's behavior. But his priesthood offered him sacrifice in only a single place—his "House of Holiness," the Temple in the sacred city of Jerusalem. This piety of the Jews toward their unique god was part of the larger body of custom that constituted their distinctive *ioudaismos.* But it did not exhaust it by any means. No more, at least, than celebrating the Mass of the Church of England exhausts what it means to be British or praying in a mosque defines the entire cultural identity of an Egyptian.

The term "Judaism," then, started as a reference to what we might call the cultural traditions of the Judeans and those descended from them. This is, broadly speaking, how we will employ it as well. We will be exploring the particularly religious dimensions of that culture during a specified period of its history. But as soon as we announce such a program of study a difficult question arises. Granting that the term "Judaism" has a certain history, is it plausible that the religious and cultural tradition defined by the term only comes into being with the term itself? If the existence of sub atomic particles surely precedes their conceptualization among modern physicists, is it not likely that Judaism existed before Greek-speaking Jews began to ponder the meaning of *ioudaismos*? Probably. But what might that Judaism have looked like? Where and when did it get its start?

The Things Called "Judaism"

Of one thing we may be sure: Judaism is not as old as its "founders," Abraham and Moses. Neither Abraham, the Mesopotamian migrant who left home at the command of God, nor Moses, who brought the people Israel to Mt. Sinai to embrace a covenantal contract with the God of Abraham, can be considered the historical founder of Judaism. The simple reason is that, as we know Abraham and Moses now, they are merely characters in a much larger epic of ancient Israel's history. If the Bible's stories about Abraham and Moses describe historical individuals, these individuals would have lived somewhere between the seventeenth and the thirteenth centuries before the emergence of Christianity, i.e., between 1600–1200 BCE. But the biblical stories that describe these individuals and the revelations they experienced do not seem to have been recorded in written form much before 1000–600 BCE. In any case, they are found in a book, the Torah of Moses (the Pentateuch: Greek for "Five Books"), which probably reached its present shape sometime closer to the fifth century BCE.

Those who produced this epic—those who created images of Abraham and Moses that would inspire centuries of emulation among the Jews—are the true founders of Judaism. We must search for them among those who may have had a hand in the literary shaping of the Torah itself. Judaism did not begin when Abraham or Moses lived, although virtually all forms of Judaism claim to embody the tradition of these and other biblical heroes. Rather, it began when a much later generation of Judeans began to probe the meaning of the lives of these servants of God.

Thus we ask: when and where did the Torah in its authoritative form first become the charter of an organized community? Who were the first people to see themselves as bound to the covenantal promises and duties described in the Mosaic writings? Most of the evidence available to historians—literary writings, archaeological remains, and other circumstantial bits of information drawn from surrounding civilizations—suggests that the "where" of Judaism's origins is the settlement of a small Israelite community living in Jerusalem under Persian protection. Around 450 BCE, this community seems to have embraced the Torah as its official history book and legal charter. Judaism begins, that is, when the Torah becomes the official constitution of the Judeans under Persian protection.

The next chapter will present a more detailed case for this view. For now, it is important to point out that, the present book, unlike many other texts for the study of Judaism, does not contain a lengthy section on "the Biblical Period" of Judaism—the period from roughly 1800–450 BCE in which most of the biblical stories are set. The idea of a "Biblical Period" is itself a remnant of a time when historians were quite confident that the Hebrew Bible accurately reflected the religious world of the patriarchs, matriarchs, priests, and prophets whose names dot the biblical narratives. It was once assumed that most of the Hebrew Bible was written down from roughly 1000–587 BCE, during which literary traditions from various sectors of ancient Israelite society were shaped in Jerusalem, either by priestly scribes associated with the Temple or other writers associated either with the court of the royal Davidic dynasty or various non-royalist groups.

Historians supposed that much of the biblical literature was based upon eyewitness sources transmitted accurately by tradition, or shaped by later writers who, much like modern historians, were interested in sifting through various types of historical evidence. In recent decades, however—

largely due to an increased appreciation of how religious descriptions of the past are composed and transmitted—this confidence has been shaken. The relation of the religion of ancient Israelites to those who composed the Hebrew Bible, as well as to all forms of Judaism, must be more cautiously described.[9]

This is not to deny, however, that what used to be termed "the Biblical Period" is the seed-bed of traditions that everywhere inform Judaism. We shall note in the following chapter, for example, that earlier forms of the stories and laws now found in the Torah of Moses circulated among some ancient Israelite priests and scribes well before the destruction of Israelite society in Yehudah in 587 BCE. Just as surely, Israelite patterns of sacrificial worship in Jerusalem's Temple, or theological themes articulated by Israelite sages, priests, or religious visionaries exercised a powerful influence long after the destruction of the Israelite society and culture that nourished such religious forms. But, the Israelite sources of Judaism must be distinguished from the later religious world in which those sources are venerated, interpreted, and transformed.

The religious worlds of the ancient Israelites surely had certain traits that survived in later forms of Judaism in the same way that certain physical traits are shared by many generations within a given family. Some traits may be submerged for a generation or two and reappear in unusual new configurations. So, too, with Judaism. As a descendant of ancient Israelite religion, it bore within itself numerous elements continuous with ancient Israelite tradition. But it also brought these into relationship with new experiences and fresh cultural acquisitions. The result was a continuously transforming tradition claiming the family name of "Judaism" for the new members born of historical circumstances.

Much of our work in this book involves tracing just such transformations. A basic question of comparative method thus arises: in our comparative efforts, how shall we decide when the objects of comparison are "Judaism" or not? Is it not possible that while some communities may have originated in Judaism, they have so altered their character as to now stand beyond its communal boundaries? Certainly Jews in ancient times charged others with forsaking true Judaism (that is, "the true ways of God"). Perhaps they were right. If so, we should be careful about just what sorts of communities we will look toward for information about Judaism.

I propose that we rely again on our definition of religion. Let me recast that definition now by weaving into it the particulars of Judaism. Broadly speaking:

Judaic worlds may be sought where communities construct disciplined ways of life that serve to heighten awareness of the personal, communal, and, indeed, cosmic implications of constituting the direct physical descendants of God's people, Israel.

The stress on physical descent is crucial. It is possible, as in Christianity or Islam, to recognize a spiritual kinship with ancient Israel as worshippers of the same god or heirs to a continuous series of revelations. But part of what makes a religion Judaism is this stress on physical, ethnic continuity. This is not to say that Judaism is comprised solely of direct physical descendants of ancient Israelites. No existing community of Jews can verify such a claim. Rather, Judaism is comprised in part by people who insist on making it. [10]

This brings us to another fundamental marker of Judaic worlds, particularly in ancient and medieval times. They all ground their claim to constitute the descendants of the people Israel on their possession of and loyalty to an authentic version of the Torah of Moses. All assume that this Torah is a direct disclosure or revelation of God's love and will for Israel, and that the path to establish a proper relationship to the God of Israel is somehow to be discovered within the Torah or in correctly guided interpretations of it. When, therefore, we encounter in Persian, Hellenistic-Roman, and Sasanian cultures a community claiming ethnic and spiritual continuity with ancient Israel on the basis of some interpretation of the Torah, we shall have the right to say we are talking about Judaism. Where the physical claim is denied or the primacy of the Torah is radically displaced in favor of some other covenantal inheritance, we shall have to look more carefully to see if we have a Judaism or not. There is, we shall see, a good deal of gray in the history of early Judaic worlds. This book sorts out the various shades.

The Plan of This Book

The theoretical questions we have just entertained will remain utterly meaningless unless they are embodied in the actual study of Judaism. The structure of this book is designed to highlight their significance. As you incrementally master more and more information about the various Judaic worlds in their historical settings, you should grow increasingly confident in your grasp of the general character of early Judaism as a distinctive formation of religious meaning.

Our discussion will unfold through a series of six chapters. The first chapter, by way of orientation, will sketch the geographical, social, and political settings of the various Judaic worlds of our period. Here we explain as well why the date 450 BCE looms so large in our estimate of the origins of Judaism and why 650 CE serves as a convenient conclusion. This chapter will also serve as a source of historical and cultural reference points to help contextualize the many details that will require sorting and interpretation in the chapters to follow.

The second chapter, "Dynamics of Texts and Traditions," traces the origins of the literary traditions, written and oral, that emerged out of and reflected the Judaic worlds we shall discuss. The Hebrew Bible and other literature intimately in conversation with it serves as important evidence for the ways in which Jews imagined the world they inhabited. As we have already pointed out, a key marker of Judaism is a claim to communal identity grounded in at least some of these writings. This chapter, therefore, exposes the remarkably diverse manner of Judaism's engagement with its sacred writings and the traditions of interpretation that continually enlivened and renewed them.

The chapter "Symbolic Vocabularies and Cosmic Structures" concerns what people usually call "theology" or, if they are skeptics, "ideology." Jewish scriptures and traditions, while diverse in style and content, were also remarkably consistent in their inventory of symbolic language and core conceptions. Indeed, throughout our period, certain symbols—God, Torah, Israel, and Messiah among others—underwent continuous redefinition and restatement, as Jews applied their treasury of traditions to the ongoing political and cultural realities that surrounded them. So we will study the interaction between Judaic religious symbols and the way Jews imagined their natural situation in time and space—the cosmos. We will give our attention to ways of thinking that were rather influential, as well as those that did not quite work out.

Religious writings carry authority, and symbolic vocabularies are communicated and reinterpreted only to the degree that historical communities engage them in their ongoing projects of socialization. Therefore, our fourth chapter on the "Social Foundations of Early Judaic Worlds" confronts an important fact about both religion and Judaism: radically different societies can be constructed out of the same scriptural heritage and dominant symbolic structures. Indeed, we shall see that the creation of distinct societies with explicit boundaries was a nearly universal Jewish preoccupation in the millennium before us. In the first place, Jews and non-Jews engaged in a centuries-long, often divisive, conversation about the relation of the Jewish nation to non-Jewish communities. We will see how Jews, confronted with images of themselves constructed by hostile or ignorant non-Jews, sought to modify or reshape those images in polemical settings. Second, we will point out that, despite the sense that the Jews were a distinct community over against various foreigners, Jews commonly found important issues that divided them from one another in profound ways. We will point out that a widespread practice of "religious conversion" in the latter centuries of our period was often connected to inner-Judaic religious polemics regarding "real" Jews and "false" Jews, and even the distinctions between Jewish men and women.

Students of religion have long recognized the key role of ritual actions and other sorts of ceremonies in maintaining social order, transmitting communal identity, and drawing powerful experiential connections between ideas of the world and actual behavior in the world. In chapters five and six, finally, we will confront this dimension of early Judaism. First, in a chapter on "Public Ritual Space and Ceremonial Performance," we explore some ways in which early Judaism created specific arenas for ritual activities that expressed and reconfirmed the Jews' sense of being a unique community, distinct from all others. Specifically, we will focus on the Temple, the synagogue, and the home as unique, but intersecting, ritual spaces for the celebration of Jewish national identity in the framework of the entire cosmos created by the God of Israel.

The concluding chapter on "Rituals of Initiation into Transformative Knowledge" moves from public rituals of national identity to the more exclusive and perhaps esoteric rituals practiced among Jews preoccupied with the cultivation of specialized, redemptive wisdom. Many such Jews, including some teachers within the emerging rabbinic communities, viewed their world as open to dramatic incursions of other-worldly angelic beings or divine creative forces. They sought in many cases to gain productive access to these beings and forces in order to penetrate worlds beyond the everyday. We examine what the Jews brought back with them from their communication with the most powerful and overwhelming presences that structured their conceptions of reality; how they shared their knowledge; and what they hoped to become by knowing what they knew.

Each chapter is equipped with fairly extensive endnotes, which fulfill three functions. The first is to depict for you, as economically as possible, the scholarly studies that have shaped my own presentation of the material. The second is to offer suggestions for helpful resources for the next stage of study. You will want and need to read other books to fill in the sketchy picture offered here. The third objective of the notes is to make you aware of controversies among contemporary scholars, particularly when I am taking one side of an interpretive issue upon which there continues to be some serious disagreement. I do have my points of view on certain matters, but I think you should know that there are others worth exploring as well. These will appear, occasionally, in the endnotes.

In sum, this book employs the interpretive methods of the modern university to firmly root one picture of early Judaism in the cultural structures of its own time and place. We will encounter in our chapters the arcane concerns of ancient peoples. Our connection to them will be grounded solely in our common humanity. Like those who lived in early Judaic worlds, we, too, must live in a world. By exploring the manner in which early Judaism constructed its own worlds, it is possible to have clearer insight into the constructed character of our own worlds. By reflecting upon the ways Jews found—or failed to find—nourishing connections to the foundations of the universe, we become ever more aware of the nature of our own gropings toward those connections.

But no world constructed by contemporary people can be equivalent to any of the worlds of early Judaism. And no contemporary scholarly portrait of the worlds of early Judaism can be identical to the thing itself. Only with difficulty can any aspect of early Judaism be selectively appropriated by the modern faithful as a foundation of their own attempts to dwell in a religious world.

This book, therefore, unlike more than a few others, makes no claim to interpret the religious truth of Judaism as contemporary ears might wish to hear it. Its sole modest goal is to ensure that the study of Judaism in the context of the contemporary university continues to find its home in the welcoming setting of programs and departments devoted to the critical study of humanity's religious traditions from a comparative and historical perspective. This is, in other words, an "academic" book for those learning how to think with the critical and interpretive tools of the comparative study of religions.

Notes

1. The first edition of this book contains an analysis of the various synonyms for "Early Judaism," on pp. 15–20. You can refer to this discussion on the website that accompanies the second edition.

2. The concept of religious world is spelled out in the work of William E. Paden, *Religious Worlds: The Comparative Study of Religion,* with a new preface (Boston: Beacon Press, 1994), pp. 51–65.

3. An excellent place to trace the development of modern European ideas of religion is J. Samuel Preus, *Explaining Religion: Criticism and Theory from Bodin to Freud* (New Haven and London: Yale University Press, 1987). This should now be supplemented with Bruce Lincoln, *Theorizing Myth: Narrative, Ideology, and Scholarship* (Chicago and London: University of Chicago Press, 1999), and Jonathan Z. Smith, "Religion, Religions, Religious," in Mark C.

Taylor, *Critical Terms in Religious Studies* (Chicago and London: University of Chicago Press, 1998).

4. The background of the definition of religion offered below can be traced in the essays of Clifford Geertz, "Religion as a Cultural System," in C. Geertz, *The Interpretation of Cultures* (New York: Basic Books, 1973), pp. 87–125; Talal Asad, "The Construction of Religion as an Anthropological Category," in T. Asad, *Genealogies of Religion: Discipline and Reasons of Power in Christianity and Islam* (Baltimore: Johns Hopkins University Press, 1993), pp. 27–50.

5. The inability of modern Western models of religion to anticipate or explain the recent resurgence of radically politicized forms of Islam, Judaism, Christianity, Hinduism, and Buddhism has become an important sub-theme of the contemporary study of religion. See, for example, Carl Juergensmeyer, *Terror in the Mind of God: The Global Rise of Religious Violence*. 3rd edition, completely revised (Berkeley, et al.: University of California Press, 2003), and Bruce Lincoln, *Holy Terrors: Thinking about Religion after September 11* (Chicago and London: University of Chicago Press, 2003).

6. A most useful attempt to compare different styles of religious activity both within and across the boundaries of discrete religious communities is that of Dale Cannon, *Six Ways of Being Religious: A Framework for Comparative Studies of Religion* (Belmont, et al.: Wadsworth Publishing, 1996).

7. D. Cannon, *Six Ways of Being Religious,* offers compelling reflections on the forms of religious experience accessible to empirical, comparative methods of interpretation.

8. The complex issue of how and when terms designating "Judeans" shifted from a purely geographical usage to denote a religious-cultural identity has been dealt with recently by Shaye J.D. Cohen, *The Beginnings of Jewishness: Boundaries, Varieties, Uncertainties* (Berkeley, Los Angeles, London: University of California, 1999), pp. 69–139. See also James D.G. Dunn, "Judaism in the Land of Israel in the First Century," in Jacob Neusner, ed., *Judaism in Late Antiquity. Part Two: Historical Syntheses* (Leiden: E.J. Brill, 1995), pp. 232–236; and Morton Smith, "The Gentiles in Judaism 125 BCE–CE 66," in William Horbury, W.D. Davies, John Sturdy, eds., *The Cambridge History of Judaism: Volume Three. The Early Roman Period* (Cambridge: Cambridge University Press, 1999), pp. 192–249.

9. Among academic historians of Judaism, Jacob Neusner is one of the few to write introductory texts that draw a sharp distinction between Judaism and ancient Israelite religion. His *The Way of Torah: An Introduction to Judaism,* 6th ed., (Belmont, et al.: Wadsworth Publishing, 1997), pp. 26–35, is an example. Most contemporary historians recognize the distinction; the debate is how sharply to draw it.

Most, like Shaye J.D. Cohen, *From the Maccabees to the Mishnah* (Philadelphia: Westminster Press, 1987), pp. 13–26, discern continuities of ideas and institutions that suggest a rather close relationship between what is often called "Israelite Religion" and later "Judaism." A few, such as Philip R.

Davies, *In Search of "Ancient Israel"* (Sheffield: JSOT Press, 1992), question whether there was ever in historical fact an ancient Israel or an ancient Israelite religion. Most students of the matter take a position somewhere between these. For an excellent account of the debate, see Marc Brettler, "The Copenhagen School: The Historiographical Issues," in *AJS Review* 27 (2003), pp. 1–22.

10. Some readers of the first edition of this book understood me to be arguing that Judaism is necessarily an "ethnic" identity defined by biological continuity with ancient Israel. See in particular, Gabriele Boccaccini, *Roots of Rabbinic Judaism: An Intellectual-History, From Ezekiel to Daniel* (Grand Rapids, Mich. and Cambridge, UK: William B. Eerdman's Publishing, 2002), pp. 12–13. Let me stress that this is not my view. There is no Jewish "ethnicity" grounded in empirical biological traits. But "Judaism," I claim, is constituted by people who for the most part claim an ethnic continuity with ancient Israel. This claim is part of their religious world. On this basis, Judaism can be distinguished from other religions, such as most forms of surviving Christianity, that claim to inherit the faith of Israel without physical descent.

CHAPTER I

Political and Cultural Settings of Early Judaism

FEW HUMAN INSTITUTIONS of any complexity, least of all religions, really begin at a specific moment. Accounts of the pristine origins of a unique community responding as one to the direct utterance of a god or the inspired preachings of a charismatic prophet belong to the realm of religious story. They express a community's sense of participating in a radical new beginning or a transformative moment of revelation. What is recalled by the faithful as a sudden reorientation toward reality usually appears to the historian of religion as the result of much prior historical preparation. Like most cultural traditions, religions normally emerge from a peculiar mixture of plan and accident, conditions imposed by the cultural-historical environment and by creative (and often unorchestrated) human responses.

As historians of religion, therefore, we cannot be satisfied with Judaism's claim to have originated in revelations to Abraham or Moses. It would be no less misleading, however, to state without qualification that Judaism began on some particular day in 450 BCE (or 449 or 451) in the territory of Yehudah. To the contrary, the origins of the religious worlds we call Judaism are diffuse. The date we have chosen is a conventional reference marker rather than an absolute point separating the past of "Israelite religion" from the future of "Judaism."

Think about the matter of Judaic origins with the help of a metaphor drawn from the textile craft. Early Judaism can be imagined as a cloth woven by many hands over a period of centuries within a broad geographical and cultural landscape. Some of the oldest fibers that dominate the patterns of the earliest identifiable Judaic cloth were surely contributed to the weave by the vanished Israelite civilization that had once thrived in the Land of Israel. But the design into which these fibers were woven comes from other hands. Basic motifs were contributed in Persian Yehudah. Yet others seem to have entered the weave through the labors of Israelites outside the ancestral territory, particularly in Mesopotamia. To the dominant patterns, set on the loom by the mid-fifth century, were added later elements of coloring and different sorts of yarn, randomly contributed by a variety of hands, in and beyond the Land of Israel, for a millennium thereafter.

The result, of course, is a rather unruly and rough weave reflecting generations of artisans employing a wide variety of styles, without a single overseer to coordinate all the weaving. To complicate matters, if this cloth was ever sewn into a completed garment, it is surely lost to us by now. What has survived, rather, are unmatched swatches of the fabric itself, their colors faded by time and their edges torn and frayed. Subsequent chapters of our book will explore some of the patterns and colors of this poorly preserved fabric in great detail. For the present it will help to identify the main artisans.

Which communities of ancient Israelites seem to have been key participants in the cultural labor that produced the fabric of the earliest Judaic worlds? Where and when did they live? Is it possible to identify the circumstances under which they worked or their specific contributions to the common (if largely uncoordinated) labor they shared with others across large stretches of time, space, and culture?

The Israelite Inheritance of Early Judaism

The geographical and cultural context of Judaic origins extends from the coastal cities of the Nile River delta in North Africa to the rich Mesopotamian urban and agricultural heartland between the Tigris and the Euphrates rivers near the Persian Gulf.

Flanked by an ancient Egyptian civilization on the west and those of Assyria and Babylonia on the east, the center stage is occupied by a land whose most ancient historical populations knew as Canaan. On this land, often the object of political designs and military invasions by the successive empires surrounding it, there arose from 1150–587 BCE the Hebrew-speaking civilization of which all forms of Judaism claim to be the successor.[1] It is this civilization that first called the land Israel (Hebrew: *'eretz yisrael*), after the name of one of its historical ancestors, known also as Jacob.

The heartland of the Land of Israel is the territory on either side of a spine of hills running north and south through the land between the Mediterranean coast on the west and the Jordan River on the east. On this territory, the ancient Hebrews—whom the Hebrew Bible calls "Israelites" (Hebrew: *bnei yisrael*)—pursued some 400 years of fractious political life. Early on, an Israelite empire established by a king named David (ruled ca. 1000–961 BCE) became a major Middle Eastern political player. According to the account in the book of Samuel, David extended his dominion to parts of what is now southern Lebanon, southwestern Syria, and western Jordan, threatening powerful neighbors on either side of his borders. But the experience of Israel

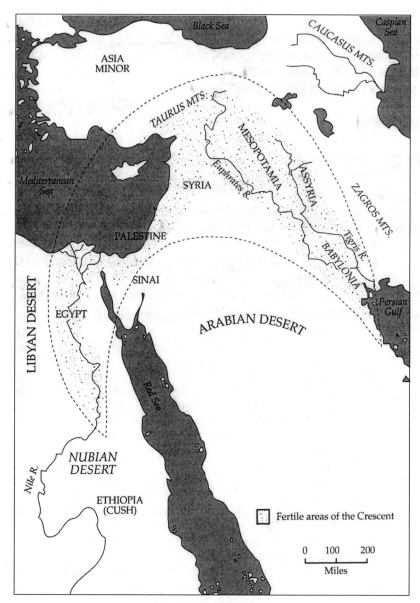

The Ancient Near East

The dotted area is usually called "The Fertile Crescent." The fertile lands watered by the Nile in Egypt and the Tigris and Euphrates in Mesopotamia enabled the development of the great civilizations that preceded by more than two millennia the earliest emergence of Israelite civilization in the Land of Israel.

as an international super-power was short-lived. The later history of the empire under David's dynastic heirs included a divisive civil war and the creation, by 922, of two bitterly contending kingdoms, frequently boxed in by superior surrounding empires.

The southern kingdom, called Yehudah (after one of the sons of Jacob), remained under the control of a Davidic dynasty; the northern kingdom, called Yisrael (Israel), suffered a series of dynastic struggles throughout its history. Both kingdoms were eventually conquered by foreign invaders. The northern kingdom of Yisrael fell to Assyrian armies in 722 BCE. Many refugees streamed southward into Yehudah and became absorbed into the closely related cultural life of the Davidic kingdom. Others, deported to various areas of the Assyrian lands, disappeared from the stream of Israelite civilization. The southern kingdom of Yehudah, for its part, wobbled on as a rather weak state for over a century after the destruction of its northern neighbor. It collapsed after a series of invasions from an expanding Babylonian Empire between 597–587 BCE. With the banishment of the last king of Yehudah, Zedekiah, to Babylonian imprisonment, the history of ancient Israelite civilization as a political and social entity confined to a single territory comes to an end.

Judaism did not exist at the time of the destruction of the Davidic state in 587 BCE. Yet nearly every aspect of Judaism resonates in some fashion with the civilization created during the life of that state. Here we can briefly point to some themes that will play an important role in future chapters.

Like many civilizations of the ancient Middle East, that of Yehudah was permeated by a sense that its land was the central point at which the heavenly world, with its divine beings, came into contact with the world of human activity. In most Middle Eastern cultures, the precise point of intersection could be located. It was on the altar of the city's principal shrine. There priests offered regular gifts of slaughtered animals and other agricultural goods to the divinities of heaven, particularly, the divine protector of the state. In Yehudah the most important shrine was the temple in the capital city of Jerusalem. Built by David's son and heir, Solomon, it was believed to shelter the Glory (Hebrew: *kavod*) of God, that element of the divine reality that could be manifested in the human world. In the temple, the Glory was served in a daily routine of sacrificial rites offered by priests descended from Aaron, the brother of Moses, who was celebrated as the founder of the Israelite priesthood. When Judaism would finally emerge among the fifth-century BCE community of Yehudah, memories of that temple and all it represented would play an important role. Indeed, the second temple was built upon the spot occupied by the first. And priests descended from the

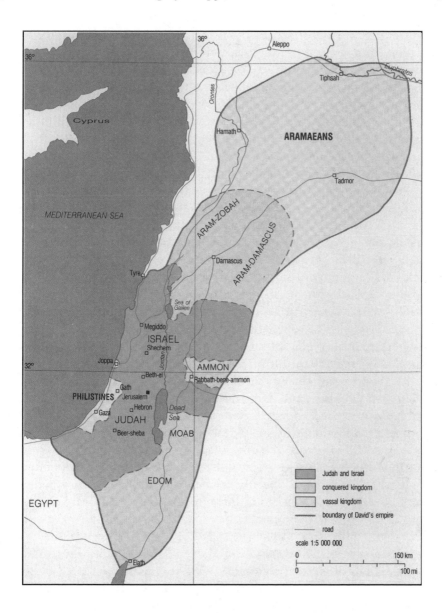

United Israelite Kingdom under David and Solomon

According to the account in the biblical book of Kings, the kingdom bequeathed by David to his son Solomon, which is described as lasting a mere forty years. But memories of its glory nourished the theological imagination of ancient Israelite prophets and, in later centuries, the messianic visions of Judaism.

various families claiming lineage from Aaron were restored to its service. At their head stood a priestly family claiming descent from Zadok, who was recalled as the chief priest under Solomon's administration.

The Solomonic temple, in addition to its function as the intersection of heaven and earth, was also a center of what might be called the national memory. Its priestly scribes kept economic records, cultivated empirical knowledge about the movements of heavenly bodies, and chronicled events in human history and national life. They also preserved a variety of ritual and legal traditions relevant to their own priestly roles as well as to the conduct of society at large. As preservers of memory, however, the Aaronide priests of Jerusalem enjoyed no monopoly. Priests out of favor with the monarchy, stemming from other priestly lineages, had been exiled, at times, to less central shrines or had been deprived entirely of cultic responsibilities. They, too, preserved their own accounts of the past. Needless to say, these did not coincide in all aspects with those of the royally empowered Aaronide priests.

The royal dynasty also preserved historical records and narratives. Quite naturally, these often identified the royal palace, rather than the official priesthood, as the key factors in the dynasty's success. While royal house and priesthood enjoyed a convergence of interests, they could nevertheless compete for primacy in the life of the state. Like the temple, moreover, the palace was also an important intellectual center. As in other Middle Eastern kingdoms, scribes, sages and poets served as appointees at the royal court, where they cultivated and preserved their own traditions of theology, cosmology, and worldly wisdom. Thus, both temple and palace collected, generated, and preserved much of the intellectual and religious culture of Yehudah. All these diverse sources of cultural tradition and, doubtless, many others which can no longer be traced by literary historians would, in the centuries after 587 BCE, nourish the formation of Judaism. In much revised form, many of these sources would find their way into the official communal literature that would take shape among the Persian Israelites of fifth-century Yehudah.

But the lines of cultural continuity were seriously interrupted by the events of 587. The Babylonian conquerors of Yehudah dealt with its inhab- itants much as they, and the Assyrians before them, had defused the political will-to-resistance of other conquered peoples. They depopulated Yehudah of its political, cultural, and economic leaders—those, in other words, who preserved the intellectual culture and owned the wealth of the national group—and transferred them to the Babylonian urban centers. Many of those escaping deportation eastward to Babylonia sought refuge in Egyptian territories to the west, securing their lives in the one empire that seemed able to withstand the Babylonian expansions. The Israelite small landholders, artisans, and herders remaining in their land were soon joined by other foreign deportees, themselves the victims of similar Babylonian depopulations of their own native territories.

In later Judaic tradition, this experience of political defeat and territorial dislocation was captured in the image of the "Exile" (Hebrew: *galut*) to Babylonia. As we shall see, the theological interpretation of the causes of this event is among the crucial markers of any religious world called Judaism. For now, however, it is enough to point out a principal social consequence of Yehudah's fall. After nearly half a millennium of continuous political life in a relatively bounded territory, the people calling itself Israel was dispersed both within its ancestral land and outside of it. Beyond Yehudah—in Babylonia or Egypt—they were defeated exiles, dislocated refugees and, at times, slaves; within it they shared pasturage, water sources, and villages with strangers under the domination of a conquering empire.

Living a national life on the Land of Israel had once been a defining aspect of what it meant to be the People Israel. With Yehudah under foreign control, its official political and religious institutions shattered, and the cultural elite scattered far and wide, it was hardly clear in the decades after 587 where a new organizing center of Israel's collective life might be found.

The Emergence of Judaism in Persian "Yehud"

Although no solutions seem to have emerged immediately, political events did begin to create opportunities. The Babylonian Empire fell in about 539 BCE to the invading Achaemenid armies under King Cyrus the Great of Persia. Unlike his predecessors, Cyrus pursued a rather benign policy regarding his subject populations, designed to curry loyalty to the Achaemenid regime. Where possible, he repatriated deportees and appointed local ethnic administrations to govern ancestral lands. Such administrations, with Persian approval and enforcement, developed legal charters grounded in local traditions. This permitted the governed to see local ethnic leaders applying local laws, while the presence of the empire, at least in everyday matters, receded into the background.[2]

Throughout the sixth to fourth centuries BCE, a series of Persian rulers encouraged the descendants of deported Israelite political and cultural leaders to engage in the repopulation and reconstruction of Israelite communal life in the district now known, in the Aramaic language of the Persian Empire, as Yehud. Centered around the ancient Davidic capital of Jerusalem, Yehud slowly became a principal center of economic and cultural life. With the help of Persian financing and military supervision, key elements of urban life in Jerusalem were restored. By around 515 BCE the central shrine of Israelite sacrificial worship had been rebuilt and rededicated. Priests claiming descent from Zadok were placed in prominent positions of temple and civil administration.

The enhancement of Jerusalem as a provincial capital had important consequences beyond its walls as well. On the one hand, much of the peasantry of the countryside enjoyed physical protection and economic benefit from its allegiance to the new order forming in Jerusalem. On the other hand, the Babylonian-born Israelites in control of that order were not natives of the land. They often had to struggle with an indigenous population that saw itself, with some justification, as the authentic preserver of Israel's traditional ways.

So, from the late sixth century BCE until well into the fourth century BCE, Yehud was the site of a tense and—from hindsight—immensely productive cultural struggle. The struggle occurred at various points of social tension: between the laws of the new state and the venerable customs of the land; between the culture of the city and that of the countryside; between native Israelite and Babylonian-born Israelite. A key conflict, alluded to clearly in the biblical books of Ezra and Nehemiah, concerned the definition of who

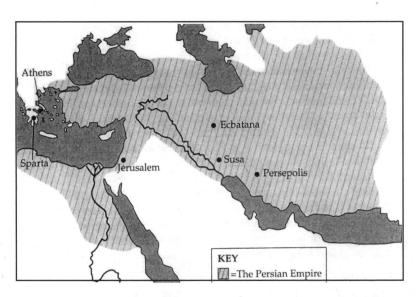

The Persian Empire of Cyrus the Great

The shaded area indicates the extent of the Achemenid Dynasty's power under Cyrus and his successors.

was actually an Israelite. Here those whom the priestly administrators of the state defined as full-blooded Israelites, primarily the Babylonian immigrants with priestly genealogical records, were privileged in relation to those, primarily home-born "people of the land," whom the newcomers regarded as being of mixed lineage (see Ezra 10:1–44 and Neh 13:23–28). Much of the struggle resolved itself to a single crucial matter: Who really belonged to the Land of Israel and how should those who truly belonged to it live upon it?

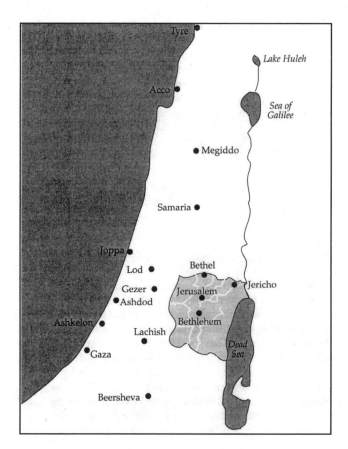

The Persian Province of Yehud

The shaded area represents the range of Jewish settlement permitted by the Persians after 539 BCE. Jerusalem was the center of the small colony, which occupied only a small portion of the former kingdom of Yehudah.

Based on T. Eskenazi and K. Richards, *Second Temple Studies, 2: The Temple Community in the Persian Period* (Sheffield, England: Sheffield Academic Press, 1992), p. 142.

Those contending over a period of centuries to define the course of the successor civilization to Davidic Yehudah are, from our present perspective, the first weavers of the fabric of Judaism. The narrative threads of that fabric were gathered from diverse memories of the glory of Israel's national past and tragedy of its collective degradation in Exile. Other threads were supplied from preserved records of priestly ritual, traditions of scribal wisdom, and documents of royal legislation. The loom was built of opportunities provided by Persian foreign policy. With these materials, the earliest generations of the Jews of Yehud wove a patterned cloth that would be added to by others in many places and times. Unfortunately, historical sources are so scarce for the earliest period that it is difficult to reconstruct much of what actually happened, either in the homeland or in Egypt and Babylonia. As we shall see in Chapter Two, most of what we can say must be grounded in inferences drawn from a single piece of cloth—some of the surviving texts of the Hebrew Bible.

Homeland and Diaspora under Hellenistic Empires

The haze covering the origins of the earliest Judaic religious world doesn't really lift until the late fourth century BCE and later. And by then, Israel found itself in a rather different cultural milieu. In 332 BCE the Persian Empire had fallen to a new world power, that of Greece, whose conquests under Alexander the Great had extended Greek control from Southern Europe and North Africa all the way to India. When Alexander died in 323, his successors divided his vast empire into more manageable spheres of influence. Under this division, the territories of Yehud and its environs fell between the spheres of two competing dynasties, the Egyptian Ptolemies and the Seleucids of Syria. The Ptolemies retained firm control of the area from about 301–201 BCE, until it was seized by the Seleucids under Antiochus III the Great. Seleucid rule was, in turn, finally overthrown by the Jews themselves in 152.

Unlike their Persian predecessor, the empires that succeeded Alexander saw themselves as more than the bringers of political and social stability. While often competing among themselves for political and military primacy, they nevertheless regarded themselves as the bearers of a civilization that constituted a kind of universal norm of culture. Grounded in Greek language, political traditions, artistic forms, and intellectual life, this cultural complex came to be called "Hellenism" after the country Hellas (Greece) from whence it spread.

Each of the Hellenistic empires developed its own particular cultural style indelibly colored by the North African or Middle Eastern political, artistic, and intellectual traditions that had preceded the Alexandrian conquests. Even within the same empire, the nature of the Hellenistic cultural world was modulated by many local influences. Urban cultures, for example, differed from one another in important ways. And everywhere in the Hellenistic world, as in our own, the urban centers were more cosmopolitan and "international" than the cultures of the countryside.

So cultural Hellenism was a highly diverse blend of Greek tradition shaped and interpreted by specific non-Greek peoples. Each Hellenized region shaped Hellenism to its own distinctive pattern; each Hellenized people created its own Hellenism. This is the case with the Israelites as well. Our introductory chapter has already observed that both native and Diaspora Israelites were identified by the geographical/ethnic term *ioudaioi*, which we have rendered as "Judeans" or "Jews." By all accounts, the Jews were widely recognized as a distinctive people. For example, the major cultural center of Ptolemaic Egypt, the coastal city of Alexandria, had an enormous Jewish population that may have reached into the hundreds of thousands. From the third century BCE until well into the second century CE, Alexandrian Jews produced a prolific literature in Greek. Including such Hellenistic genres as drama, poetry, philosophy and history, these writings demonstrate the degree to which the Jews of this Egyptian oasis of Hellenistic culture absorbed it as their preferred form of creative expression.[3]

It was once assumed by historians of Judaism that the Hellenization of the Jewish Diaspora could be contrasted to the relatively pure, uncontaminated Judaic culture of the Land of Israel. That opinion is no longer tenable.

Tracking Hellenism in the Land of Israel
Some Key Dates

323 BCE	Death of Alexander the Great
301	Land of Israel absorbed into Egyptian Ptolemaic Empire
201	Syrian Seleucids establish authority in Land of Israel
175	Onias III replaced by Jason as high priest in Jerusalem
168	Maccabees begin "anti-Hellenistic" resistance
167	Antiochis IV Epiphanes intervenes against Maccabees
164	Jerusalem placed under Maccabean authority
152	Jonathan appointed as first Hasmonean high priest
152–63	Succession of Hasmonean high priests/kings

The main reason is that archaeological studies show that Jews living in their ancestral land possessed more than a passing knowledge of Greek language, architectural styles, theories of urban planning and other markers of Hellenistic culture. Jewish archaeological remains in the Land, that is, are rather similar to Jewish and non-Jewish archaeological remains throughout Hellenistic North Africa, Italy, and Asia Minor. So the Hellenization of the Jews must be imagined as a matter of various degrees and styles.

In both the Diaspora and in the homeland, Judaism functioned in two ways: it served to distinguish the Jews from their cultural surroundings; but it also helped them to make an identity for themselves within that multi-ethnic environment as part of it. So various Diaspora "styles" of Judaism might certainly differ from those of the homeland (as they might differ from each other), but all bore significant traits of Hellenistic culture.

In the Diaspora, as we have already pointed out, the Jews seem to have eagerly absorbed the literary and intellectual traditions of the Greeks and to have made them their own. But in the course of doing so, they preserved their ethnic cohesiveness. Reports about the Jews of Hellenistic Alexandria, for example, dwell on the propensity of these Jews to live in their own parts of the city, to preserve customs and laws regarded by non-Jews as either

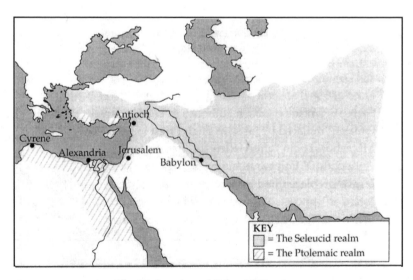

The Ptolemaic and Seleucid Empires

For over a century after the death of Alexander, the Ptolemies of Egypt and the Seleucids of Syria contested for control of the Land of Israel. This map shows the territory of the two empires prior to 201 BCE.

noble and wise or parochial and irrational, and, notably, to insist upon exemptions from certain acts of citizenship that involved sacrifice to local deities. Apparently, Jews used the forms of Egyptian Hellenistic culture to create their distinctive Judaic style within that culture. They defined themselves—and others recognized them—as a distinctive people within the larger collection of groups making up the various subcultures of Egypt.

This type of self-definition within the setting of a larger cultural tradition occurred among Jews throughout the Hellenized Diaspora, in such centers as Rome and Sardis. It is nothing more than what the Jews of the homeland were doing as well. Throughout the third and second centuries BCE, the face of Coele-Syria (as the Greeks called Yehudah and its environs west of the Jordan River) had been transformed by trade and immigration. Both stimulated the establishment of the characteristic form of Hellenized urban life, the city composed of free citizens (Greek: *polis*). As a result of such demographic and social changes, Aramaic-speaking Jews routinely rubbed shoulders with Greek-speaking foreigners, both Jews and non-Jews. They learned to speak their language and grasp their particular ways of understanding the world. Political leaders of native Jewry—appointed by imperial decree from among the hereditary priesthood of Jerusalem—became familiar with the court styles and diplomatic protocols of the Ptolemaic or Seleucid powers, and moved easily within them. In general, Jews in positions of social and economic power reproduced in their own country patterns of social, economic, and political life that were the acknowledged norm throughout the civilized world.[4]

But for all that, the Hellenization of important groups within native Jewry took a different form from that common in the Diaspora. In the homeland, Judaism carried with it almost necessarily a political meaning that was only implicit in the Diaspora. Language was an important factor here. Jews living in their land knew Greek, which they used in the Hellenized cities, but they spoke in their homes and towns a Jewish dialect of Aramaic acquired during the Persian era. Greek-speaking Jews of the Diaspora defined their distinctiveness within the sphere of Greek language. Judeans, by contrast, did so with an ancestral language that preceded the Greek experience. No longer associated with Persian domination, it came to seem quintessentially Jewish—no less so than the ancient Hebrew to which it was closely related.

Even though they moved rather comfortably in the Hellenized environment of their country, Jews nevertheless retained awareness of being natives in a land under foreign, imperial domination. One of the most important political events of this period involved a powerful conflict among

Yehudah's priestly elites over the meaning of Hellenism and of the place of Judaism within the larger Hellenistic world. The event started as a civil war among Jews and turned into a Jewish war of liberation against the Seleucid Empire. It resulted in the creation of a Jewish kingdom under the Hasmonean family. That kingdom was to be the last independent Jewish state in the Land of Israel until the founding of the State of Israel in 1948.[5]

The terms of the struggle that helped to create the Hasmonean kingdom deserve our attention, for they highlight the way in which terms like "Hellenism" and "Judaism" took on political as well as cultural meanings. Throughout the period of Ptolemaic rule, the Jews of Coele-Syria had been governed from Jerusalem by Zadokite high priests who served as provincial administrators responsible to the Ptolemaic king. These high priests served a dual role. Wearing the priestly robes, they were representatives of public religious tradition, responsible for supervising the sacrificial rites of the Jerusalem temple. But they were also political figures, charged with supervising the routine affairs of government through a bureaucracy of professional civil servants or scribes.

As in other territories, this upper level of local leadership grew increasingly at home in the international cultural scene, and looked to the imperial government to preserve its standing and privilege. It also represented to the peasantry, urban artisans, and tradespeople a prestigious local power charged with protecting their interests. This apparently peaceful local situation began to suffer disruption after the Seleucid conquest of the land in 201 BCE. Circles associated with the high priest continued to remain loyal to the Egyptian Ptolemaic dynasty. By 175, the reigning high priest, Onias III, was removed from office by the Seleucids and exiled to Ptolemaic Egypt, where he (or, perhaps, his son, Onias IV) helped to establish a temple to the God of Israel at Leontopolis that would survive as a Jewish sacrificial site into the first century CE.[6] In the meantime, the new king, Antiochus IV Epiphanes, sold the office to Onias' brother, Jason. In return for this gift of power, Jason expressed his loyalty to the new king by embarking upon an ambitious campaign to reform the official culture of Jewish Coele-Syria along more internationalist lines.

Jason's policies included the transformation of Jerusalem into a polis. By granting the rights of citizenship to selected Jewish aristocrats and property holders, the Greek constitution of the polis enabled them to become full citizens of the empire and significantly enhance their social and economic horizons. Jerusalem's new status transformed as well the status of distinctively Greek institutions—such as athletic contests and public baths. They were no longer private activities but took on the character of public works, official institutions of the city. Jason's policy of reform drew attention to an issue that had until then been only implicitly addressed. It was one thing for Hellenistic culture to informally take root almost imperceptibly in the folk-ways and economic life of the country. But to make such acculturation an official policy of the local Jewish government and afford it ideological primacy in the official life of the community was another matter entirely.

Jason's policies, and the more extreme measures proposed by his successor, Menelaus (ruled 171–167), drew a sharp response among Jews in the countryside in particular. Hellenism came to be identified by many opponents of the priestly Jerusalem elites as the cultural weapon of Greek political domination, wielded in this case by Jewish turncoats. Judaism, by contrast, was now represented as a pristine tradition wholly alien to the international culture of the time, a banner around which to organize political resistance to Hellenism. From the perspective of hindsight, however, it is clear that the debate was not between Judaism and Hellenism as opposing forces, but really over the degree to which a Jewish culture, already deeply enmeshed in Hellenistic cultural traditions, would self-consciously conform even further to international cultural norms. But hindsight is the luxury of historians, not of historical actors. The fact is that the ideological struggle created a climate of opinion in which it was possible to imagine Judaism and Hellenism as radically opposed spiritual entities. The forces of tradition, standing for Judaism, found themselves in pitched battle against the Hellenizers, who represented irreverence and innovation.

By 168 BCE, a full-scale civil war had broken out between the supporters of the high-priestly administration and various opposition groups, led by Judah the Maccabee ("the Hammer") of the non-Zadokite priestly Hasmonean family. The goal of the Maccabean forces was to depose the sitting high priesthood and to reverse its policies of official Hellenization. Naturally, the civil war required Antiochus to intervene on behalf of his Jewish loyalists. Thus a civil war became an international incident, a war against reformers became a war against a foreign oppressor. This war against the Seleucids ground on for years until 152, when internal affairs among the Seleucids convinced them to abandon the fight and concede political independence to the Jewish rebels. In that year Jonathan, brother of Judah the Hammerer, officially accepted the title of high priest. He inaugurated the Hasmonean dynasty that, within a half century, would style its priestly leader as both "King" and "Priest of the Most High God." This dynasty of non-Zadokite priests with royal titles ruled Judea as an independent kingdom until the Roman conquest of 63 BCE.[7]

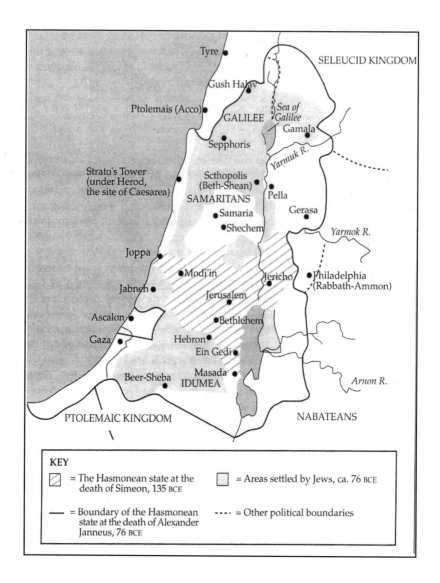

Tyre

SELEUCID KINGDOM

Gush Halav

Ptolemais (Acco)

Sea of Galilee

GALILEE

Gamala

Sepphoris

Yarmuk R.

Strato's Tower
(under Herod,
the site of Caesarea)

Scthopolis
(Beth-Shean)

SAMARITANS

Pella

Gerasa

Samaria

Yarmok R.

Shechem

Joppa

Modi'in

Jericho

Philadelphia
(Rabbath-Ammon)

Jabneh

Jerusalem

Ascalon

Bethlehem

Gaza

Hebron

Ein Gedi

Masada

Arnon R.

Beer-Sheba

IDUMEA

PTOLEMAIC KINGDOM

NABATEANS

KEY

▨ = The Hasmonean state at the
death of Simeon, 135 BCE

▨ = Areas settled by Jews, ca. 76 BCE

—— = Boundary of the Hasmonean
state at the death of Alexander
Janneus, 76 BCE

···· = Other political boundaries

The Hasmonean State, Second to First Centuries BCE

The boundaries of the Hasmonean kingdom fluctuated in relation to the
state's need to accommodate the dictates of powerful imperial neighbors. The
Roman conquest of 63 BCE removed any pretense regarding the actual control
of the country.

The Hasmonean experience was to have a profound impact upon Judaism in Judea and its environs. The bitterness spawned in the battle against Hellenism did not dissipate with the Hasmonean victory. To the contrary, as the Hasmonean dynasty wore on, it was routinely accused by outsiders to power of betraying the original ideals of the anti-Hellenistic revolution, of outdistancing even the ancient Hellenizers in diluting the pure essence of Judaism. Opponents could easily question the legitimacy of Hasmonean political leadership from two perspectives: as kings, the leaders were not Davidic; as high priests, they were not descended of Aaron through Zadok.

From the mid-second century BCE and after, native Jewry gave birth to a variety of groups calling for one or another form of religious revitalization or political reform. The temple and its priesthood became a source of conflict and controversy rather than a factor promoting political unity and ideological uniformity. Some of the groups involved in this controversy, such as the Pharisees and the Dead Sea community, will figure prominently in later chapters of our description of early Judaism.[8]

We can now sum up the situation of the Jews in the Hellenistic world. Nearly all Jews came into rich contact with Hellenistic culture and shaped it in ways distinctive to their own situations. The Hellenized Judaism of the Diaspora retained a rich sense of its ethnic distinctiveness and traditions within a comprehensive mastery of all aspects Greek cultural expression. Jews of the homeland adapted to the Hellenistic environment on rather different terms, conditioned by the particular political pressures of living in their ancestral country. Defining themselves in opposition to what they identified as Hellenism, they cultivated literary and cultural traditions that they perceived as more ancient than those of Greece. To put it in other terms, the most articulate Diaspora Jews—and many in the homeland as well—tended to see their Judaism as an expression of all that was best in Hellenism. Other native Jews, however, were inclined to view their Judaism as an antithesis of everything represented by Hellenism. But however Jews perceived their Judaism, none of them inhabited the insular Judaic world created in Persian Yehud centuries earlier. The Persian cloth had been taken up by a whole new team of weavers whose skills and tastes were profoundly shaped by the experience of living in cosmopolitan Hellenistic culture.

Political Experience under Roman Domination

The Roman legions of the general Pompey entered Jerusalem in 63 BCE to resolve a dynastic struggle between two Hasmonean brothers, Hyrcanus II and Aristobulus II. Hyrcanus was appointed high priest and executor of

Roman political power, so the dynastic question was resolved. But the Romans—except for a brief period of rule by Parthian invaders from 40–37 BCE—never left. Their conquest of the land they later called Palestine (Latin: *palaestina*) was part of a larger expansion of Roman control throughout the territories of Alexander's heirs, an expansion that gave birth to the Roman Empire. The cultural consequences of Roman domination of Diaspora and Palestinian Jewry were relatively minor, for Roman civilization was itself a thoroughly Hellenized cultural tradition. Despite important changes in the political administration of the Jews in Palestine, Diaspora and Palestinian Jews continued to develop long-standing patterns of culture.[9]

In order to solidify its control, Rome thoroughly reorganized the administration of Palestine into various districts, installing the Hasmonean heir Hyrcanus as a high priest without any effective political power. The regime remained unstable. Within a short time an Idumean nobleman named Antipater had insinuated himself into effective administrative control. With Roman support, he appointed his sons, Herod and Phasael, as district governors. Antipater was poisoned in 43 BCE, preparing the path for the Parthian invasion of 40. Antipater's son Herod was instrumental in leading a force that repelled the Parthians in 37. As a reward, Herod was appointed king of Judea with the full support of Roman military might. For perhaps the first time since the restoration of Persian Yehud, Jews were governed in their own country by a non-priestly royal administration.

Herod was, by all accounts of the period, a vicious and despotic ruler. He routinely ordered the murders of political enemies and even family members in order to consolidate his power. But he was also a man who liked a fine marble building and was willing to pay for it out of his public works budget. His reign was distinguished by the inauguration of impressive construction projects throughout the country. A special beneficiary of his attention was Jerusalem. He built aqueducts, stadiums, and an elegant race track in downtown Jerusalem. He presided over a lavish overhaul of the temple, transforming it into an enormous and exquisite compound. In short, he made Jerusalem an international city on a scale it had never enjoyed—the pride of Jews throughout the Roman Empire and a symbol of their "arrival" as integral members of world civilization.

With Herod's death in 4 BCE (only a few days after he had had his son, Antipater, executed), the Romans once again reorganized the administration of Palestine. Archeleus, one of Herod's surviving sons, was named successor over the largest part of Herod's territory, the districts of Judea, Samaria, and Idumea. More despotic than his father, Archeleus' appointment caused great unrest among the Jews, leading to his removal by Roman authorities in 6 CE. Thereafter Rome dispensed with any pretense to autonomous Jewish rule. It placed the entire territory under the control of a series of Roman procurators, or governors. Each had to deal with an increasingly restive and resentful Jewish population longing to rid itself of the domination of foreigners and their despotic local puppets.

The most famous of these procurators, of course, was Pontius Pilate (ruled 26–36 CE). His execution of Jesus of Nazareth on charges of political agitation had consequences for Rome that Pilate could never have imagined. The last of the procurators was Gessius Florus (ruled 64–66). His particularly stupid blunder was to forcibly expropriate from the temple treasury a rather large sum of gold in compensation for back taxes. Since temple funds were considered sanctified and could be put only to the purposes of the temple itself, the act was seized upon by the Jews as an idolatrous desecration. Anti-Roman riots naturally ensued. The riots turned into a full-scale war to expel Rome from the Land of Israel. The war, from the Jewish point of view, was a disaster. It dragged on, with much loss of life and property, until 73, with the fall of the last Judean fortress, Masada. But the fatal wound had already occurred in 70, with the Roman destruction of Jerusalem and the burning of the Herod's magnificent temple.

For Diaspora and Judean Jews, the pillage of Jerusalem and the burning of the temple recalled the horrors of a half a millennium earlier. The religious consequences of these events will occupy us in detail in future chapters. But for now, the political and economic dimensions of the catastrophe are themselves worthy of note. The temple served, even under Roman domination, as a potent international symbol of Jewish political identity. Its violation was not only a sacrilege, but a statement of utter contempt for the Jewish nation. It was a political as well as a religious humiliation. Moreover, the temple, like other Middle Eastern religious centers, functioned as a financial hub of the country's economic life, a center for banking and the exchange of currencies. Its destruction, along with the mass burning of productive agricultural lands, threw the peasantry, artisans, and merchants of the country into desperate financial straits.

It appears that Judean as well as Diaspora Jews could not reconcile themselves to what had occurred. After a generation of relative calm and regrouping, Jewish political unrest once again emerged, this time in the traditionally pacifist Diaspora. From 115–117 CE, under the reigns of the emperors Trajan and Hadrian, Diaspora Jews from North Africa to Mesopotamia took up arms in what appeared to be a coordinated series of riotous outbreaks. Very little is known of the motives of these disturbances; but they were severe enough to engage Rome's best military tacticians in their suppression.[10]

Palestinian Jewry seems to have sat out this period of unrest, but it re-entered the anti-Roman battle in 132. Sparked by a charismatic guerilla leader, Shimon bar Kosiba, this war clearly had as its objective the expulsion of Rome from Palestine and the recreation of an independent Jewish kingdom in the Land of Israel. Bar Kosiba called himself "Prince" (Hebrew: *nasî*), a title that had clear royalist implications. He also was given the punning nickname, "bar Kokhba" ("Son of the Star"). This recalled the prophecy from the Torah about a star that would "proceed from Jacob" to establish dominion (Num 24:17). All this suggests that he and his followers viewed their rebellion as the political stage of a larger world drama that would culminate with divine intervention on behalf of Israel. For a short time, at any rate, bar Kosiba's forces managed to regain Jerusalem and restore sacrificial services in the temple ruins. A government was formed, coins dated "Year One of the Liberation of Israel" were struck, and taxes were collected. Despite the excitement, an exhausted Diaspora seems to have been unable to muster much enthusiasm for bar Kosiba's war, and did little to detract Rome's military attention from Palestine. Eventually, superior Roman military power and economic resources prevailed. By 135 the last of bar Kosiba's forces fell at the battle of Betar.

The victorious Emperor Hadrian punished Jewish survivors of the rebellion with brutal punitive measures. These included deportations from Judea, mass executions, and the prohibition of Jewish customs regarded as politically subversive. By 135 the face of Judea had been transformed. Nearly all the Jewish population was gone, deported into the northern province of the Galilee or finding a haven as refugees in the Parthian provinces of Mesopotamia. Jerusalem itself had become the site of a new Roman city, Aelia Capitolina. And what remained of Herod's temple housed an altar dedicated to Jupiter, the chief god of the Roman imperial religion. With Jewry's political and economic center destroyed, its Diaspora populations in disarray, and its homeland depopulated, there is every reason for Rome to have been confident that the Jews would soon cease to be a significant factor in the life of the Empire.[11]

Reconstituting Jewish Society in Palestine and Babylonia[12]

Rome was correct in its political judgment. Neither Palestinian nor Diaspora Jewry would ever again become a political flashpoint. But Rome did not anticipate that its own policies toward the Jews would set in motion processes that, over the next three centuries, would lead to dramatic transformations of the Jews as a political community and of Judaism as a religious

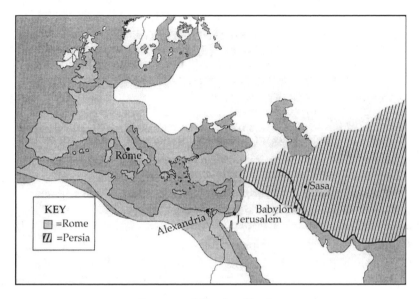

Roman and Persian Empires

The great Mesopotamian empires of the Parthians and, from 224 CE, the Sasanians constituted a powerful threat to Rome's Middle Eastern holdings, including Palestine. The dark area to the right contained heavy pockets of Jewish population, particularly in the areas between the Tigris and Euphrates.

world. Two factors were at work here. The first was indigenous to Palestinian Jewish culture: the rise to prominence of a community of Torah scholars who called themselves "sages" (Hebrew: *khakhamim*) and often bore the title "rabbi" ("master"). We discuss these rabbis in great detail in later chapters. For now, we simply observe that their distinctive interpretations of Jewish history and law proved immensely influential among Palestinian and Babylonian Jews in particular. Taking up the charred fabric of Hellenistic Jewish culture in Palestine and the Diaspora, the sages preserved what they could of the inherited weave and added to it patterns of their own strikingly original design.

The rabbis' new cloth, however, would have found few Jewish buyers without their corresponding success in establishing a market for its display. This brings us to the second crucial factor in the post–70 survival of Judaism: the success of the sages in persuading first Roman and, later, Babylonian imperial authorities that they could be effective in governing a numerous and politically volatile Jewish population in both empires. Our survey of the social and cultural setting of early Judaic worlds concludes, therefore, by

Roman Presence in the Land of Israel
Some Key Dates

63 BCE	Pompey invited into Jerusalem to resolve Hasmonean dynastic struggle in favor of Hyrcanus II
40–37	Parthian occupation
37	Herod appointed king of Judea by Romans in reward for anti-Parthian activities
20	Work begins on Herodian temple renovations
4	Death of Herod
6 CE	Herod's successor, Archeleus, deposed; Coponius appointed first Roman procurator
26	Pontius Pilate appointed procurator
30	Crucifixion of Jesus of Nazareth
66	Palestinian Jews revolt against Roman occupation
70	Herodian temple destroyed by Romans
73	Fall of Judean resistance at Massada
ca. 95	Rabban Gamaliel II appointed patriarch by Romans under Emperor Domitian
115–117	Anti-Roman diaspora rebellions; decimation of Alexandrian Jewish community by Emperor Trajan
132	Bar Kosiba leads rebellion against Rome; takes title of patriarch
135	Emperor Hadrian suppresses Bar Kosiba's revolt
138	Hadrian's death ends measures to suppress Judaism
140	Rabban Shimon b. Gamaliel II appointed patriarch under Emperor Antoninus Pius
170	Rabbi Judah b. Shimon b. Gamaliel appointed patriarch under Emperor Marcus Aurelius
212	Edict of Emperor Caracalla confers Roman citizenship on all empire's residents, including Jews
313	Emperor Constantine's Edict of Milan establishes Christianity as a legal religion in Roman Empire
361–363	Emperor Julian initiates attempts to rebuild Jerusalem temple; his death signals end of project
425	Emperor Theodosius declines to appoint successor to Gamaliel VI as patriarch; patriarchate ends

tracing the role of rabbinic figures in shaping Jewish political life in the later Roman Empire and in the Sasanian Empire of Babylonia.

The fundamental patterns of Rome's policy regarding Jewish self-government in Palestine were sketched within a generation after Rome's suppression of the war of 66–70. The bar Kosiba episode constituted only a brief interruption of a process that had gotten underway sometime during the reign of the Emperor Domitian (81–96). Rome's administration of Jewish Palestine was calculated to pacify the Jews not by persecution and humiliation, but rather by offering them significant privileges of self-government in return for political quiescence. Jews in Palestine could preserve their ancestral customs, as long as these were compatible with Roman law and did not lead to social unrest. As Persian policy had done centuries earlier in Yehud, Rome's intentions in Palestine were to cultivate local leaders who could directly administer Jewish affairs and distance the imperial hand from everyday life.

Rome pursued this policy by placing Palestinian Jewry under the authority of a Jewish appointee who bore the official Greek title of *ethnarch* ("Leader of the People") or *patriarch* ("Leader of the Fatherland"). The Hebrew title by which the office was known, *nasi* ("Prince"), drew upon biblical memories of great tribal leadership and, especially, the prophet Ezekiel's vision of a future leader of restored Israel (Ezek 46:1–18).

The role of the patriarch as a Roman official was a complex one with international significance. For Jews outside of Palestine—in Egypt, Asia Minor, and Italy—the office eventually became an important symbol of Jewish ethnic autonomy within the polyglot environment of the empire's diverse peoples. What the temple and its high priest had represented before 70—the national dignity of the Diaspora's Jews—the patriarchate itself stood for by 200. In the homeland, of course, the holder of the office embodied the last vestiges of Jewish political independence, administering a delicate balance of political submission and cultural autonomy. By 200 the holders of the office claimed matrilineal descent from the ancient Davidic royal family. Once and for all, Jewish self-government in the Jewish homeland had passed from the hands of high priests who ruled as non-Davidic kings, to a leader who claimed the prestige of Davidic origins without the advantage of priestly lineage.

The patriarchal office seems to have been hereditary, passed on within a single rabbinic family named Gamaliel. The office remained in the Gamaliel family throughout its entire history in an unbroken chain of fathers, sons, and grandsons. It remains unclear why Rome chose a rabbinic family for this powerful position. Nor is it certain why, among rabbinic families, that of Gamaliel was selected. Nevertheless, the results of placing a rabbinic sage in charge of administering Jewish affairs in the homeland were largely foreseeable. Wherever patriarchal influence extended in Palestine or the Diaspora, rabbinic interpretations of Jewish traditions could stake a claim to enjoy the status of Jewish civil law and ritual custom. To be sure, patriarchs often had to negotiate with other powerful non-rabbinic groups —for example, priestly landholders—in allocating political and social authority within the Jewish polity. So it was not possible to flatten other Jewish interests under a rabbinic steamroller. Nevertheless, the Judaic world in which the rabbis lived came increasingly to intersect with other patterns of Judaism that had survived the wars. By the end of the first Judaic millennium, rabbinic custom was increasingly accepted in many sectors of Jewish society as Jewish tradition *per se*.

A pioneering figure in this transformation was the most famous patriarch, Judah b. Shimon b. Gamaliel, who ruled in the late second and early third centuries. He loomed so massively in later rabbinic memory that he remained the only rabbinic authority referred to simply as "Rabbi," without a proper name to identify him. Rabbi ensured that rabbinic legal tradition would become the main source of law in Jewish courts under patriarchal jurisdiction. It was under his reign, and those of his successors, that a compilation of rabbinic traditions called the Mishnah ("Repeated Tradition") became the central nourishment of rabbinic intellectual life, spawning the tradition that would eventually issue into the vast talmudic literature of later centuries. We will discuss this literature at length in the next chapter.

The Palestinian patriarch, as the sole legal representation of the Jewish polity in the Roman Empire, enjoyed enormous influence and prestige. But from the early fourth century on, the patriarchate became somewhat problematic. The principle reason was the sudden rise to political prominence of Christianity. Beginning as a Jewish messianic movement focused on the first-century CE teacher, Jesus of Nazareth, Christian communities had by the end of that century begun to move beyond Jewish communal boundaries. Focusing now on the vast missionary possibilities of the non-Jewish peoples of the Roman Empire, Christianity had become by the third century a successful, but controversial, religion. As monotheists, Christians refused to participate in Roman imperial religious rituals that included offerings to the emperor as a divinity. Jews had long been exempted from such rites. But Christians, many of whom took pains to explain that they were not Jews, were suspected of harboring seditious political views. The second and third centuries saw frequent and vicious Roman persecution of Christianity.

Things changed, however, in the fourth century. In 313, the Emperor Constantine, who had strong sympathies with Christianity, issued the Edict of Milan, which established Christianity as one of the tolerated religions of the Roman state. After Constantine, with the exception of the brief reign of Julian (361–363), the Roman Emperor himself was a Christian. Especially in the eastern territories of the Byzantine Empire, this had important consequences for the Jewish political prominence represented by the Palestinian patriarch. It had been one thing for Imperial Rome, the persecutor of the Church, to acknowledge the political and cultural integrity of a subdued Jewish ethnic minority. It was quite another for Christian Byzantium to tolerate expressions of Jewish royal nostalgia among the people who had rejected the kingship of Christ. The patriarchate survived the transition of the Roman Empire to Christianity for about a century. By 425, with the death of the incumbent, Gamaliel VI, the Emperor Theodosius allowed the office to lapse. An unseemly expression of pride among a people who were privileged to survive in Christendom only in conditions of subordination, the patriarchate was an office whose time had passed.

During the centuries of the patriarchate, a parallel institution, the exilarchate, was developing in Mesopotamia, under the Parthian and, from 226, the Sasanian Empires. Called in Aramaic the *resh galuta* ("Head of the Exiles"), the exilarchate had its roots in the mid-second century under the Parthians. It appears to have been born from that empire's calculations regarding the possible role of the Jews as allies in its foreign policy relating to Rome, its chief rival for control of the Middle East.[13]

The Parthians had never forgotten their nearly successful conquest of Palestine in 40–37 BCE, and hoped to regain the country. Accordingly, they carefully cultivated the loyalties of the substantial Jewish communities within their own borders. These communities had grown, by the mid-second century, through significant migrations of Jews from war-ravaged Palestine, among whom were numbered many rabbinic disciples. Such refugees were hardly supporters of Rome. The Parthian appointment of a prominent figure, Huna, as exilarch in 170 was at least in part an effort to demonstrate to Palestinian Jews the sympathies of Persia for their plight. If anti-Roman Jewish unrest could be fomented in Rome's Palestinian eastern frontier, this might serve as a pretext for a Persian invasion and a restoration of Palestine (with its fertile fields, rich cities, and valuable coastal ports) to its ancestral Persian political constellation.

The Parthian goals ultimately went unfulfilled, and even the Sasanian successors to the Parthian territories were frustrated in their own designs against Rome. Nevertheless, the exilarchate proved to be an institution of crucial importance for Mesopotamian Jewry. The great Sasanian Emperor, Shapur I, significantly enhanced the authority and standing of the exilarchate after 242. Although never, like its Palestinian counterpart, the familial perquisite of a prominent rabbinic house, the exilarchal families nevertheless claimed even stronger connections to the Davidic House than the Palestinian Gamalians. The patriarchate claimed matrilineal descent from David, whereas the exilarchate claimed a more prestigious patrilineal relationship.

A series of exilarchs, relatively poor in rabbinic learning but rich in power conferred by the Sasanian state, tried to work with the increasingly influential rabbinic masters then establishing centers of learning in the empire. Requiring rabbinic legal expertise for their own operations, and seeking scholarly confirmation of their Davidic legitimacy, the exilarchs were crucial in establishing rabbinic legal and ritual custom as the binding traditions in Mesopotamia's Jewish courts and schools. Thus Palestinian rabbinic contributions to the fabric of Judaism were taken up and enhanced among the rabbinic circles of Babylonia.

As long as the Palestinian patriarchate remained in existence, the exilarch cultivated a posture of submission to the prestigious institution emanating from the Land of Israel. Patriarchal prerogatives in such crucial matters as establishing the religious calendar in accord with calculations of the phases of the moon and the ordination of rabbinic disciples as teachers were readily acknowledged. After 425, however, the vacuum in Palestinian leadership enabled the exilarch to emerge for a time as the premier political figure in the Jewish world. In the late fifth century, however, the very existence of the exilarchate was threatened by governmental policies against Judaism and Christianity. The Exilarch Huna V was executed in 470, and the office lapsed temporarily, until it was restored early in the sixth century. Thereafter it remained tightly controlled by imperial policies.

Rabbinic attitudes toward the exilarch, recorded in the talmudic literature, were complex. During the existence of the patriarchate, which joined an impeccable rabbinic family to the prestige of Davidic lineage, Mesopotamian sages owed their primary allegiance to the patriarch. Yet in order to pursue rabbinic religious goals in Mesopotamia, it was necessary to work with the exilarch. Thus, while rabbinic sages lampooned his relative ignorance of their traditions, or otherwise questioned his competence to rule, they were bound to the exilarch in a marriage of political convenience. The heads of the rabbinic schools (Hebrew: *yeshivot*) of the cities of Sura and Pumbedita were cultivated by the exilarch, and they in turn enhanced their prestige by their relationship to him.

Unlike the Palestinian patriarchate, the exilarchate received enough support from its imperial sponsors to survive radical political and cultural changes in the empire. When Muslim armies gained final political control of the Byzantine and Sasanian lands by the mid-seventh century, the exilarchate appeared an eminently useful tool for governing the Jewish masses under Islamic social policies. The office thrived especially after 661 under the Umayyad dynasty. But the history of the exilarchate in the Islamic world takes us far beyond the scope of this book.

Conclusion

Our social and political survey of the first Judaic millennium has focused upon the attempts of Jews to secure their social and political interests under the domination of Persian, Hellenistic, Roman, and Sasanian empires. We have seen that the continuous Jewish habitation of the Land of Israel (under various names), and of important Diaspora centers such as Egypt and Babylonia, served as the setting for major developments in the way Jews defined themselves as a group and expressed that collective self-understanding.

In the homeland itself—from the earliest expression of Judaism in Persian Yehud to the last years of the Palestinian patriarchate under Rome—Judaism continuously reshaped itself in conversation with the occupiers of the land and the cultures they brought to it. So, too, in the Diaspora, a continuous communication between the surrounding cultures and the Jewry of the homeland fostered important modulations of what could be meant by the term "Judaism" at any particular time. *Ioudaismos* might have seemed rather uniform to outsiders; but among the Jews themselves it took many forms.

We have, then, pointed out some of the key weavers of the cloth that became Judaism, identified some of the materials they used in their work, and described the cultural settings in which they labored. But what did they make? We begin now to look more closely at the threads themselves and the larger patterns into which they were woven.

Babylonian Jewry
under Achemenids, Seleucids, Parthians, and Sasanians
Some Key Dates

597–587 BCE	Successive waves of Jewish deportees transported from the Land of Israel to Babylonia
540	Babylonian Empire under Nabonidus falls to Cyrus the Great of Persia, first major ruler in the Achemenid Dynasty
539	Cyrus permits repatriation of Jewish exiles
ca. 450–398	Emperor Artaxerxes I or Artaxerxes II encourages restoration of Yehud under guidance of Babylonian Jews, Ezra and Nehemiah
331	Alexander the Great conquers Persian Achemenid Empire and establishes control in Babylonia
323	Babylonia claimed for Seleucid Empire
ca. 240	Arsaces I founds Arsacid dynasty in Parthia
120	Parthian Arsacids establish control of Babylonia
ca. 135 CE	Rabbinic refugees from Palestine establish a center in Huzal
ca. 170	Huna I appointed exilarch under Parthian Emperor Vologases III
226	Sasanian dynasty establishes control in Babylonia
242	Sasanian Emperor Shapur I enhances exilarchate of Mar Ukba I
455	Zoroastrian persecutions of Jews and Christians under Sasanian Emperor Yezdegerd I
ca. 470	Execution of Exilarch Huna V under Sasanian Emperor Firuz
520	Execution of Exilarch Mar Zutra II under Sasanian Emperor Kovad I
634	Sasanian Empire falls to Islam during exilarchate of Bustenai

Notes

1. The historical scholarship on the history and religion of ancient Israel is enormous, complex, and filled with controversy. For a synthesis by an experienced, respected, and judicious scholar, see Patrick D. Miller, Jr., *The Religion of Ancient Israel* (Louisville, Ky.: Westminster/John Knox, 2000). A more controversial, but stimulating alternative is available in Ziony Zevit, *Religions of Ancient Israel: A Synthesis of Paralactic Approaches* (London: Continuum, 2001).

2. Guidance for the study of Persian Yehud can be found in the following: Philip R. Davies, ed., *Second Temple Studies: 1. Persian Period* (Sheffield: Sheffield Academic Press, 1991), Tamara C. Eskenazi and Kent H. Richards, eds., *Second Temple Studies: 2. Temple Community in the Persian Period* (Sheffield: Sheffield Academic Press, 1994), and Charles Carter, *The Emergence of Yehud in the Persian Period: A Social and Demographic Study* (Sheffield: Sheffield Academic Press, 1999).

3. The works of Erich Gruen are indispensable for the study of Hellenistic culture amongst the Jews of the ancient world. See Erich S. Gruen, "Hellenistic Judaism," in David Biale, ed., *Cultures of the Jews: A New History* (New York: Schocken Books, 2002), pp. 77–132, and Gruen, *Heritage and Hellenism: The Reinvention of Jewish Tradition* (Berkeley: University of California Press, 1998). A detailed study of the styles of Hellenization in various parts of the Jewish Diaspora is elegantly presented in John M.G. Barclay, *Jews in the Mediterranean Diaspora: From Alexander to Trajan (323 BCE–117 CE)* (Edinburgh: T & T Clark, 1996).

4. Albert I. Baumgarten, *The Flourishing of Jewish Sects in the Maccabean Era: An Interpretation* (Leiden, et al.: E.J. Brill, 1997), pp. 80–113 offers an excellent account of the patterns and forms of Hellenization within the Jewish communities of the homeland prior to the first century CE.

5. For guidance in interpreting the complex sources of information regarding the origins and history of the Hasmonean state, see Lester L. Grabbe, *Judaism From Cyrus to Hadrian. Volume One: The Persian and Greek Periods* (Minneapolis: Fortress Press, 1992), pp. 221–311. A recent, and iconoclastic, interpretive analysis has been offered by Seth Schwartz, *Imperialism and Jewish Society, 200 BCE to 640 CE* (Princeton, N.J.: Princeton University Press, 2001), pp. 32–42.

   We will discuss Schwartz's ground-breaking book more extensively below.

6. Useful information about the temple at Leontopolis is offered in Grabbe, *Judaism From Cyrus to Hadrian. Volume One*, pp. 266–267.

7. An excellent, but demanding, account of the tensions aroused by the Hasmonean attempt to unite the role of king and high priest is offered by David Goodblatt, *The Monarchic Principle: Studies in Jewish Self-Government in Antiquity* (Tübingen: J.C.B. Mohr [Paul Siebeck], 1994), pp. 15–29.

8. For further sociological reflection on Jewish sectarianism, see A. Baumgarten, *The Flourishing of Jewish Sects in the Maccabean Era.*

9. Here I follow Seth Schwartz's judgment in *Imperialism and Jewish Society, 200 BCE to 640 CE*, p. 43: "Scholars often treat the arrival of the Romans in Palestine in 63 BCE as a watershed in Jewish history. But little changed for the first 140 years of Roman rule."

10. See the summary of evidence in Grabbe, *Judaism from Cyrus to Hadrian. Volume Two: The Roman Period*, pp. 596–599.

11. Consult the details in Grabbe, *Judaism from Cyrus to Hadrian. Volume Two*, pp. 601–605.

12. Authors of introductory texts normally feel obliged to present a clean, uncomplicated historical narrative that conforms to the views of a scholarly consensus. When I wrote the following section of this book in the middle 1990s, there did in fact seem to be something of a consensus regarding the emergence of the sages in post-70 Palestine and their accession to power through the Roman institution of the patriarchate. I found that consensus expressed in the basic studies of David Goodblatt, *The Monarchic Principle*, pp. 131–231 and Lee I. Levine, *The Rabbinic Class of Roman Palestine in Late Antiquity* (Jerusalem and New York: Yad Izhak Ben-Zvi and Jewish Theological Seminary of America, 1989), pp. 134–191 This consensus, however, has been seriously challenged by the work of Seth Schwartz, *Imperialism and Jewish Society, 200 BCE–640 CE*, already referred to above. Schwartz is highly skeptical in particular about the Roman role in the creation of the office of the patriarch, and argues that the period of the patriarchate's greatest influence coincides with the fourth-century Christianization of the Roman Empire. Since Schwartz's book has still to receive a full scholarly debate, I have decided to make only minor changes to the narrative I composed for the first edition of this book. But I also warn readers that before long the Schwartzian narrative may have won many adherents in academic circles. In any event, readers of this volume should consult with care Schwartz's chapter, "Rabbis and Patriarchs on the Margins," on pp. 102–128 of his book.

13. Jacob Neusner, *Israel's Politics in Sasanian Iran: Jewish Self-Government in Talmudic Times* (Lanham, Md.: University Press of America, 1986), is the handiest discussion of the history of the Babylonian exilarchate and its relations with the main rabbinic schools.

CHAPTER 2

Dynamics of
Texts and Traditions

THE UMAYYAD MUSLIMS established their dynasty in the Syrian city of Damascus in 661, commanding many of the former territories of the Christian Byzantine and Zoroastrian Sasanian empires. Those territories, of course, encompassed the large Jewish populations of Egypt, Palestine, and Babylonia. It was a population that had become, over the past centuries, increasingly familiar with the religious world taking shape among the rabbinic sages and their growing numbers of disciples.

This is not to say that the majority of Jews in the Umayyad lands would have considered themselves disciples of the sages. To the contrary, rabbinic writings are quite clear that the sages often met resistance to their authority over the private lives of Jewish townspeople. But whatever Jews might have thought of the sages' teachings, they had little choice but to abide by the rabbinic laws applied in the Jewish courts of the empire or to recognize the authority of the rabbinic appointees in the exilarch's administration. Whether Jews encountered a rabbinic sage as a neighbor, a fellow worshipper, a business partner, a preacher, or a local official, it would have been impossible to miss a striking fact. Whatever the sage did—how he ate, dressed, prayed, sold his goods, or tried cases—he was guided by rather distinctive understandings of the Torah of Moses, understandings he regarded as ancient traditions of all Israel.

Central to the training of rabbinic disciples was a peculiar discipline of memory, particularly in the memorization of literary texts. Some of these texts, such as those recorded in the Hebrew Bible, had existed long before the rise of the rabbinic movement and formed a crucial imaginative resource for numerous worlds of Judaism. Sages knew them by the particular name, "Written Torah." In addition, a disciple would also have mastered a complementary body of rabbinic teachings called "Oral Torah." He proved his worthiness as a scholar by holding forth upon this entire textual tradition of Written and Oral Torah in extended public disquisitions on legal and theological topics.

49

This explicit theory of a dual Torah as written scripture and oral tradition was unique to rabbinic Judaism. For the half millennium prior to the emergence of rabbinic Judaism, the demarcation between scriptural writings and non-scriptural traditions had been far less clear-cut. Much of the present chapter, accordingly, is devoted to the problem of scripture and tradition in non-rabbinic Judaic worlds. We begin with an account of the origins of the Hebrew Bible itself, the collection of writings that Jews throughout our period referred to as "Scripture." Then we explore some of the ways in which different Judaic communities interpreted the relation of these writings to other authoritative literary works in their tradition. By the end of this chapter, it will be possible to appreciate what was at stake in the rabbinic division of all sacred learning, Torah, into "Written" and "Oral" sources.

Our story, then, is largely about the sacred writings of early Judaism and their echoes in Judaic tradition. It is important, therefore, as a kind of prelude, to discuss one of the central problems that all students of the history of religions must confront sooner or later. What are "sacred scriptures" and how do they differ from other sorts of writings that also enjoy authority in religious communities? Working through this question will prepare us to discuss the nature of the scriptural collection of early Judaism and the interpretive traditions that transmitted its meaning.

The Hebrew Bible as a Scripture

The Hebrew Bible has been known by many names. Among the Jews of our period, and the earliest generations of Christians, "Scripture" was perhaps the most common designation. Jews since the Middle Ages have commonly referred to it as the "*Tanakh.*" Christians, of course, have known it as their "Old Testament" since the late second century CE. The very term "Bible" is an inheritance from Greek-speaking Jews who referred to their scriptures as *ta biblia ta hagia*, "the holy books." Just about every name for this book, it seems, testifies to a particular religious community's reverence for it. In order to speak about it as an historical object, we shall use the neutral term "Hebrew Bible." The noun "Bible" allows us to acknowledge this work's authoritative status in diverse religious groups; the adjective "Hebrew" identifies the ancient language in which most of it (but for some Aramaic sections) was originally written.

By whatever name it is called, however, today it looks like a modern book. The appearance is deceptive. Most modern books are written by authors who are proud to identify themselves with their work, regard it as their personal creative statement, and want to protect their writing from being used by others without due credit. Authors (or publishers) choose the titles, the author's name is emblazoned on the cover, and the finished product is marketed by advertising. So a modern book, like the one you are holding this very moment, represents a specific kind of cultural object. Copyright lawyers call it "intellectual property."

The Hebrew Bible originated as a very different kind of object. In the first place, although it has composers—a literate elite known as "scribes"[1]—none of them took responsibility for their work. Rather, many whom we might regard as "authors" regarded themselves as mere "scribal arrangers" who organized and recounted what they had received as ancient tradition. If, in preserving for the future the wisdom of the past, writers changed what they received, they did so, in their view, in order to enhance it, not necessarily to falsify it.

Authorship, in this sort of world, belonged to the person who inspired the written book, not to the one whose pen had produced it. Therefore, when ancient books were linked to authors, these were rarely the actual composers. More commonly, the "author" was the ancient figure of the past—Moses, or some other figure deemed close to God—whose inspired communications were believed to have been preserved in tradition long enough to be recorded by later writers in the book bearing his name. Thus, ancient scribes could, quite honestly, claim an inspired or revealed status for a book of their own composition. They viewed themselves as mere vehicles through which the revelations given to the inspired ancient author spoke to the present and future.

Throughout the history of Persian Yehud and well into the Hellenistic period, Jewish scribes composed many such books. The Hebrew Bible is a very selective collection culled from this larger literary tradition. These books have many different authors (none of them known for certain). Until well into the early centuries CE most Jews would never have seen all these books gathered together in a single place. The entire collection of writings would be found only in particularly sacred settings, such as the archive of the Jerusalem temple. And few people outside the priesthood or trained scribes would have had occasion to consult all of them. It was, in fact, early Christian missionaries who, in the late first century CE, first brought Greek translations of these books together into a single volume between covers. For centuries, Judaism resisted the Christian innovation of the bound book (Latin: *codex*) as a form for preserving scriptural texts.

Jews knew these writings primarily as separate, rather unwieldy, scrolls. Written on papyrus or treated hides, some could be dozens of feet long. For centuries there was little universal agreement about precisely how many such scrolls were included in the scriptural collection, which writings should enjoy scriptural status, or which versions of the texts were the authentic versions. Very few people would have owned the entire collection or ever have studied it all on their own. Most people would have learned to read and write by copying out crucial passages of some of the scriptures. More commonly, they would have known many of the writings only as something heard in the course of public addresses of a religious, educational or political kind. Even for the thoroughly literate, scripture was primarily something heard in the exposition of a teacher much more than something read by oneself.

In all, for most of the history of early Judaism scripture was a rather more fluid reality than the solid, printed modern versions might suggest. In its cultural origins it was not a "book" at all, but a rather diverse anthology. As a medium of knowledge it was mostly heard in public as an evocative utterance from a teacher rather than read in private as a source of personal instruction.[2]

Scripture, Tradition, and Canon

This last point about the communal setting for communicating knowledge of the Hebrew Bible gets us into the heart of our discussion. Throughout this chapter you will meet familiar concepts like "scripture," "tradition," and "canon." But we will use them in the specialized sense developed by recent historians of religion in their efforts to clarify just what is at stake when venerable writings, such as the Hebrew Bible, are found at the center of a community's collective life.[3]

Let's begin with "scripture." *A scripture is a writing preserved by a religious community as an authoritative source of teaching, reflection, or worship*. The great attention devoted to scriptures derives in part from conceptions of their origins. Scriptures are not understood to be "authored." Rather, they are "received." Although the texts are preserved by human memory and inscribed on permanent surfaces in human languages, they are believed to have originally been delivered to the communal ancestors complete and perfect. Very commonly, they are believed to originate as communications from a god or heavenly messenger.

The matter of origins is crucial. There is an important difference between a writing received by a particular composer as an inspired revelation and a writing received by a religious community as its scripture. The former need not necessarily attain the recognition of the latter. Texts normally do not become scriptures simply because the latest composer claims to have received it. Rather, writings become scriptures only because communities have at some point agreed to place them at the center of the common life.

Reading from a Scriptural Scroll

Until well into the Common Era, Jews preserved their most important literary texts on scrolls of animal skin or papyrus. Illustrated here is a fresco representing a Jew reading from such a scroll. The fresco was found in the remains of a third-century CE synagogue in the Syrian archaeological site of Dura-Europos. It is possible that the painter intended this to be a portrait of the prophet Moses or of the post-exilic leader Ezra.

Any text regarded as scripture came to be so because a community, formally or informally, gave it a central place in the pattern of communal life. Often, the precise role of a given text in the common life is a source of conflict. Different segments of a larger community might dispute whether this or that writing is truly authoritative for all members. Thus, it often happens that a text that is "scripture" in one community is simply a "writing" in another. Disputes within religious communities over what is and is not scripture is a common theme in the history of religions.

The communal consensus that regards a text as scripture brings into play the second term we have introduced, "tradition." *Tradition is simply that which has been handed down from the past for preservation in the present.* This can include writings. In the history of religions, it is tradition that sustains writings in the life of a community long enough for them to acquire the exalted status of scripture. There are relatively few examples of writings penned by a single known author who intended to write a scripture and saw his intentions realized. The works of the Hellenistic teacher Mani and of the nineteenth-century founder of Mormonism, Joseph Smith, are rare exceptions. Even the Quran of Islam, delivered as oracles by the prophet Muhammad over a period of decades, was not accepted by the Islamic community as its sole and complete scripture until a generation after Muhammad's death. This is a remarkably swift transition. Usually, a writing has been transmitted for some generations—or even centuries—before achieving its scriptural place in a community's life.

In this sense, scripture and tradition are mutually intertwined realities. A particular writing must first have been an oral or written tradition before it could become a scripture. Once a traditional literary work became scripture, it was usually preserved in a fixed text that could not be changed or emended. Traditions originally formulated and transmitted without writing, such as epic poetry or legal traditions, eventually were transcribed, in whole or in part, in written copies that served as aids to the collective memory. In many cases, as in the Hebrew Scriptures, great effort was invested in ensuring that copies of the text were reproduced word for word and letter for letter, for nothing in the holy writing could be lost or altered. Such writings normally coexisted for a long time with the orally transmitted versions, which were mastered by professional memorizers trained in sophisticated mnemonic techniques.

In the long ages prior to the printing press, scribes were entrusted with the crucial mission of producing letter-perfect copies of scriptural texts. But even the most careful scribe is capable of error. Especially in cases where a community might have only one manuscript of its scripture, even the occasional errors of scribes could be copied and recopied as part of the sacred scripture. Ancient scribes and other authorities were aware of this possibility, and took measures to determine which version of their scripture was the authentic "received" version. Often drawing upon the literary science of Hellenistic scholarship, Judaism, Christianity, and Islam developed very sophisticated critical standards for determining the correct versions of their scriptural texts.

This is where the term "canon" enters the picture. In one sense, *a canon is a norm by which a community determines which version of a scriptural text is authentic or authoritative.* That is, the canonical version of the text is the one used as the standard for making copies. Thanks to the discovery of the Dead Sea Scrolls, which we shall discuss from a variety of perspectives, historians are able to demonstrate significant variety in the texts of ancient versions of the Hebrew Bible. Apparently, prior to the canonization of the present received text of the Hebrew Bible, there were other versions of the text in circulation. Which, if any, were canonical beyond the boundaries of the communities that preserved them is difficult to say. Most probably, different Jewish communities preserved their own traditions of the canonical text. There may have been a great deal of overlap both in the contents and textual versions of these canonical collections; but there would have been significant diversity as well.

The term "canon" also has a second meaning: *a collection of scriptures.* The norms for determining whether a given writing is canonical or not vary. Some communities test the content of a writing in light of doctrinal or legal content; others in terms of its antiquity or supposed authorship. The canon of any community's scripture is that collection that passes the scrutiny of these various norms.

The canon of the Hebrew Bible, for example, shifts in different communal settings. Some early Jewish—and most Christian communities until the sixteenth century—had a canon of writings rather larger than the canon accepted within rabbinic Judaism since the early centuries CE. The Greek translation of the Hebrew Bible, known as the Septuagint, is an important example, for it became the foundation for the Old Testament of Christianity. But even today there is no universal Christian agreement upon the precise content of the Old Testament canon. The point to grasp now is that the canon of scripture is the product of various communal negotiations.

It is very helpful to view scripture, tradition, and canon as complex processes that represent the results of interpretive reflection within historically specific communities. Only rarely, as in the Indian Vedic tradition, is the sacredness of a scripture bound up with its preservation in a dead

language understood by few. In Judaism, Christianity, and Islam in particular, interpretation is the very life of the scriptural process. As scriptures are
handed on from generation to generation in canonical versions, they must
be interpreted so that the unchangeable text continues to penetrate the lives
of those who revere it.

The question of the text's meaning becomes central. Unfamiliar words
cannot be replaced with more up-to-date terms; rather, they must be
defined. Obscure concepts or perplexing episodes cannot be ignored;
rather, they must be explained. In many cases translations must be made for
those who are unfamiliar with the original language of the scriptural texts.
All this work of transmitting the meaning of scriptures is another kind of
tradition—the tradition of interpretation. In many cases differences of opinion about the meaning of a shared scripture can become very controversial.
If such differences of tradition are not reconciled, they can justify religious
divisions, the birth of competing communities or sects, and even religiously
motivated violence.

We can summarize this discussion of scripture, tradition, and canon by
resorting once again to metaphor. Think of canonization as a snapshot of
a sweeping motion, say, that of a dancer's leap. That leap is the historical
transmission and growth of literary tradition. Like a photograph, the canon
represents a momentary freezing of a continuous process that began before
the snapshot was taken and that continues long afterward. This frozen
image—the dancer suspended in the air—becomes the official portrait of a
community's tradition, its scripture.

Note that the canonical freezing of scripture is accurate and false at once.
It is accurate in that it captures perfectly a single moment. It is false in that
it separates that moment from all that preceded and followed it in time. The
dancer is always in mid-motion. Earlier forms of the tradition are no longer
visible to the community as part of the canonical scripture. They drop from
memory or survive as embellishments of the canonical scripture. Similarly the
subsequent life of tradition—the next step of the dance—is also lost or is
preserved beyond the borders of the canonical portrait of scripture and begins
to frame it. Knowing the dancer's entire performance, however, can enhance
one's appreciation of the photograph of part of it. This is our task here. Let's
try to put some flesh on the bones of this rather puzzling metaphor.

The Emergence of Scripture in Persian Yehud

To be candid, historians of Judaism are not in total agreement about when
the first canonical snapshot was taken. No single historical reconstruction
of the origins of Judaic scripture commands universal acceptance. This,

however, is to be expected. Historians reach their opinions on the basis of their interpretations of evidence. And in the present case, not everyone agrees about what counts as evidence. Moreover, the evidence agreed upon is slender, and its interpretation is very difficult. The issue, to oversimplify a bit, is one of literary history.

Few historians of Judaism doubt that Israelites living in Yehudah prior to the Babylonian deportations of 597–587 BCE possessed well-developed literary traditions, in both written and oral form. The disputed historical question, rather, has to do with the relationship of the present contents of the Hebrew Bible to those traditions, on the one hand, and to the religion of ancient Israel, on the other. Two issues are involved. One is to what extent the present writings gathered in the Hebrew Bible are an accurate representation of Israelite traditions as they existed prior to the destruction of Yehudah in 587. The second is whether the present writings (or the traditions that preceded them) ever represented and shaped the religious world of Israelite civilization *as a whole* prior to 587. In other words, was there some form of the Bible in biblical Israel and, if there was, did it enjoy authoritative standing for the population at large?

Each of these questions is hotly debated. Some scholars see most of the Bible already complete as early as the seventh century BCE; others argue for the composition of most biblical writings as late as the Hellenistic period.[4] We cannot enter too deeply into that debate here, although the footnote to the preceding sentence will give you some guidance to further reading. Our own discussion follows the views of those contemporary historians of Judaism who regard the writings of the Hebrew Bible in their scriptural form as a literary tradition originating primarily with the Jews of Persian Yehud. These writings reached their current textual form among the scribal groups of Persian Yehud who reshaped the earlier literary tradition in light of their own experience and in view of their own social, political, and religious interests. Accordingly, the Hebrew Bible testifies first of all to the religious world of those Jews, rather than to that of the ancient Israelite civilization, whose traditions they selectively retrieved, composed, and interpreted.

To continue our textile metaphor, the literary strands of the Hebrew Bible were contributed, in large measure, by ancient Israel, but the weaving was done on a Persian loom. For this very reason, our point of view is that the scriptural form of the writings in the Hebrew Bible represents the religious world of Jews who lived from the Persian through the early Hellenistic periods. Biblical Judaism, paradoxically, comes into existence in the Persian period.

The Canonical Shape of the Hebrew Bible

But even an answer to the question of the origins of the Hebrew Bible does not explain its present form. Here, the snapshot metaphor we used to understand the idea of canon is helpful. The Hebrew Bible is a snapshot of Jewish scriptural tradition. The snapshot was taken in the early centuries CE, probably by rabbinic photographers.

In order to understand the picture that they composed for us, we might best attend to the key parts of the composition. We have already mentioned that a common Jewish term for the Hebrew Bible is "*TaNaKh.*" This is an acrostic that refers to the three major divisions in which the collection is preserved: *Torah* ("Teaching"), *Nevi'im* ("Prophets") and *Ketuvim* ("Writings"). Each of these canons is a kind of peg upon which hang the narrative strands of the biblical story. This story will occupy us for the next few pages, because it contains the primary clues that will guide us to Persian Yehud as the point of its earliest circulation as scripture.

The Torah describes the origins of the world and the history of the Israelite nation from its beginnings with Abram to the death of its great leader, Moses. The central focus of the Torah is the description of a series of covenants, or contracts, sealed between God and Israel. Abram (soon renamed Abraham), his son Isaac, and his grandson Jacob (also known as Israel) receive the earliest of these. The culmination of these covenants, however, comes centuries after Jacob's death, in a collective covenant agreement between God and all Israel at Sinai. Moses plays the key role in mediating the covenantal terms between God and Israel. In return for Israel's obedience, God promises to grant it a rich land and protection from its enemies.

The narrative continues in *Nevi'im*, particularly the books of Joshua through Kings. These describe the history of Israel's life in the land chosen for it by God and the events surrounding their loss of that land at the hands of Assyrian and Babylonian invaders. The major thesis of *Nevi'im* is that the land was lost because of Israel's repeated violations of its covenant agreement with God. With few exceptions, the kings of Yisrael and Yehudah led the people away from the teachings of God's prophets. Exile was the result.

The story concludes in the books of Chronicles and Ezra-Nehemiah, the last books of *Ketuvim*. They depict the eventual resettlement of the land by a remnant of the original people, under the guidance of a priest named Ezra and Nehemiah, a provincial governor appointed by the Persian emperor. In the Bible's interpretation, that Persian emperor—scholars debate whether it was Artaxerxes I or his son, Artaxerxes II—was a mere vehicle of God. The return to the land was made possible only by Israel's sincere repentance of its earlier disobedience and its commitment to comply with all aspects of the original covenant set forth in the Torah.

The basic plot of the *Tanakh*, then, is quite simple: it narrates the history of a covenant. That covenant is made between God and Israel in the Torah, broken by Israel in *Nevi'im*, and restored by God in *Ketuvim*. In addition to this basic narrative line, the Bible contains a wide variety of writings that, in one way or another, supplement or amplify the plot. These are distributed throughout *Nevi'im* and, in particular, *Ketuvim*. The former supplements the sad history of Israel's loss of its land with a series of books of poetry and narrative about the faithlessness of Israel and the covenantal loyalty of God, ascribed to ancient social critics known as prophets. *Ketuvim*, for its part, introduces its optimistic image of Israel's return to its land with a diverse collection of writings. These include prayers and religious meditations (the book of Psalms), reflections on the meaning of suffering and happiness (Job and Ecclesiastes), and stories about ancient heroes and heroines (Daniel, Ruth, and Esther).

In its canonical form, then, the Hebrew Bible is essentially a three-act drama containing its own commentary—a very sophisticated piece of literary work. The Torah sets the fundamental theme, which is then amplified in exquisite detail in *Nevi'im* and *Ketuvim*. In order to see how this dramatic structure of the canon took shape, we must first ask when its basic story line might have originated.

We begin with a simple observation. The Hebrew Bible ends its story with the return of small groups of Jews to the Land of Israel from exile in Babylonia. If, like all stories, this one begins with the end already in mind, we may conclude that much of its depiction of early Israelite history is told from the perspective of those who are seeing the story whole from the perspective of their own day. Accordingly, the core narrative of the Hebrew Bible in its canonical form was conceived sometime after the return, in 539 BCE, of Israelite exiles to their ancestral territory under Cyrus.

The plot of the Hebrew Bible, after all, raises and answers questions which were fundamental to those who had resettled the Land of Israel and wished now to abide safely upon it. The story they told was essentially a confession of guilt and a resolution to atone for it. It explained how God's special people was descended from a great hero of absolute obedience, Abraham, born in the Babylonian city of Ur. The Torah's first introduction of Abraham is telling. Without any forewarning at all, God begins speaking to Abraham, ordering him to leave his family, birthplace, and everything familiar to him "for the land that I will show you." There, God promises, "I will make you a great nation, and I will bless you. I will make your name

---

The Literary Coherence of the Scriptural Canon

In the form transmitted in Judaic tradition, the scriptural canon is a carefully structured whole containing a narrative and various works that comment on or otherwise amplify the narrative.

The narrative is organized into three thematic sections as follows:

TORAH	*NEVI'IM*	*KETUVIM*
Covenant Making	*Covenant Breaking*	*Covenant Renewal*
Genesis-Deuteronomy	Joshua-Kings	Chronicles and Ezra-Nehemiah
	Isaiah	Psalms
	Jeremiah	Proverbs
	Ezekiel	Job
	The Twelve	Song of Songs
		Ruth
		Lamentations
		Ecclesiastes
		Esther
		Daniel

In this context, the books of Isaiah, Jeremiah, Ezekiel, and the Twelve Minor Prophets interpret the Covenant Breaking narrative of Joshua-Kings and predict the Covenant Renewal narrative of Chronicles and Ezra-Nehemiah. In the same way, the books of Psalms through Daniel look backward toward the tragedies of the past and define the sorts of covenantal loyalty that will lead to the renewal of the covenant.

---

great, and you shall be a blessing ... and all the families of the earth shall bless themselves by you" (Gen 12:2–3). And Abraham follows. Abraham's obedience is his dominant trait. A few chapters later (Gen 22:1–19), God tells Abraham to offer his favorite son, Isaac, as a sacrifice. Abraham, without saying a word, obeys, sparing Isaac only after a heavenly voice orders him to desist.

In many ways, the Torah's Abraham is both a model of what Israel ought to be and a confession of what it had failed to become. Through persistent violation of Abraham's example, Israel came to suffer the loss of its political independence and homeland. What would it mean in the setting of Persian Yehud to begin the history of Israel with the now-famous stories of Abraham's obedience and end it with the return of the exiles? Quite simply, Israel's origins and destiny are bound up with each other.

The image of Abraham's silent submission to God's will in leaving his native Babylonia for an unknown land implies that the restoration of Jews from Babylonian captivity is more than an arbitrary action governed by the Persian emperor. Rather, it is under the control of the very God whom Abraham obeyed. The descendants of the exiles, most of whom had known no other home than Babylonia, modeled their own repopulation of the land of Israel after that of Abraham, and saw in Abraham's obedience to the divine call a way of expressing their own. The present generation sought to secure the promise to Abraham—of progeny, land and blessing—by re-enacting his obedience and perfecting the life of obedience once and for all.

It is in this sense that the origins of the biblical narrative and those of Judaism are closely bound up together. The basic story of the Hebrew Bible emerged in the century following 539. Exactly who the storytellers were is almost impossible to say. But what they did is clear. They reshaped the diverse narrative and legal traditions of ancient Yehudah into a carefully plotted literary epic. Through the figures of ancient Israelite heroes, that epic told the tale of its tellers.

As they saw things, the history of the world provided the setting of Israelite history in the past and the future. Yehud's program for national survival was given thereby a cosmic significance. The daily confirmation of Israel's setting in cosmic history was the ancient sacrificial center of the Davidic dynasty, the Jerusalem temple. Restored in successive building projects from about 520, its sacrificial service was reconstituted in line with traditions preserved by the surviving priesthoods of Persian Yehud. Now the Creator of the World could be served as he desired, conferring his blessing upon his people.

All the elements of a coherent religious world—the placing of self and community in a relationship to the fundamental structures of reality—were fully in place. These elements, in various combinations and emphases, would be carried forward by all versions of Judaism for the next millennium.

The Torah of Moses

The charter for Yehud's reconstruction—its epic of Israelite origins and compendium of national law—was a collection of five scrolls called the Torah of Moses. A document with this title is mentioned many times in the book of Deuteronomy, where it is associated with a collection of laws. In its canonical version, however, the Torah is much more than a legal collection. It is, in fact, a history of the universe from the moment of its creation by the God of Israel down to the death of the people's greatest prophet and leader, Moses.

The one clear reference in the Hebrew Bible to a Torah of Moses that contains just such an historical vision is not, however, in Deuteronomy. Rather, it is found in the account of the post-exilic restoration recorded toward the end of the book of Nehemiah. The composer of this work describes the efforts of Persian-Jewish repatriates, sometime between 450–380 BCE, to rebuild Jerusalem's walls and restore proper observance of God's covenant among the population of Yehud.

A central figure in his account is the priest and scribe Ezra. He is portrayed (Nehemiah 8–9) as reading the Torah of Moses to an assembly of Jerusalemites in the restored temple and guiding them in their early attempts to repent for their sins and to reconstitute a proper covenantal relationship with the God of Israel. Ezra's summary of the Torah of Moses in these chapters agrees with the scope of the canonical Torah.

Accounts of Ezra's activity may be almost as legendary as those of Moses. In many ways, as a mixture of law-giver and priest, he is portrayed as a more perfect leader than Moses, whom God made concede priestly duties to his brother, Aaron. Nevertheless, the description of the Torah read by Ezra establishes that, by the fourth century BCE, a book like the present Torah in overall scope and argument was used as the basis of historical thought, religious teaching, civil administration, and sacrificial ritual in restored Jerusalem.

Some historians have suggested that it was drawn up in Babylonia precisely for this purpose. Given the opportunity to restore limited Jewish self-rule in Yehud, Babylonian Jewish leaders such as Ezra compiled the Torah of Moses as their charter. This is a possible, but as yet unproven, scenario. At the very least, however, the Torah of Moses soon passed beyond the purely political status of being a charter of Babylonian-born Israelite expatriates. It became a public tradition sustaining the social and religious institutions of Yehud. It rooted in the distant past the new community governed by it. It also linked that community's destiny to the Creator of Heaven and Earth. By the end of the Persian period, the Torah of Moses had become a Judaic scripture.

The main concerns of Persian Yehud's Judaism can be surmised from the single-mindedness of the Torah's retelling of the past. No matter what sort of ancient Israelite traditions it gathers together, it makes sure to structure the narration around a single theme: God's overpowering love for his creation is constantly rebuffed by the rebellious desires of humanity. Thus, for example, legends about pre-Israelite human history are told in such a way as to foreshadow and predict the later rebellious behavior of Israel under its covenant with God.

The well-known story of the first man and woman in the Garden of Eden is a case in point (Gen 2:4–3:24). Given by God everything they could possibly require by way of material comforts, Adam and Eve are commanded only to refrain from certain forbidden fruits in the center of the Garden. This they prove unable to do; neither do they show any genuine remorse when God discovers their act. As punishment, God expels the humans from his Garden, making it impossible for them ever to return. As the story tells it, this is the moment that pain, suffering, and death enter the world. At the very origin of human history, then, the Torah finds a spirit of human rebellion that incurs the divine punishment of exile.

The Torah, moreover, sees Israel's history as a reenactment of human history within the confines of a single people. The covenant making event at Mt. Sinai is described in the scroll of Exodus (18–25) as a moment of close bonding between God and Israel, with Israel eagerly entering into agreement to observe all the laws of God. Yet forty days later, with Moses still on the mountain communing with God, Israel begins to pine for a substitute deity and pressures Aaron into molding a golden calf to worship.

As the Torah describes it, only Moses' active intervention on behalf of his people prevents God from destroying them in punishment (Exodus 32). Then God permits the Israelites to build a wilderness Tent of Meeting in which God promises to make his presence available among the people. From that Tent he reveals all the laws by which he is to be worshipped and through which Israel will express its love of him (the Leviticus scroll). Yet what is Israel's response? Much of the fourth scroll of the Torah, called Numbers, records stories in which Israel complains against the rigors of its desert wanderings, yearns longingly for its period of Egyptian servitude and in other ways forgets or evades its responsibility to God.

The Torah ends in Deuteronomy with a long speech by Moses in which he predicts that if this spirit of disobedience continues after Israel is brought into its land, the promise of the land will, indeed, be revoked. The stark choice offered by Moses here is only one of many examples (Deut 30:15–20):

> See, I set before you this day life and prosperity, death and adversity. For I command you this day, to love the LORD your God, to walk in his ways, and to keep his commandments, his laws and his rules, that you may thrive and increase, and that the LORD your God may bless you in the land that you are about to enter and possess. But if your heart turns away and you give no heed, and are lured into the worship and service of other gods, I declare to you this day that you shall certainly perish; you shall not long

endure on the soil that you are crossing the Jordan to enter and possess. I call heaven and earth to witness against you this day: I have put before you life and death, blessing and curse. Choose life—if you and your offspring would live—by loving the LORD your God, heeding his commands, and holding fast to him. For thereby you shall have life and shall long endure upon the soil that the LORD your God swore to your ancestors, Abraham, Isaac, and Jacob, to give to them.

The fifth scroll of the Torah ends with this choice ringing in the ears of its audience. Obedience or rebellion; life or death? The history of early Judaic religious worlds is the history of those who defined that obedience and how life would reflect it.

Toward a Uniform Canon

The Torah of Moses received pride of place in the Judaism that developed around the temple in Jerusalem. But it was still part of a larger national epic that included accounts of centuries of living under kings on the Land of Israel, of being swept off of it and of returning to renew covenantal life upon it. This epic in its entirety—Genesis to Deuteronomy, Joshua to Kings, and Chronicles/Ezra-Nehemiah—existed by the fourth century BCE at the latest. Nevertheless, the present literary division of that story into three formal divisions—*Torah*, *Nevi'im*, and *Ketuvim*—and the inclusion of supplementary writings did not become commonplace until the middle of the second century BCE.[5]

Indeed, it is remarkable that any uniform collection of Jewish scriptures emerged at all. As we have seen in detail in Chapter One, Judaic civilization after the fourth century BCE was anything but homogeneous. In addition to a small community centered around Jerusalem and other locations in the ancient homeland, most Jews of the Hellenistic period were scattered in lands as far apart as Egypt and Babylonia. Despite the superficial uniformity of a shared Hellenistic culture, Jews lived under competing and often warring political empires and spoke a variety of languages. The restored temple in Jerusalem and its priesthood enjoyed high prestige among most of the dispersed Jewish world, but no authoritative religious or political institution extended from Jerusalem to legislate on such matters as the nature and content of scripture.

By the third century BCE, Greek-speaking Jews of Egypt began to translate the Torah and other Hebrew writings into Greek. Whether this was a sign of their fading grasp of Hebrew or an effort to promote the merits of their own ethnic literature in the circles of higher Egyptian culture—or a little of both—is not clear. This translation, the Septuagint mentioned earlier, eventually gathered together not only translated versions of Hebrew scriptures, but some works originally written in Greek, such as one called the Wisdom of Solomon. Alexandrian Jews in particular treasured this collection of writings as their own distinctive national classic, analogous in prestige and in wisdom to the philosophical, dramatic, and poetic literature celebrated by Greek-speaking Egyptians as the classical models for all literary and intellectual activity.

An often told Alexandrian story about the origins of the Septuagint reveals the high regard in which Jews held this scriptural translation. In its essential outlines, the story speaks of a powerful Ptolemaic king who, hearing of a book of philosophy preserved among the Jews of Jerusalem, resolved to have it translated for his famous library in Alexandria. The book is the Torah of Moses. The king sent for seventy Jewish scribes to produce the translation and sequestered them in seventy isolated rooms for seventy days. In the end, each emerged with the identical translation of the Torah. Clearly, the story's point is that the Greek rendering of the Torah, like the Hebrew original, is divinely inspired. The date of the completion of the translation was a widely celebrated holiday among Alexandrian Jewry. And the very name "Septuagint," which means "Seventy," preserves the significance of the translation.[6]

Aramaic-speaking Jewish communities of Palestine preserved as well a wide variety of writings in Hebrew and Aramaic that seem to have enjoyed scriptural prestige, even though they are not found in the present canon. Some of these writings, such as the Wisdom of Joshua ben Sira, were eventually translated into Greek and preserved in versions of the Septuagint. Inherited by Greek-speaking Christians, they remain part of some collections of the Old Testament. Others, such as the book of Jubilees (which we discuss in detail further on), a collection of visionary texts called the book of Enoch, and the many Aramaic and Hebrew writings found in the Dead Sea Scrolls also seem to have been frequently copied and circulated. But, however much these diverse writings might have been valued by some Jewish groups of this period, or by later Christians, they did not find their way into the canon of scripture transmitted by rabbinic Jews in the era of Christianity.[7]

To conclude, the process by which certain books attained scriptural status while others enjoyed it for a time and then ultimately lost it is very difficult to trace. It is clear, however, that the process of defining a scriptural canon extended over a period of centuries. For the first several centuries of its existence the Hebrew Bible was a scripture whose canonical boundaries remained open. Only in rabbinic writings from the third century onward

Tradition and the Shaping of Judaism's Scripture

The Hebrew Bible did not happen all at once. The chart that follows attempts to isolate key stages in the transformation of pre-scriptural traditions of ancient Israel into the canonical collection accepted by rabbinic Judaism.

Principal Sources of Ancient Israelite Tradition, ca. 1000–587 BCE

Primarily Oral Traditions
1. Heroic epics
2. Priestly ritual practices
3. Public oratory

Primarily Written Traditions
1. Civil and ritual law codes of royal scribes
2. Civil and ritual law codes of priestly scribes
3. Royal archives
4. Histories of royal deeds

Persian Period, ca. 539–323 BCE

1. 450–400: Selected oral and written traditions composed into the "Torah of Moses"
2. 450–400: Completion of written histories of pre-exilic monarchies (Joshua-Kings)
3. 450–350: Systematic compilation of prophetic oracles
4. 450–350: Early collections of psalms and proverbs
5. 400–350: Completion of written history of post-exilic restoration community (Chronicles and Ezra-Nehemiah)

Hellenistic Period, ca. 323–63 BCE

1. 350–160: Composition of Esther, Ruth, Job, Ecclesiastes, Song of Songs, Daniel
2. 250–200: The Torah and other Hebrew writings are translated into Greek by Egyptian Jews
3. 200: Canon of Nevi'im circulates with Torah as a scriptural collection
4. 200–100 CE: Jubilees and other works compete with Torah and Nevi'im as authentic scriptures

Roman Period, ca. 63 BCE–320 CE

1. 100 CE: Rabbinic tradition defines present boundaries of Jewish canon
2. 200 CE: Rabbinic tradition begins to claim exclusive legitimacy as the true meaning of scriptures
3. 300 CE: Septuagint is abandoned by Jews and becomes basis of Christian Old Testament
4. 300 CE: Surviving pre-rabbinic traditions of scriptural interpretation absorbed into interpretive traditions of rabbinic Judaism and Christianity

do we find the names and even the sequence of scriptural books corresponding more or less closely to the present canon.

The rabbinic connection to the present canon cannot be overlooked, although the precise impact upon the canonical boundaries is difficult to define. Did the sages merely tinker with the fine points of an inherited canon common to most Hebrew or Aramaic-speaking Jews (as some rabbinic traditions suggest)? Or did they, to the contrary, wield a ready scalpel in excising from their canon works highly regarded in the larger Palestinian setting? Scholars hold divergent views, and we can not debate the matter here.[8]

It is clear, however, that any definition of the canon of scripture is part of the larger process of interpreting its meaning. As we shall now see, this process of scriptural interpretation had been underway for centuries, even prior to the closing of the rabbinic canon itself.

The Problem of Scripture's Meaning

Our usual habit of thought is to imagine scriptures as writings that give rise to interpretations and commentaries. First there is the scripture, then there comes the explanation of its meaning. Things are not that simple. We have already observed that Judaism's earliest scriptural text—the Torah of Moses—is an interpretation of still earlier traditions of ancient Israel. We must now point out yet another important matter. Ancient Jews did not wait for the completion of their scriptural canon before beginning to interpret the books within it. Moreover, they did not always wait for the completion of the books before interpreting them. In more than a few cases books in the present scriptural canon contain within them commentaries on earlier versions of those same works. The commentary was included in the work before the text was "photographed" in its present canonical form.

Interpretation Within the Canon of Scripture

A prime example, pointed out by many biblical scholars, can be found in the canonical book of Psalms. Psalms is a collection of poetry, usually in the form of prayers and songs. Historians regard some of these as versions of poetry sung during the sacrificial services of the first and second temples; others are of uncertain origin. The canonical book has 150 of these poems. They include some of the most well-known passages of the Hebrew Bible, such as the famous Psalm 23: "The LORD is my shepherd, I shall not want..."

Of interest to us in the present context are the various introductory comments to individual psalms. These relate specific psalms to certain events in the life of David or other heroes. These events, invariably, are described at length in other portions of the scriptural canon. Consider the first stanza of Ps 51:3–4:

> Have mercy upon me, O God, as befits Your faithfulness;
> in keeping with your abundant compassion,
> blot out my transgressions.
> Wash me thoroughly of my iniquity,
> and purify me of my sin;
> for I recognize my transgressions,
> and am ever conscious of my sin.

Consider now the way the following introductory lines illumine what you have just read (Ps 51:1–2):

> For the Leader.
> A psalm of David.
> When Nathan the prophet came to him after his intimacy with Bathsheba.

Without the introduction, the anonymous psalm is a prayer of contrition for an unspecified transgression against God. It proclaims the psalmist's trust in divine forgiveness (see verses 17–19).

The introduction, however, does three things. First, it provides a notation guiding the use of the psalm in communal worship ("For the Leader"). This is functionally similar to the phrase "stage left" in the printed script of a play. It's an instruction about how to perform the work, but it is not part of the performance. The second part of the introduction identifies the anonymous author as King David. That is, this element explains the authority of the poem—it goes back to the great king of Israel. Most important, for our purpose, is the third part, which relates the creation of the psalm to an event in David's life.

That event would be familiar to anyone who knew the history of David's early reign as described in the scriptural book of Samuel. Found in the canon of *Nevi'im* between the books of Judges and Kings, Samuel describes the events leading up to the coronation of David as king and the history of his reign. In its canonical form it is divided into two scrolls, I and II Samuel. II Samuel 12 recounts how Nathan, a court prophet of David, disclosed to the king his knowledge of a grotesque amorous plot.

The plot involved David's own scheme to possess a married woman named Bathsheba. The king had one day observed Bathsheba from his window bathing on the roof of a nearby house. Obsessed with her beauty, David had arranged for Bathsheba's husband, a soldier named Uriah, to be placed in the front line of battle. Upon Uriah's death, David married Bathsheba, who bore him a son. As the story is told in II Samuel, David received a curse from Nathan for this behavior, which resulted in the death of the child born to Bathsheba. David is pictured as fasting and petitioning God all night long to avert the curse.

This is the background assumed by the introduction to Psalm 51. In light of II Samuel 12, the scribal commentator who introduced the psalm wants his readers to know two things. First, David's petition during that terrible night included more than a prayer to spare his son. It included as well a petition for forgiveness. More importantly, this psalm is that very prayer.

The interpretive achievement of the few words of this introduction is remarkable. First of all, they have enriched an appreciation of II Samuel's picture of David. By reading the psalm into the story of II Samuel, we appreciate the depths of David's remorse for what he now recognizes as a horrible sin. So, by commenting on Psalm 51, the scribe has also commented on a story that he supposed would be in the minds of his audience.

The introduction also enables the psalm to have yet more profound significance. It can no longer be interpreted as an anonymous hymn. Rather, it now expresses a national hero's utterance of trust in the midst of profound emotional turmoil. The implication is that the reader can express his or her own response to similar life crises in the inspired words of David. Scripture is not only a record of past events, but a text that can be incorporated into life in its most intimate settings.

This sort of instructional introduction occurs frequently in the book of Psalms. They were added while the psalm texts were relatively unfixed in a canonical version. Their immediate purpose, apparently, was to link the psalm texts more closely to other works already regarded as scripture. But they also enhanced the power of the psalms to address the inner life of their audiences. As the psalm texts were received as canonically fixed writings, the interpretive introductions became part of scripture itself. Words that began their life as a commentary on scripture became, in the end, scripture.[9]

Interpretation Beyond the Scriptural Canon

The canonical "photograph" of the Hebrew Bible's scriptures, obviously, masks a good deal of interpretive motion in ancient Judaism's literary tradition. That motion is even livelier beyond the borders of the received canon.

Historians have long known of early Judaic writings that revise, retell, or otherwise offer interpretive renderings of passages now preserved in the Bible. Translations of some of these works into languages such as Amharic, Armenian, and Slavonic were for centuries preserved in ancient Christian monastic libraries, where they were revised in line with Christian ideas and treasured as prophetic testimonies to Christian belief. Others, preserved in Greek or Latin translations, were accorded a kind of quasi-scriptural status as "apocrypha" in the Old Testament canons of various Christian communities. The existence of yet others was entirely unsuspected until they were discovered, over several years beginning in 1947, in pottery jars secreted in caves in the Dead Sea wasteland of Qumran.

Each of these texts exhibits its own complex relationship to the scriptural works of the *Tanakh*'s canon. Some are clearly dependent upon scriptural writings in nearly their present form. In not a few cases, however, it is difficult to be sure exactly how the composer or readers of the work understood its relationship to other writings presently part of the canon. These are the occasions that make life interesting for students of early Judaism. They allow us to see how writings, ignored by rabbinic Judaism for nearly 2000 years, once competed with the present works of scripture as authoritative expressions of the religious worlds of those who produced and preserved them.

Let's look at one such work, usually entitled the book of Jubilees.[10] It presents itself as a record of what really happened when Moses spent forty days with God on Mount Sinai. The book was probably composed in Hebrew in the middle of the second century BCE, during the early Hasmonean dynasty. Until the twentieth century, the only copies to survive the Roman destruction of Jewish Palestine were monastery translations in ancient Christian languages. But other Hebrew copies were recently found among the Dead Sea Scrolls. So before us is a work that apparently enjoyed rather wide ancient circulation among Palestinian Jews.

Jubilees' anonymous compiler lived some three centuries after the Torah of Moses had become the central scriptural text of Yehud. For at least a century, that Torah in Greek translation had dominated the scriptural canon of Diaspora Jews. Against this background, Jubilees must make us wonder: if its compilers and audience regarded the Torah of Moses as an authoritative text recording authentic Mosaic teaching, how did they square it with the picture of Mosaic teachings offered in Jubilees? And more curious still, if they regarded the picture offered in Jubilees as authoritative, how did they understand the authority of the canonical Torah of Moses?[11]

Jubilees' distinctiveness can be appreciated only by first glancing at the Torah of Moses. There the actual revelation of God's covenantal law at Sinai to Moses and Israel occurs in Exodus 19–24. The Ten Commandments are pronounced in Exodus 20. Then Exodus 21–24 presents a large compendium of rules and regulations for the conduct of society and the maintenance of proper relations with God. Finally, at the end of chapter 24, a thick cloud encasing the presence of God appears "as a consuming fire on the top of the mountain. Moses went inside the cloud and ascended the mountain; and Moses remained on the mountain forty days and forty nights" (Exod 24:17–18). There he received the actual stone tablets of the covenant as well as explicit instructions on how to build a movable sacrificial tabernacle (Exodus 25–31). The tabernacle, also called the Tent of Meeting, is subsequently constructed (Exodus 34–40) and, according to the books of Leviticus and Numbers, serves as the site for further revelations of God to Moses and his priestly assistant, Aaron.

The composer of Jubilees depends upon the reader's knowledge of this scenario. But his independent point of view is forecast in the extended title that heads most copies of the text:

> This is the account of the division of days of the Torah and the testimony for annual observance according to their weeks of years and their Jubilees throughout all the years of the world just as the LORD told it to Moses on Mount Sinai when he went up to receive the tablets of the Torah and the commandment by the word of the LORD, as he said to him (in Exod 24:12), "Come up to the top of the mountain."

This heading's reference to "the division of days...for annual observance" signals the book's overall purpose. This is to establish a calendar for regulating the schedule of scripturally mandated festivals. In contrast to the Hasmonean and later rabbinic linkage of the lunar and solar years, the calendar of Jubilees links all temple observances to a solar, rather than a lunar, calendar. In this scheme, each year has exactly 364 days and is divisible exactly into fifty two weeks of seven days. Each of the year's twelve months has exactly thirty days and each New Year begins on a Wednesday. The four remaining days belong to no month at all. They serve as seasonal markers, dividing summer from fall and winter from spring. This regularity ensures that every festival will fall on exactly the same day of the week each year rather than wandering unpredictably from one year to the next.

Jubilee's interest in organizing the solar year in terms of multiples of seven has implications beyond the creation of a regular festival cycle. As the book unfolds, it becomes clear that the composer views all history as a series of fifty immensely long epochs (Jubilees), each composed of seven weeks of seven lengthy years. Against this chronological system he plots all the events of history from Creation until Israel's entry into the Land of Israel. He then links all the sacred seasons of the temple calendar to events that occurred in that historically crucial period of wilderness wandering.

The mysterious language of "weeks of years" and "jubilees" is part of the computational system he uses to determine the dates upon which those observances were established in the past. In such a meticulous work of historical scholarship, we should not be surprised that the book of Jubilees itself consists of 50 chapters. Why all this is so important to Jubilees will become clear momentarily.

The actual giving of the Torah to Moses, which Jubilees describes in detail, occurs nine years ("one week and two years") into the fiftieth and final jubilee (Jub 50:4). So presumably the composer of the work believed himself to be standing at some crucial turning of world history, the end of the fiftieth and final jubilee. But that matter need not concern us here, for he does not dwell upon it himself. The point for us is what the composer of Jubilees does with the Torah of Moses.

First, as we have seen, he constructs a solar calendrical system (unmentioned in the Torah) that mathematically rationalizes the Torah's festival calendar. Secondly, he situates the Torah's rather simple historical chronology within a vastly expanded temporal framework of eons. Most importantly, in order to fit the Torah's contents into his historical system, he offers his own conception of the origins of the Torah's various festival laws. Many of the sacrificial and festival laws in the canonical Torah are recorded in the book of Leviticus (e.g., Lev 23:1–44). There the context of the revelation to Moses and Aaron is the Tent of Meeting—outside the explicit framework of the revelation at Sinai. In Jubilees, to the contrary, they are all revealed to Moses during his forty days on the mountain. In sum, Jubilees represents a view of the history of revelation that revises the sequence chosen in the Torah of Moses.

And that's not all. Jubilees makes no effort to downplay its revisions of the canonical Torah's historical record. Rather, it challenges any possibility of viewing the canonical Torah of Moses as a complete and authoritative record of revelation. According to the composer of Jubilees, there was a witness on Sinai who saw what actually transpired between God and Moses. This witness, a mysterious figure called "the Angel of the Presence," is also a participant in the revelation. In fact, he appears to be the narrator of most of the book of Jubilees from the second chapter on.

Commissioned by God to "write for Moses from the first creation until my sanctuary is built in their midst forever and ever," (Jub 1:28), the angel does so. Here is how Jubilees describes the beginning of the angel's commission:

> And the Angel of the Presence, who went before the camp of Israel, took the tablets of the division of years from the time of creation of the Torah and the testimony according to their weeks of years, according to the jubilees, year by year throughout the full number of jubilees, …until the sanctuary of the LORD is created in Jerusalem upon Mount Zion…And the

Angel of the Presence spoke to Moses by the word of the LORD, saying, "Write the whole account of creation, that in six days the LORD God completed all his work and all that he created. And he observed a Sabbath the seventh day, and he sanctified it for all ages. And he set it as a sign for all his works.

For on the first day he created the heavens, which are above, and the earth, and the waters and all the spirits that minister before him: The angels of the presence, and the angels of sanctification, and the angels of fire, and the angels of the spirit of the winds, and the angels of the spirit of the clouds and darkness and snow and hail and frost, and the angels of resoundings and thunder and lightening, and the angels of the spirits of cold and heat and winter and springtime and harvest and summer, and all the spirits of his creatures that are in heaven and on earth... (Jub 1:29–2:2)

It seems that the angel is reading to Moses from the "tablets" originally written by God. If so, Moses writes in his own hand what God wrote in his, mediated through the recitation of the angel. In any event, the Angel of the Presence narrates and Moses records in writing, a rather different Torah from the one that circulated among most Jews as the canonical text of Mosaic teaching. The book of Jubilees is presented as the record of that Torah, the authentic one, to which angelic presence provides final testimony.

Let's consider what kind of statement Jubilees represents at the time of its composition, early in the Hasmonean period. Its main preoccupation is with structuring the sacrificial rites of the Jerusalem temple so that the dates of all holidays fall in a regular sequence. Jubilees's advocacy of this ritual calendar seems to be a direct response to the Hasmonean priests' use of a system of leap years to solve the Torah's calendrical puzzle. We must assume, therefore, that those who composed Jubilees or regarded it as persuasive were critical of the Hasmonean regime. Jubilees expresses that criticism through its account of revelation. Instead of confronting the Hasmonean regime explicitly, it undermines its religious legitimacy by presenting a new account of how Moses received the Torah and an alternate version of what that Torah contained. If Jubilees is an account of the revelation to Moses, then the interpretation of the Torah of Moses housed in the Hasmonean temple is not.

We would, of course, love to be able to interview the composer or sympathetic readers of Jubilees to find out exactly how they understood the relation of this work to the Torah of Moses known to the Hasmoneans and others throughout the ancient Jewish world. Perhaps they would have said that Jubilees was an authoritative explanation of the Torah of Moses, verified by the angelic transmitter. So the mandate of the Torah of Moses could be best followed in accord with the instructions provided in Jubilees. Perhaps they would have gone further, claiming that Jubilees was the true Torah. But we can't interview them. And their conversations with their contemporaries about the matter are essentially lost. We know only that the proponents of Jubilees did not prevail in that conversation.

Jubilees failed to displace the Torah of Moses. The rabbinic canon, indeed, made no room for it. While certain of its perspectives did indeed survive in later expressions of Jewish scriptural interpretation, the book as a whole disappeared from Jewish tradition. Perhaps the community that claimed Jubilees as Torah was suppressed by the Hasmoneans and marginalized in the Palestinian community. The presence of Hebrew copies among the Dead Sea Scrolls may suggest as much, since (as we shall see in Chapter Four) the community at Qumran appears to have rejected the Hasmonean regime as corrupt. It also seems to have accepted a calendar much like that of Jubilees. Perhaps, then, in the religious world of Qumran, Jubilees was read as an amplification of the Torah of Moses and an authoritative statement of how its calendrical system should be applied.

But all explanations at this historical distance are speculative at best. The point for us is that in Jubilees we see the remarkable motion behind the picture-perfect canonical surface of the received biblical canon. Jubilees opens up to us a Judaic world that existed in close contact with the emerging scriptures of Judaism, competed with other visions of Judaism for primacy, but ultimately was not to survive. Ultimately, the arbiter of what could and could not survive as a Judaic world was the shifting character of Judaic interpretive tradition itself.[13] And this brings us, at last, to the rabbis.

The Sources of Rabbinic Tradition

As you'll recall from Chapter One, scholars with the title of "rabbi" played in important organizational role in Palestinian Jewry's recovery from the catastrophic consequences of Bar Kosiba's uprising in 132–135. Within a generation after 135 the program of the sages was being vigorously pursued by the Patriarch Rabban Shimon ben Gamaliel with the help of a growing body of disciples. We have already noted that, by the late second or early third century, the Mishnah, the rabbinic movement's principal compilation of legal and religious tradition, had become the platform of Palestinian Jewish autonomy under the Patriarch Rabbi Judah.

One of the most perplexing historical questions of the post–70 period concerns the origins of a group that, eventually, came to represent itself as the authoritative expression of everything that Judaism would call Torah.

Where were the rabbis before the war against Rome and what, in the centuries following, brought this group to its eventual prominence?

The Pharisees

It is not easy from our present standpoint to identify the social origins of these rabbis. But there are clues. For example, rabbinic texts from the third and fourth centuries CE record the names of Shemaiah, Avtalion, and an early–first-century Gamaliel as transmitters of teachings during the time of the second temple. Greek forms of two of these names—Samaias and Polion—are mentioned in the writings of the late–first-century Jewish historian Flavius Josephus. A teacher named Gamaliel, likewise, appears in the late–first-century Christian work, the Acts of the Apostles, now part of the New Testament canon. Samais, Polion, and Gamaliel are all identified with a group known in Greek as the *pharisaioi*, Pharisees. Later rabbinic sources refer to this group as *perushim*, a Hebrew word that might mean "separatists" or "ascetics."[14]

By all accounts, these Pharisees were rather important participants in the political and religious life of Jerusalem prior to the destruction of the temple. Although rabbinic Judaism cannot be equated with the Judaism of the Pharisees, it is likely that at least some Pharisees were instrumental in the formation of the Judaic world transmitted within the later communities of rabbinic sages. This is, at least, the perspective of many passages of rabbinic literature. As we shall see, the earliest examples of rabbinic historical writing make a point of linking rabbinic traditions to the Pharisees and scribes who lived while the temple still stood.

Just who the Pharisees were is not an easy question to answer. They have left no writings of their own, so there is no first-hand evidence from which to imagine the details of their religious world. We are entirely dependent upon what ancient writers, nearly all of whom wrote well after the heyday of the Pharisees, chose to record about them. Readers of the Christian Gospels encounter the Pharisees as religious hypocrites who challenged Jesus' authority and who may have had a hand in his crucifixion. Fanatically loyal to what the Gospel of Mark calls "traditions of the elders" (e.g., Mark 7:1ff.), the Pharisees are said to have been more concerned with having clean hands and tithed food than with true love of God and humanity.

Other first century CE writings, particularly those of Josephus, portray the Pharisees as a popular political party concerned with fostering deep loyalty to the Torah among the masses as well as to teaching certain ancestral traditions not included in the Torah itself. Whether the Pharisees were hypocrites, as the Gospels claim, or religious democrats, as Josephus holds, is not for us to determine, for we have no other evidence than these partisan depictions. But what does seem certain—because it is the only thing upon which our otherwise irreconcilable sources agree—is that the Pharisees placed a great premium on something called "ancestral tradition."

Even though such tradition was not written in the Mosaic Torah, it does seem to have governed pharisaic understandings of how to live in light of the Torah's requirements. We know very little of what this pharisaic interpretive tradition might have contained. All we have is the testimony of later rabbinic Judaism, which claimed the teachings of at least some Pharisees as its own. In the rabbinic versions of these teachings, however, the term "tradition" is not particularly prominent. Instead, the term "Torah" appears repeatedly as something far richer than the physical scroll of Mosaic writings; richer even than the entire collection of scripture itself. In the Judaism of rabbinic sages, Torah comes to stand for the entire body of Jewish religious tradition, both what is written in the Torah of Moses as well as the interpretations needed to embody it in life.

Pharisaic Tradition and Rabbinic Torah

History has not preserved any first-hand writings from pharisaic sources. Therefore, any attempt to draw lines of continuity between the pharisaic "ancestral tradition" and the sense that "Torah" conveys in the later rabbinic world must be speculative. That said, let us attempt one disciplined speculation.

The Gospels' Pharisees, you'll recall, are accused of always washing their hands and tithing their food. Jesus is said to have complained that the food they put into their mouths was more important to them than the words that came out of them (Mark 7:14–15; Matt 15:10–11, 23:23–29). Josephus, our other main source of information about Pharisees, doesn't mention this aspect of their tradition. But early rabbinic literature is also deeply concerned with laws governing the purity of foods and their proper tithing. It devotes as well much attention to the conduct of the meals in which food is eaten and drink consumed. Perhaps this common interest in rituals surrounding food can help us think about the connection between pharisaic "ancestral tradition" and rabbinic "Torah."

The Gospels have little interest in generous interpretations of the Pharisees' dietary compulsions. Rabbinic literature, by contrast, develops a rather full theory of what is at stake in such dietary laws. The purity of food, its proper tithing, and the specific decorum of the meal itself were believed to contribute to a most remarkable transformation of the dining table.

Under the appropriate circumstances, common food properly preserved in purity could serve as a vehicle for invoking a sanctifying divine presence upon the dinner tables of the sages' families. In early rabbinic tradition, in other words, the rituals of the meal penetrated the otherwise firm barrier between the world of ordinary experience and the world of Heaven. Eating a meal was a religious activity.

This was especially so at holy occasions. The Torah of Moses, for example, enjoins Jews to "sanctify" the Sabbath. It offers, however, few explicit instructions on how such sanctification is to be achieved. The Mishnah, for its part, assumes this is done by taking a meal. It records a series of disputes— transmitted by the followers of two early–first-century Pharisees named Hillel and Shammai—regarding precisely how to sanctify the Sabbath at the Friday evening meal that inaugurates the holy day. It is done by uttering a blessing called the *kiddush* ("sanctification").

The followers of Shammai and Hillel, as the Mishnah represents them, agreed upon many things concerning the *qiddush*. For one, the wine must be produced in purity and properly tithed before it is suitable for the meal. This common agreement, sets the stage for their disagreements. They dispute, for example, whether the person making the blessing must cleanse the hands before or after mixing the wine in the cup. At issue is whether unwashed hands might convey uncleanness to the cup, thus invalidating the wine. Another dispute concerns whether a benediction is recited first in honor of the Sabbath day and then over the cup of wine drunk at the dinner, or vice versa.[15]

The disputes of the Shammaites and Hillelites regarding mealtime rituals provided generations of rabbinic disciples with food for thought. For our purposes, the interesting thing is not the theory behind each opinion, but the remarkable assumption shared by both parties. Each assumes that the Sabbath must be sanctified with blessings at a Friday night meal that includes wine. You will look in vain throughout the Torah of Moses for any such requirement. But it is assumed as a firm and noncontroversial fulfillment of a divine commandment to sanctify the Sabbath. The conflict concerns only the details of the procedure.

This dispute about the conduct of the Sabbath meal, and many similar disputes on related matters, may serve as a link between pharisaic notions of tradition and what later rabbinic sages understood as Torah. To complete our speculative experiment we offer the following proposal. Pharisaic tradition and rabbinic Torah share, at the very least, an interest in ritual actions. Some of these rituals, like the specific procedures for inaugurating the Sabbath, probably entered rabbinic Torah via the route of earlier pharisaic tradition. Others represent rabbinic developments beyond explicitly pharisaic origins.

It is highly unlikely that all aspects of rabbinic ritual life originate in pharisaic traditions. In most cases, at any rate, the lines of connection are too blurred to trace. Common to both Pharisaism and rabbinic Judaism, however, is an attitude toward the nature of these ritual actions. Even though they may not be explicitly stated in the Torah of Moses, they are conceived as the fulfillment of the divine will. The Gospels, clearly enough, regard this as an absurdity and mock it as a sign of pharisaic hypocrisy. But it is certainly central to the rabbinic movement after the destruction of the temple.

During the same post–70 decades in which the Gospel traditions were forming the image of the early–first-century Pharisees, the founders of the rabbinic movement were attempting to redefine the ritual life of Judaism. Rabban Yohanan ben Zakkai, a witness to the destruction of the temple, is singled out in rabbinic writings as the originator of a number of ritual innovations. These made it possible to perform in the home or in public prayer services, ritual acts once central to the services of the temple. It was also in the post-temple period that rabbinic traditions recorded a burgeoning interest in structuring prayer services that could serve as a replacement for the suspended temple sacrificial offerings.

Neither of these matters—performance of temple rites in homes or the recitation of prayers instead of sacrifices—has any clear foundation in the Torah of Moses. For the Torah, the service of God was what Aaron and his priestly descendants did at the altar (e.g., Exod 29:1–46) or what ordinary Israelites did by preserving the memories of God's redemptive acts (e.g., Deut 6:1–25). But in rabbinic communities a host of ritual practices was developed and accepted as received tradition, part of what it meant to live in continual conversation with the covenantal obligations imposed by the Torah.

If God required absolute obedience, and if the destruction of the temple made many of his commandments impossible to fulfill, then it was only through traditions preserved outside the textual confines of scripture that Jews could begin to reconstruct their covenantal relationship with the god of Abraham, Isaac, and Jacob. It is in this sense that "tradition" and "Torah" become inseparably bound up with each other.

The Rabbinic Written and Oral Torah

The question, of course, is *whose* tradition? We have learned—and ancient rabbinic sages surely knew—that various traditions of interpretation and practice had for centuries shaped Jews' understanding of the Torah of Moses. Rabbinic sages would have had no perception of the book of Jubilees as tradition despite its antiquity, for they rejected its schedule of holidays.

An important rabbinic attempt to define a legitimate family tree of tradition is recorded in a third-century CE rabbinic work, the title of which is probably best translated as "The Founders" (*avot*). It begins with the following assertion:

> Moses received Torah on Sinai, and passed it on to Joshua, Joshua to elders, and elders to prophets. And prophets handed it on to the men of the great assembly. They said three things: (1) Be prudent in judgment. (2) Raise up many disciples. (3) Make a fence around the Torah.

This passage continues with a lengthy list of later sages, living well after the return from Babylonian exile, each of whom receives "Torah" from his predecessor and passes it on to disciples. This list of teachers, which includes pharisaic figures as well as rabbinic sages known to have lived as late as the early third century CE, makes two intertwined claims. First, the tradition passed on as Torah by the rabbis begins with Moses and remains intact for well over a thousand years. Second, tradition is Torah *only* if it is transmitted by a rabbinic sage. So much for Jubilees and a host of other texts deemed by sages to fall beyond the framework of Torah.[16]

This list makes an extraordinary claim for the continuity of Mosaic teaching through the sages. But even more interesting is the way in which Torah, received by Moses and passed on to his disciples, is distinguished from *the* Torah of Moses, the actual document recording the Mosaic legislation. One builds a fence around the *textual* Torah of Moses with the *interpretive tradition* of Torah preserved by the rabbis. Indeed, in rabbinic perspective it is precisely tradition that constitutes the "fence around the Torah" (Avot 3:13).

As *Avot* views things, traditional Torah passed on in rabbinic teaching constitutes a systematic safeguard against the violation of the scriptural Torah of Moses. Rabbinic Torah, as ancient tradition, enables Jews to properly embody laws, values, and norms of the scriptural Torah in their own pattern of life, even where these have no apparent warrant in Moses' book. That tradition, transmitted in rabbinic teaching and practice, is nothing less than Torah itself. It embodies in public and private life what God wanted for Israel when he revealed its basic outline, the Torah of Moses, to the entire community on Sinai. Thus, according to rabbinic Judaism, *rabbinic tradition and scripture together constitute Torah*; indeed, each requires and presupposes the existence of the other.

Mishnah Avot's Chain of Transmission Linking
Mishnaic-Rabbinic Tradition to Sinai

The Prophetic Chain of Transmission:

Moses ↳ Joshua ↳ the Elders ↳ the Prophets

This chain carries the tradition of Torah through the period from Moses to the destruction of the First Temple (587 BCE).

Transmitters of the Early Second Temple Period:

Men of the Great Assembly
  ↳Shimon the Righteous
    ↳Antigonus of Sokho

This chain carries the tradition of Torah from roughly the time of Ezra (450–400 BCE) to the early second century BCE. The Men of the Great Assembly and Antigonus of Sokho are known only from rabbinic texts.

The Age of the Pairs (Late Second Temple Period):

Yose b. Yoezer and Yose b. Yohanan of Jerusalem
  ↳Joshua b. Perakhyah and Nittai the Arbelite
    ↳Judah b. Tabbai and Shimon b. Shetakh
      ↳Shemaiah and Avtalion
        ↳Hillel and Shammai

Rabbinic tradition views the "Pairs" as holding the offices of patriarch and Supreme Court justice respectively throughout the Hasmonean and early Roman Period in the Land of Israel (150–10). They are known primarily from rabbinic texts.

The Age of the Mishnaic Sages (Late Second Temple–Post Temple):

Rabban Gamaliel I
  ↳Rabban Yohanan b. Zakkai
    ↳Rabban Shimon b. Gamaliel I
      ↳Rabban Gamaliel II
        ↳Rabban Shimon b. Gamaliel II
          ↳Rabbi Judah b. Shimon b. Gamaliel

The title "Rabban" (Our Master) is a form of "Rabbi" (My Master) and appears first with these figures. All but Rabban Yohanan b. Zakkai are recalled in rabbinic tradition as having served as patriarch. Rabban Yohanan is recalled as reconstituting the study of Torah in a coastal town called Yavneh after the destruction of the temple in 70 CE.

This perception of the inseparability of rabbinic tradition and the Mosaic scripture is expressed in rabbinic writings of the fourth and fifth centuries in a remarkably apt image. These writings, which we shall shortly discuss more extensively, speak from time to time of two Torahs having been revealed on Sinai. One of these, called the Written Torah, is the actual scroll of Mosaic teachings preserved as scripture and read in the synagogues. The written Torah includes as its written extension and amplification the entire canon of the Hebrew Bible as the rabbis defined it. The second, called the Oral Torah, is claimed to have been transmitted to Moses by word of mouth alone and memorized. This orally preserved Torah has accompanied the Written Torah since the very beginning and, indeed, constitutes the authentic interpretation of the Written Torah's many commandments. Most important of all, the only way this Oral Torah can be learned is by long and diligent discipleship to a rabbinic sage, who has committed the entire Torah, Written and Oral, to memory.

It is small exaggeration to say that the crucial human relationship of early rabbinic Judaism was between the sage and his disciple. The disciple, a kind of apprentice rabbi, served his master as a butler and companion, much like his non-Jewish contemporary in the Hellenistic world might serve a philosophical teacher. In return, the disciple had the opportunity to study the sage's every word and gesture as an exemplification of what it means to fully embody Torah. The essence of the sage's teaching was his words of Torah and the way his behavior embodied Torah.

Rabbinic tradition, then, worked in two ways. As a pattern of behavior learned by imitation, it was tradition transmitted simply by example. As an intellectual tradition, it was learned by studying and mastering the rabbi's oral teachings. To the degree that many sages argued that their patterns of behavior were themselves based upon interpretation of the Torah of Moses, these two types of tradition were often fused into one and seen as continuous with the Mosaic revelation. It is for this reason that the actual literature of rabbinic Judaism, when it came to be composed into written texts, consisted almost entirely of words of Torah ascribed to specific rabbis and depictions of how these words were exemplified by their deeds.[17]

The Literature of the Oral Torah

Sages routinely referred to the content of their traditional learning by the words *mishnah* (Hebrew) or *matnyta* (Aramaic). The best rendering of either term is "Repeated Tradition." By the early third century there seems to have circulated a rather large Hebrew compilation of such repeated tradition. It was associated with the editorial work of the Patriarch Rabbi Judah.[18]

Scholars still debate the degree to which this "Mishnah of Rabbi" existed in a written form. There is no doubt, however, that it was commonly memorized by rabbinic disciples, and that much of their training was bound up in oral discourse about the interpretation of this text. This is what was "oral" about Oral Torah—it was performed in the course of its interpretation. Something very much like this early Mishnah is, at any rate, preserved in the copies of the Mishnah found in rabbinic manuscripts from the Middle Ages and onward into the printed books of the modern world.

The work called *Avot*, from which we quoted a while ago, is included in the Mishnah, along with over sixty other treatises on various aspects of Jewish law. Each treatise, in whole or part, is devoted to a specific legal topic and presents diverse rabbinic discussions about how to best implement the divine commandments contained in the Torah of Moses regarding that topic. The basic assumptions governing the compilation of the Mishnah are clear: God spoke once in the Torah of Moses and revealed his commandments; he continues to speak through the traditional Torah of the rabbis, which explains how to perform his commandments. These rabbinic explanations are called *halakhah* or "procedure," that is, procedure for implementing the commandments. To follow the rabbis' halakhic procedures is to do God's will as transmitted to Moses on Sinai.

The interpretive tradition of Oral Torah did not stop with the Mishnah, but continued to grow in subsequent centuries as the Mishnah spawned later schools of technical interpretation. One important method of halakhic research was to identify and explicate those passages of the Written Torah that served as the basis for the specific procedures of Oral Torah. But the interests of rabbinic students of the Written and Oral Torah ranged far beyond strictly halakhic matters, and soon included extended reflection upon other concerns central to the interpretation of the Bible—ethical issues, historical recollections, and theological speculation. These fell under the category *aggadah*, "teachings" designed to foster a desire to serve God in obedience to the rules of *halakhah*.

Eventually, these two types of interpretive tradition were gathered together into immense, encyclopedic compilations of rabbinic teaching,

Terminology and Chronology of Rabbinic Literature

In rabbinic literature it is convenient to distinguish among types of tradition in which knowledge was transmitted, forms of their transmission prior to their editing into finished compilations, and, finally, the works into which these traditions are compiled.

Types of Tradition

1. *Halakhah*: tradition about legal or ritual practice.
2. *Aggadah*: tradition about history or theology.

Forms of Transmission

1. *Midrash*: halakhic or aggadic tradition transmitted as an explanation of a biblical verse.
2. *Mishnah*: halakhic or aggadic tradition transmitted without reference to a biblical verse.
3. *Talmud*: analysis of a halakhic tradition.

Major Compilations of Rabbinic Tradition

1. *Mishnah*: The halakhic collection supervised by Rabbi Judah the Patriarch in the Galilean city Sepphoris, ca. 200–225.
2. *Tosefta*: A halakhic collection similar to, but larger than, the Mishnah, edited anonymously by 300 CE in Palestine. Tosefta means "supplement," that is, to the Mishnah.
3. *Mekhilta of Rabbi Ishmael*: A third- to fourth-century Palestinian midrashic compilation in which the legal portions of the book of Exodus are provided with both halakhic and aggadic comment. All rabbinic authorities mentioned in this compilation are from the first to early third centuries.
4. *Sifra*: An almost exclusively halakhic midrash on Leviticus. It is probably from third- to fourth-century Palestine. All rabbinic authorities mentioned are from the first to early-third centuries.
5. *Sifre*: A pair of midrashic works on Numbers and Deuteronomy, mixing both halakhic and aggadic types of tradition. Most authorities are identical to those of Sifra and Mekhilta.
6. *Bereshit Rabba*: An enormous compilation of aggadic traditions that comment on every verse of Genesis. It is rich in traditions in the names of third- and fourth-century sages, and was probably edited in Palestine by the fifth century.
7. *Vayiqra Rabba*: This aggadic midrash focuses on Leviticus, using the first verses of the scriptural chapters as occasions for long homiletic discourses. Like Bereshit Rabba, it is probably from fifth-century Palestine.

8. *Talmud Yerushalmi*: The "Palestinian Talmud," a mostly halakhic commentary on the Mishnah (Palestine, ca. 375).
9. *Talmud Bavli*: The "Babylonian Talmud," compiling halakhic and aggadic materials into an encyclopedic commentary on the Mishnah (Mesopotamia, ca. 525).

talmud (Aramaic: "learning"). The most famous and important of these compilations are called the Talmud of the Land of Israel (edited ca. 375) and the Talmud of Babylonia (ca. 525). Both Talmuds are designed as Mishnah commentaries, offering line by line explorations of the Mishnah's halakhic applications and implications. Routinely, however, the Talmud's discussions include as well vast amounts of aggadic commentary on the Hebrew Bible. The Babylonian Talmud remains today the most revered classic of rabbinic teaching among observant Jews.

Other rabbinic teachings, on biblical interpretation in particular, were gathered together from the third to the seventh centuries in yet other large collections of lore called *midrash*, "interpretation" or "commentary." Unlike the Talmud, which is organized as a Mishnah commentary, works of midrash are normally organized around books of the Hebrew Bible or scriptural readings assigned in the synagogue for specific holidays. Substantial collections of midrash focus upon the halakhic connections between the Written and Oral Torah. Most of the surviving midrashic compilations, however, are dominated by aggadic discourses in which verses of the Written Torah are amplified by the traditions of the sages' Oral Torah.

In all, a half millennium of rabbinic literary scholarship radically transformed the inheritance of the first 500 years of Judaic literary creativity. Midway in the first Judaic millennium, the collection of the Judaic scriptures received its final canonical stamp and the task of fixing the texts of its various books began in earnest. As a consequence, any literary works of Hellenistic Palestine and the Diaspora that might have competed for canonical inclusion were suppressed. This was the fate of Jubilees. Others, such as the Wisdom of Joshua ben Sira, enjoyed a quasi-scriptural status. It is routinely cited in rabbinic literature, but is officially excluded from the scriptural canon. Yet others, particularly if they were composed in Greek, were officially ignored. As we shall see in another context, however, theological and interpretive traditions found in them seem to have survived in rabbinic oral tradition as teachings of sages.

Halakhic inquiry, for its part, had constructed a system of religious discipline that served as a whole to replace the ancient temple's sacrificial media of atonement. Applying the textual tradition of the Written Torah to their lives through the ritual traditions of the Oral, rabbis and the Jews they influenced experienced an intimate sense of continuity between past and present, a trust that their pattern of life now conformed self-evidently to the original pattern handed by God to Moses. Suppressing or transforming other worlds of Judaism, rabbinic Judaism created a religious world that, for many centuries, would appear to be the obvious embodiment of the world of the Mosaic Torah. By the early Middle Ages, any non-rabbinic Judaic world would have to define itself in categories provided by rabbinic Judaism itself.

Conclusions

We have argued three basic points in this chapter. The first is that the main scriptural texts of Judaism—the Torah of Moses and the epic that it introduces—emerged in the Persian period as part of a larger attempt to organize the Jews of Yehud around a program of religious-political regeneration. During the centuries after the return to Yehud, all the inherited lore and law of ancient Israel was rethought and reinterpreted to produce a national history. This history was not motivated by neutral curiosity about the past. Rather, the image of the past was shaped to interpret the present. In light of the past, the current historical moment appeared as the god-sent opportunity to once and for all correct the course of Israel's history.

The development of the scriptural canon unfolded through the successive attempts of Jews to interpret that covenantal history and apply it to their own situations. This constitutes our second main point. Judaic scripture did not happen all at once. The final canon resulted from centuries of reflective activity within various Jewish communities and did not achieve final resolution until roughly 500 years or so after the Torah of Moses began to dominate Jewish life in Persian Yehud.

Finally, we have stressed that the scriptures of Judaism were never rigidly distinct from the processes of tradition that gave them life in the various worlds of Judaism. All scripture started out as tradition; some literary traditions then became scripture, while others lived on as "commentary" or died away. The rabbinic tradition of Written and Oral Torah serves as a prime example.

It was rabbinic tradition itself that created the categories of Written and Oral Torah to distinguish scripture from tradition. Yet the rabbinic marriage of Written and Oral Torah enabled the sages to portray the entire complex of rabbinic culture as stemming from the originating moment of

Sinai. The rabbinic project, in hindsight, is not unlike that of Jubilees—to restate the Torah of Moses so that a body of interpretive tradition could determine its application. The rabbis, however, were in a position to make their revision part of the public policy of powerful empires.

Notes

1. For a rich description of Israel's scribal culture, see Philip R. Davies, *Scribes and Schools: The Canonization of the Hebrew Scriptures* (Louisville, Ky.: John Knox Westminster Press, 1998), pp. 74–88.

2. The consequences of realizing that "scripture" has both a written and oral dimension have only recently been considered at length by students of religion. An excellent place to begin is with William A. Graham, *Beyond the Written Word: Oral Aspects of Scripture in the History of Religion* (Cambridge: Cambridge University Press, 1987). For excellent studies of scriptural orality and its relationship to writing in the context of the Jewish scriptural tradition, see Susan Niditch, *Oral World and Written Word: Ancient Israelite Literature* (Louisville, Ky.: Westminster John Knox Press, 1996) and William M. Schniedewind, *How the Bible Became a Book* (Cambridge: Cambridge University Press, 2004).

3. For an overall introduction to the meaning of sacred writings in the comparative study of religion, see Frederick M. Denny and Rodney L. Taylor, eds., *The Holy Book in Comparative Perspective* (Columbia, S.C.: University of South Carolina Press, 1993).

4. See, for example, Richard Elliott Friedman, *Who Wrote the Bible?* (New York: Harper & Row, 1987); James A. Sanders, *Torah and Canon* (Philadelphia: Fortress Press, 1972); R.N. Whybray, *The Making of the Pentateuch: A Methodological Study* (Sheffield: JSOT Supplement, 1987); and W. Schniedewind, *How the Bible Became a Book*. For an analysis of the views of the Copenhagen School in particular, see Marc Brettler, "The Copenhagen School: The Historiographic Issues," in *AJS Review* 27 (2003), pp. 1–22.

5. An excellent brief introductory treatment of the history of the canon of the Hebrew Bible is the essay by Roger T. Beckwith, "Formation of the Hebrew Bible," in Martin Jan Mulder, ed., *Mikra: Text, Translation, Reading and Interpretation of the Hebrew Bible in Ancient Judaism and Early Christianity* (Assen/Maastricht and Philadelphia: Van Gorcum and Fortress Press, 1988), pp. 39–86. This should be supplemented by James A. Sanders, "Canon," in David Noel Freedman, ed., *The Anchor Bible Dictionary*, Volume I (New York: Doubleday, 1992), pp. 837–852.

6. Everything you will probably ever want to know about the Septuagint can be conveniently found in Emanuel Tov, "The Septuagint," in Mulder, *Mikra*, pp. 161–188.

7. Sample translations of this literature with helpful introductions and explanations can be found in M. De Jonge, ed., *Outside the Old Testament* (Cam-

bridge: Cambridge University Press, 1985); Michael A. Knibb, *The Qumran Community* (Cambridge: Cambridge University Press, 1987); and George W.E. Nickelsburg and Michael E. Stone, eds., *Faith and Piety in Early Judaism: Texts and Documents* (Philadelphia: Fortress Press, 1983).

8. An accessible discussion of the rabbinic role in defining the canonical boundaries is that of Sid Z. Leiman, "Inspiration and Canonicity: Reflections on the Formation of the Biblical Canon," in E.P. Sanders, ed., *Jewish and Christian Self-Definition. Volume Two: Aspects of Judaism in the Greco-Roman Period* (Philadelphia: Fortress Press, 1981), pp. 56–63. Those with a knowledge of Biblical Hebrew can consult his masterpiece on the subject, *The Canonization of Hebrew Scripture: The Talmudic and Midrashic Evidence*, 2nd ed. (New Haven: The Connecticut Academy of Arts and Sciences, 1991).

9. For other examples of conversations between writings within the scriptural canon, see Michael Fishbane, *The Garments of Torah: Essays in Biblical Hermeneutics* (Bloomington, Ind.: Indiana University Press, 1989), pp. 3–18. Fishbane's enormous book on this phenomenon, *Biblical Interpretation in Ancient Israel* (Oxford: The Clarendon Press, 1985) is technical. But no one who works through it will ever again think that biblical writings came to be "just so."

10. A good edition of this text for students is in the translation of O.S. Wintermute, "Jubilees," in James H. Charlesworth, ed., *The Old Testament Pseudepigrapha*, II (Garden City, N.Y.: Doubleday & Company, 1985), pp. 52–142. Wintermute's introduction to the translation is on pages 35–51. I have adapted Wintermute's translation in the quotations below.

11. Since the appearance of the first edition of this book, much important work has been done concerning the ways in which the authority of Moses is appropriated by Second Temple scribes and authors for their own works. Jubilees is one of many examples, the most important of which is, in fact, the biblical book of Deuteronomy. See Bernard M. Levinson, *Deuteronomy and the Hermeneutics of Legal Innovation* (New York and Oxford: Oxford University Press, 1997). An important overview of the phenomenon of Mosaic authority in literary works of the Second Temple period is now available in Hindy Najman, *Seconding Sinai: The Development of Mosaic Discourse in Second Temple Judaism* (Leiden and Boston: E.J. Brill, 2003).

12. The problem of the relationship of the Jubilees calendar to those of the Zadokites, the Hasmoneans, and the sectarian community behind some of the Dead Sea scrolls, is hotly debated. My interpretation of the material depends upon the work of Sharyahu Talmon, "The Calendar of the Covenanters of the Judean Desert," in Talmon, *The World of Qumran From Within* (Jerusalem and Leiden: Magnes Press and Hebrew University Press, 1989), pp. 147–185; James VanderKam, *The Dead Sea Scrolls Today* (Grand Rapids, Mich.: Eerdmans, 1994), pp. 114–116; and Gabriel Boccaccini, *Beyond the Essene Hypothesis: The Parting of the Ways between Qumran and Enochic Judaism* (Grand Rapids, Mich.: Eerdmans, 1998), pp. 114–115.

13. There isn't space enough in this chapter to do justice to the history of Jewish

scriptural interpretation in this early period. I recommend the texts mentioned in n. 7 and the very fine overview in James L. Kugel and Rowan A. Greer, *Early Biblical Interpretation* (Philadelphia: The Westminster Press, 1986), pp. 13–106. These should be supplemented by the extraordinary collection of ancient biblical exegesis by James L. Kugel, *The Bible as It Was* (Cambridge, Mass.: Harvard University Press, 1997).

14. Because of the connection of rabbinic Judaism with earlier pharisaic traditions, discussions of rabbinic origins are often veiled ways of arguing for the truth of Christianity over Judaism or vice versa. An important attempt to see the question of the Pharisees and the rabbis with clarity was begun a generation ago by Jacob Neusner. It is presented conveniently in Jacob Neusner, *From Politics to Piety: The Emergence of Pharisaic Judaism*, 2nd ed. (New York: KTAV, 1979). For a good summary of the current thinking on pharisaic issues, see Anthony J. Saldarini, "Pharisees," *Anchor Bible Dictionary*, vol. 5, pp. 289–303. The rabbinic inheritance from the Pharisees is assessed by Jacob Neusner, *From Testament to Torah: An Introduction to Judaism in Its Formative Age* (Englewood Cliffs, N.J.: Prentice Hall Inc., 1988), pp. 15–65.

15. The discussion comprises the eighth chapter of the mishnaic tractate Berakhot ("Blessings"). You can follow it, and its later career in talmudic tradition, in Jacob Neusner, *Invitation to the Talmud: A Teaching Book*, rev. ed. (San Francisco: Harper & Row, 1984).

16. The most useful undergraduate introduction to the development of the idea of Oral Torah and the nature of its texts is Jacob Neusner, *The Oral Torah: The Sacred Books of Judaism. An Introduction* (San Francisco: Harper & Row, 1986). The exact nature of rabbinic oral literature is still debated by scholars. One view, which holds that texts of Oral Torah were transmitted for centuries without writing, is represented by the influential study of Birger Gerhardsson, *Memory and Manuscript: Oral Transmission and Written Tradition in Rabbinic Judaism and Early Christianity*, trans. Eric J. Sharpe (Lund: Gleerup; Copenhagen: Munksgaard, 1961). My own view, argued at length in *Torah in the Mouth: Writing and Oral Tradition in Palestinian Judaism, 200 BCE–400 CE* (New York: Oxford University Press, 2001), is that written and oral versions of rabbinic teaching circulated together from a very early point.

17. The most detailed portrait of the Palestinian rabbinic sages is now offered by Catherine Hezser, *The Social Structure of the Rabbinic Movement in Roman Palestine* (Tübingen: J.C.B. Mohr [Paul Siebeck], 1997). For the later Babylonian masters, see Jacob Neusner, *There We Sat Down: Talmudic Judaism in the Making* (New York: KTAV, 1978), pp. 44–128, which should be supplemented by Richard Kalmin, *The Sage in Jewish Society of Late Antiquity* (London and New York: Routledge, 1999). For a description of the role of Torah in the master-disciple relationship among the sages, see Martin S. Jaffee, "A Rabbinic Ontology of the Written and Spoken Word: On Discipleship, Transformative Knowledge, and the Living Texts of Oral Torah," in *Journal of the American Academy of Religion* 65 (1997).

18. For detailed discussions of the nature of the editing of the Mishnah and other rabbinic documents, the best introductory work is Guenter Stemberger, *Introduction to the Talmud and Midrash*, 2nd edition, trans. Marcus Bockmuehl (Edinburgh: T & T Clark, 1995), pp. 35–49. This is the best authoritative work for scholarly opinion about the history and literary characteristics of all genres of rabbinic literature.

CHAPTER 3

Symbolic Vocabularies and Cosmic Structures

RELIGIOUS WORLDS posit various orders of reality and help individuals and groups to negotiate their relations with those orders. This is true for the worlds of early Judaism as well. All of them were grounded in more or less explicit conceptions of the cosmic order. They articulated these conceptions in terms of a clear vocabulary of core symbolic ideas. We shall discuss what we mean by "symbolic vocabularies" momentarily. For now we point out that, even though Judaic conceptions of the world's order were hardly uniform throughout our period, the symbolic vocabulary used to articulate these conceptions migrated with remarkable regularity throughout the entire millennium.

The present chapter traces that migration. It explores the ways in which a limited repertoire of symbols and ideas were incorporated into comprehensive Judaic conceptions of reality. First, we must isolate the surprisingly small cluster of such symbols or ideas. We can then better appreciate how Jews used them to think about and organize the various kinds of knowledge they had of the world. This knowledge was often congruent with what surrounding non-Jewish populations knew about reality. What made the Jews' worlds Judaic was the distinctive symbolic vocabulary through which their own knowledge was expressed.

The Judaic Symbolic Vocabulary

We begin with the common word "symbol." For the present purpose, a symbol is a word or an object around which multiple meanings seem to gather, like filings around a magnet. Just as magnetic fields are visible only in terms of the patterns made by the filings, the meanings of symbols are intelligible only in terms of the way humans actually use them. In general, religious symbols are words or objects that serve as highly compressed expressions of entire conceptions of reality.[1]

Think of the symbol of a cross (+). It has meanings that can be rather circumscribed. In a mathematical context it indicates a certain way of combining numbers. To those who read the Latin alphabet it represents the letter "t," and thus stands for a certain sound. But take the cross and enlarge it to the height of six feet or so; place the enlargement on the narrow wall of a rectangular building. It will be hard not to "read" the symbol as standing for the Savior revered by Christianity.

In its new context the cross is the Cross; it addresses the most comprehensive conceptions of the world that Christians may entertain. Among different Christian worlds, moreover, there are real differences about what that shared symbol means. All these different meanings—even though they may be in conflict—are the "real" meanings of the symbol. As historians of religion, our job is not to determine which Christians are using the symbol "correctly." This is for Christian theologians to determine. Rather, we try to understand the symbolic meanings in each Christian setting.

This begins our exercise in interpreting symbolic meanings. We shall explore the crucial symbols through which Judaic worlds have expressed their most comprehensive understandings of reality. We can focus upon five fundamental symbolic ideas. All of them, in varying degrees, figure prominently in early Judaic conceptions of the world. In their simplest forms these ideas are: the God of Israel, Torah, the People Israel, Exile, and Messiah.

Since more than one symbol seems always to figure in Judaic conceptions of reality, we can think of them together as constituting a kind of vocabulary. They are a small repertoire of symbolic terms through which Jews conventionally expressed their various conceptions of the world. This basic vocabulary of symbols made its first appearance clustered together in the writings of Persian Yehud, playing an important role in the canonical narrative that structures the Hebrew Bible. It remained central as well throughout the ancient Jewish literature that competed with the scriptures for the attention of Diaspora and Palestinian Jews.[2]

God-Torah-Israel.

The story at the heart of the Hebrew Bible concerns a single and sovereign god, the Creator of Heaven and Earth, who called into being a special people, Israel, to build for him a dwelling place in the world that he created. The means of communication between God and Israel was, of course, Torah, the divine instruction. It was disclosed in stages: first to Abraham, then to Moses and Israel on Mt. Sinai. During the years of desert wandering, it was heard in the Tent of Meeting. Later, it sounded forth from the temple in Jerusalem, God's dwelling place, to priests and prophets. Israel's compliance with the teachings of Torah sealed the covenantal relation of God and his people. In the name of that relationship, Israel called upon God for protection and sustenance as it tried to create, in the Land of Israel, the kind of social order desired by God.

The triad of God-Torah-Israel is a fundamental assumption of any ancient Judaic world. In such worlds, God is rarely understood apart from his simultaneous relations with the world as its creator, with Torah as its revealer, and with Israel as its covenant partner or redeemer. Likewise, Torah rarely stands solely for a piece of wise or useful guidance. Rather, it is something that comes from God as a message for Israel. Israel, to complete the triad, is rarely simply the name of an ethnic group. In Judaic usage, it commonly denotes a people living in covenantal relation to God through the guidance of Torah.

Messiah and Exile

In light of this triad, we can appreciate the significance of the final key terms. Just as God-Torah-Israel represents an interrelated complex, so, too, do Messiah and Exile. The English word "messiah" renders the Hebrew *mashiakh*. In its simplest meaning, it denotes "one who is anointed with oil." More expansively, it identifies a person consecrated to a divinely appointed task. In the Torah of Moses, particularly in the book of Leviticus, this term is used quite frequently of Aaron, the officiating priest charged with conducting the sacrificial service in the Tent of Meeting.

In the ceremony consecrating him to his task, specially prepared olive oil was poured onto his head (Lev 8:12) and other parts of his body. So in the priestly sense, the messiah is the priest whose sacrificial service in accordance with Torah sustains the covenantal relationship between God and Israel. This sense of the term was retained in a number of Jewish writings from Hellenistic Palestine in particular. But more often it was overshadowed by a more prominent connotation.

This is the meaning of the term "messiah" in the historical and visionary writings collected in *Nevi'im* as well as some of the Psalms of *Ketuvim*. In these writings the priestly usage of Leviticus is supplanted by a royal image. Messiah refers to one anointed to serve as king over the Israelite people in its land. The original anointed was Saul, the first man appointed as king over Israel (I Sam 8–10). The most famous messiah was David, remembered in the historical writings of *Nevi'im* and *Ketuvim* as the standard against which all future kings would be evaluated (e.g., I Kings 11:5–13, II Chr 29:1–3).

By extension the term also refers to all descendents of David's line who themselves sat on his throne. All were Anointed Ones, sanctified by the oil poured upon them for the sacred task of governing Israel on its land in loyalty to God's Torah. All enjoyed and benefited from the vow that God is said to have made to David himself, a covenant no less binding than the general covenant with Israel: "Your line on the throne of Israel shall never end, if only your descendants will look to their way and walk before me as you have walked before me" (1 Kings 8:25).

Now, as the historical books of Kings and Chronicles tell the story of Israel's kings, it becomes clear that most of them did not "look to their way and walk before" God as David is said to have done. All but a few are depicted as morally unworthy of the covenant promise in their trust. One after the other, these books recall, Israel's kings sinned against God, introduced idolatrous worship into his temple, polluted the land with wickedness, and caused (or permitted) Israel to go astray. Indeed, as the writings in *Nevi'im* tell the story, Israel became so utterly estranged from God under such anointed ones that he raised up the Babylonian Empire to destroy the kingdom begun by David.

Israel, to use a colorful image from Leviticus 18:28, was "vomited out of the land," shipped in captivity to Babylonia. The failure of messiahs to fulfill their covenant tasks explains the powerful role of our final symbolic term, Exile, in the Judaic symbolic vocabulary. Messianic corruption resulted in Exile; the reversal of Exile, in turn, was associated with the restoration of a proper royal messiah who would once and for all fulfill the Davidic role.

Some prophetic visionaries, such as the exiled priest Ezekiel, held out hope for a future day when an anointed Davidic heir would once again sit on the throne of a just Israelite kingdom. Speaking on behalf of God, Ezekiel promised that then "my servant David shall be king over them; there shall be one shepherd for all of them. They shall follow my rules and faithfully obey my laws...I will be their god and they shall be my people. And when my sanctuary abides among them forever, the nations shall know that I the LORD do sanctify Israel" (Ezek 37:24–28).

Neither the scriptural canon nor other early streams of tradition offer a consistent image of how the messiah will draw Exile to a close or even of who that messiah might be. Not all scriptural or non-scriptural traditions even imagine that a messiah of any kind will figure in the conclusion of Exile. We explore this diversity of conception in detail later in this chapter. For now we observe that the basic symbolic vocabulary of Judaic worlds draws the imagination in two quite different directions.

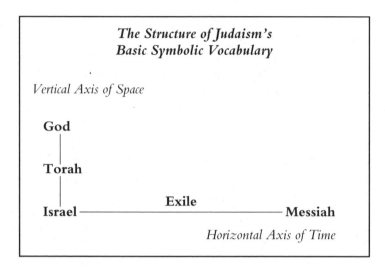

God, Torah, and Israel constitute the *vertical* or *spatial axis* of Judaic worlds. Exile and Messiah complement this with a *horizontal* or *historical axis*. Within these symbolic axes early Judaism identified and defined the significance of everything else in the cosmos. Along one of these lines, all things of importance found their place and their meaning. Sometimes, Judaic worlds articulated rather harmonious syntheses of these two directions; at other times, the imagination of early Judaism focused upon one to the neglect of the other.

We consider now how specific worlds of early Judaism used the vocabulary we have described and how broadly they applied it. As the words of a dictionary of the English language can be used to make fresh statements, all of them different but all English, so too this particular vocabulary was used to describe many types of worlds, all different but all Judaic. Moreover, not all elements of the vocabulary issue into meaningful statements in every Judaic world, just as no English book uses every word in the dictionary. But normally, the presence of one symbolic element implies and evokes at least implicit judgment about the meaning of the others.

Worlds Constructed along the Vertical Axis

Judging from the surviving literary sources, some groups within early Judaism showed a marked tendency to imagine the world almost exclusively in terms of the vertical axes of the Judaic symbolic vocabulary. In these worlds, the structure of the created order and the beings that populate it were of much greater interest than its temporal dimension. If time proved interesting at all, the past, rather than the future, dominated discussion.

The most interesting past was generally not the immediate past, counted in decades or even centuries. More commonly, it was the distant past described in ancient writings, canonical and otherwise, that were believed to have been recorded in times when God still spoke directly to human beings like Moses and other prophets. The interesting past, in other words, was disconnected from historical time. Leading to no future, its relevance for the present was as a source of moral instruction. The past was a fable.[3]

In the worlds of early Judaism, two different but often complementary traditions of knowledge regarding the nature of the created order and the meaning of the past captured the attention of reflective Jews. We will discuss each and then trace the ways in which they shaped each other in the construction of concrete Judaic images of the cosmos.

The Wisdom Traditions of Middle East

One tradition, richly represented in Persian Yehud and later Palestine, had deeply informed the priestly and scribal cultures of ancient Yehudah. Its historical roots extended back beyond Israelite culture to the great city-states and empires of Egyptian and Mesopotamian civilization—a tradition that celebrated wisdom (Hebrew: *khokhmah*) and revered the image of the sage (*khakham*) or the elder (*zaqen*).[4]

This Middle Eastern tradition of wisdom treasured authoritative teachings from past sages as reliable sources of knowledge and guidance. Much of this knowledge took the form that moderns might call a mixture of science and ethics. It was fascinated by the phenomena of the created order, cataloging their various relations, seeing in them intimations of the wisdom of the Creator of the World. It held out the promise, moreover, that understanding the design of the Creator could enable one to negotiate all of life's moral and intellectual challenges. Upon the basis of such authoritative traditions and penetrating observations, a wise and just society could be built under the guidance of sages and righteous kings.

In ancient Israel, the main bearers of this tradition of wisdom were probably priests associated with religious shrines and the temple, scholars associated with royal courts, and scribes. The results of their work was transmitted in a variety of literary genres. Chief among these were stories about the acts of ancient heroes, pithy observations on the human condition, catalogs of the various phenomena of the natural order, and, to an important degree, compendia of wise and just laws.

Parts of the Torah of Moses itself reflect this tradition. The stately description of the creation process in Gen 1:1–2:3, for example, establishes the world as an ordered realm in which all things have their proper place and role. God's comprehensive wisdom, furthermore, is contrasted to the imperfect, but perfectible, wisdom of humans. The human struggle toward wisdom is embodied in the story of Joseph, a gifted, but immature, dream-interpreter who grows in self-knowledge and compassion on his way to becoming a principal deputy of the Egyptian pharaoh (Gen 37–50). The book of Deuteronomy, for its part, proclaims that the laws of God constitute Israel's "wisdom before the nations" (Deut 4:6).

The Middle Eastern scribal tradition of wisdom appears in other scriptural writings as well, most of which reached their canonical forms well before the first centuries CE. Many psalms, of which Psalm 119 is the most prominent example, celebrate God's commandments and teachings as an unfailing source of wisdom for those who obey: "How I love your Torah! It is my speech the entire day!" (Ps 119:97). The first six chapters of the canonical book of Daniel focus in large part on the deeds of a hero noted for wisdom and piety. Similarly, the canonical collection of proverbial wisdom (Proverbs) and its sole example of abstract reflection upon life's meaning (Ecclesiastes) are both associated with Solomon, reputed by tradition to be the wisest of Israel's kings. Job, another ancient wise man, is the central figure in the canon's most sustained attempt to confront the problem of why righteous people suffer.

Beyond the scriptural canon, a number of Hebrew and Aramaic writings continued the tradition of compressing the practical wisdom of a lifetime into memorable epigrams. One of the best known is the Wisdom of ben Sira, attributed to an early second-century BCE scribe named Joshua ben Sira. In Greek translation, it became part of the canon of the Septuagint. In it sentiments like the following are common: "To fear the LORD is the root of wisdom, and her branches are long life" (Sir 1:20). The third-century CE rabbinic compilation of proverbs, *Avot*, is a rather late expression of the same tradition of proverbial wisdom: "Rabbi Hananiah ben Dosa says: He whose fear of sin dominates his wisdom will preserve his wisdom; he whose wisdom dominates his fear of sin will not preserve his wisdom" (Avot 3:9).

The Philosophical Traditions of Greece

But for all its influence, the tradition of Middle Eastern wisdom competed and combined with another. This second tradition linked the Judaic imagination to the Mediterranean world west of Egypt. It originated among the fifth-century BCE Ionian philosophers (*philosophos* means "wisdom lover") and extended to the various philosophical and rhetorical schools of the Hellenistic world, such as those of the Stoics, Cynics, and Epicureans.

Moral wisdom was for the Greek philosophers, as for their Middle Eastern counterparts, of primary importance. Where philosophy differed was in its emphasis. The Middle Eastern tradition saw the highest expression of wisdom in the capacity to master and act upon knowledge transmitted from the past. Greek philosophy, in contrast, celebrated the use of one's rational powers as a way of criticizing received wisdom.

Philosophical teachers such as Socrates and his most famous disciple, Plato, developed ways of using logical argument as an antidote to the false beliefs transmitted as tradition. More than a purely psychological power, reason was viewed as a central element of all reality—an eternal and unchanging substance, the abiding foundation of all things that came into and passed out of being in the empirical world. Using reason to deduce the principles of reality, the philosopher united himself with the source of all things. He then knew how to act ethically in accord with cosmic norms. On the basis of such norms, moreover, just laws could be legislated by wise political leaders for the creation of an orderly society.

The literary expressions of Greek philosophical wisdom are diverse. In addition to fragmentary records of teachers who preceded Socrates, they include Plato's descriptions of Socrates' philosophical dialogues, as well as the systematic treatises of Plato's disciple, Aristotle. A common literary pursuit among the Hellenistic heirs of Plato and Aristotle was to compose philosophical commentaries on ancient poetic works. A prime subject of such commentaries were the great epic works of Homer, the *Iliad* and the *Odyssey*. These epics were, indeed, the canonical texts of Hellenism, analogous in their own way to the Torah's place in the cultures of Judaism.

The goal of such commentaries was to demonstrate that the apparently irrational, naive myths and legends of the great Homer expressed profound truths about nature and morality. Allegory was the preferred method of interpretation. The allegorist would show how each troubling passage of a mythic episode could be connected to a suitable lesson taught by philosophical tradition. In this way, the allegorist saved the prestige of the Homeric epic by showing its integral connection to the best traditions of philosophical wisdom.

Greek philosophy, especially the allegorical method of interpreting ancient writings, played a profound role in the cultural lives of Greek-speaking Jews and was particularly influential in shaping the way they translated and interpreted their growing canon of scriptural texts. The Judaic form of philosophical tradition culminated in the first century CE in the writings of perhaps the first systematic philosopher in the history of Judaism, Philo of Alexandria. He was, as well, a master allegorist of the Torah. He applied the best of his skills to uncover the philosophical message behind the stories and laws written by Moses, whom he regarded as the first and greatest of the philosophers. We shall meet him again further on.[5]

Syntheses of Middle Eastern and Greek Traditions

Both of these traditions of knowledge stemmed from independent cultural resources. Yet patterns of cross-fertilization within various Hellenistic Judaic settings are everywhere apparent.

Recall, for example, the Septuagint, the Greek translation of the Bible. This translation consistently rethinks Hebrew conceptions within the philosophical terminology of Greece. A telling passage is the translation of the divine name in Exodus 3:14. When Moses confronts the presence of God in a burning bush, he inquires after the name of the divinity who sends him to bring Israel out of Egypt. The Hebrew text records the divine answer as *ehyeh asher ehyeh*, an obscure reply that seems to mean, "I will become what I will become." The Septuagint, however, translates the Hebrew as *ho on*, "I am Being." Hellenistic readers understood this term as a reference to the eternal Source of All Being, beyond the decaying matter of existence, discussed by the philosophers. Thus, the philosophical concept of divinity as a single source of all empirical reality, essentially uninvolved in the shifting events of human history, was joined to the Israelite conception of the God of Israel as the unique and only god who acts to redeem his one and only people. It was "Being" who redeemed Israel from Egyptian slavery.[6]

Just as Greek-speaking Jews adapted Greek terms to the expression of Hebrew ideas, so, too, did Aramaic and Hebrew speakers make their own the Greek intellectual heritage. The advice of the first-century BCE sage, Hillel: "What is hateful to you, do not do to your friend" (BT Shab 31a), is a bit of practical wisdom that circulated throughout the Jewish Mediterranean. It appeared as early as the third or fourth century BCE in a Hellenistic Jewish novel entitled *Tobit* (4:15). Tobit's Greek version, it seems, stands behind Philo's (uncredited) quote of this very proverb in his *Hypothetica* 7:6 centuries later. The most famous version, of course, is preserved in Jesus of Nazareth's name by Christian tradition, but it is also found in the writings of the fifth-century BCE Greek historian, Herodotus, as follows: "I will not myself do that which I account blameworthy in my neighbor." In this and other examples, wise sayings recorded in the names of Jewish teachers resonate richly with the background, if not the exact words, of the Greek literary tradition.[7]

Thus Greek culture was "nativized" by Jews and became a medium for expressing their own unique perspectives on reality. The combining of such traditions of wisdom in the worlds of Judaism was, for the most part, entirely unconscious. Few, apart from political ideologists, set out self-consciously to unify—or separate—Judaism and Hellenism. Rather, Jews simply assumed that whatever is held to be true by reasonable people and is good for a person to know and do was disclosed within the revered texts transmitted from the Jewish past.

Whether represented as Greek *sophia* or Hebrew *khokhmah,* wisdom in ancient Judaic worlds found its concrete expression in the symbolic figure of Torah. Torah, as these traditions imagined it, transcended the scriptural Torah of Moses, although Torah was certainly exemplified there. Torah, rather, was a principle of cosmic order. The canonical book of Proverbs (chapters 8–9) portrays wisdom as being God's companion from the beginning of time. The image was refracted throughout the worlds of ancient Judaism. It informed many of Philo's descriptions of Torah as a divine *logos* ("word," "principle") or *nomos* ("law," "structure") through which Being conceived the world into existence. All that exists is as it should be because the world's structure is undergirded by divine thought, Torah.

For their part, non-philosophical Hebrew writers, such as Joshua b. Sira, often equated *hokhmah* with a cosmic principle placed into the particular care of Israel: "Before time he created me, and I shall remain forever. In the sacred tent I ministered in his presence, and so I came to be established in Zion" (Sir 24:9–10). The tradition moved directly into rabbinic thinking as well. In a famous comment on the first verses of Genesis, a rabbinic sage described Torah as a blueprint of reality that even God must consult before creating the world. We shall discuss this text later in this chapter. In Mishnah Avot, one of the first pieces of wisdom the reader encounters is: "On three foundations does the world rest: on the Torah, on the temple service, and on acts of human generosity" (Avot 1:2).

The Space of the Cosmos and Its Inhabitants

Judaic forms of Greek and Middle Eastern wisdom traditions incorporated the symbols of God, Torah, and Israel into larger understandings of the cosmos as a unified whole.

Both wisdom traditions agreed in imagining the God of Israel as a divine king who reigned over an enormous cosmic realm. The same way human emperors had counselors and ministers who effected their will, so, too, God was served by a staff of heavenly ministers and messengers. Scripture, of course, mentions at times a "divine council" convened by the God of Israel (e.g., Ps 89:6–8). It often describes as well divinely appointed messengers, such as the mysterious *malakh* ("messenger") who announced the good news of Samson's conception to his barren mother (Judg 13:3). Here and elsewhere, the Septuagint translated the Hebrew term *malakh* as *angelos*, the Greek word for "messenger." In the worlds of early Judaism, however, these divine counselors and angelic messengers were imagined against a cosmic canvas much broader than that articulated in most of scripture.

In the polytheistic pantheons of Hellenism, cosmic rulers routinely deployed a retinue of less powerful gods as their emissaries. Jews articulated this understanding of things within their own symbolic vocabulary, introducing the necessary modifications. The God of Israel, accordingly, filled the position occupied by Zeus or other cosmic rulers, such as the goddess Isis. Angels played a role very much like that of the minor gods in non-Jewish Hellenistic worlds.

The distinction between Greek gods and the angels of the God of Israel, however, was of crucial importance to many philosophically oriented Jews. They joined Stoics and others in denigrating the immoral behavior of the gods who populated the religious worlds of Hellenism. Few Jews, of course, would invest any effort in allegorical sanitizations of tales of divine lust and patricide. Similarly, few would have been prepared to offer angels the sacrificial forms of worship that non-Jews offered to their gods. Nevertheless, Jewish monotheism, grounded in the very structure of the Judaic symbolic lexicon, blended well with the philosophical monotheism of non-Jews, who regarded worship of the lesser gods as superstition, even if it served a patriotic purpose.

Unlike the gods of the Greek myths, the angels of the Judaic worlds were for the most part beyond moral reproach. Jews indeed knew of rebellious angels. Satan or related figures such as Samael and Belial loomed increasingly large in the Judaic worlds of antiquity. In some cases a mere heavenly advocate, Satan or analogous figures could also appear as a malevolent source of opposition to God's power.

But for the most part, the angels populating Judaic worlds did only what their king commanded them to do and carefully avoided the embarrassing moral lapses of Hellenistic gods. Some angels might have once fornicated with human women (Gen 6:1–4), but, unlike the randy drunkard, Dionysius, they had since learned to restrain themselves.[8]

Despite this difference with regard to the gods, Jews agreed with their neighbors that all divine and angelic activity took place against the backdrop of vast cosmic spaces. God's dwelling was at the apex of a cosmic structure that began with the twelve astral constellations of the Zodiac. Beneath the stars was a series of seven heavenly spheres, each governed in its workings by the power of one of the seven fixed heavenly bodies. Angelic messengers populated these spheres and moved up and down the cosmic ladder on their various tasks. Humans, for their part, lived down at the bottom, on earth.

Most humans stayed on earth until their bodies died, at which time their souls would confront one of two destinies. Souls devoted in life to wisdom and good works would float effortlessly up the cosmic ladder to return to the source of their being in the divine world. Others, coarsened by a life lived in the pursuit of folly or sin, would descend beneath the earth, cut off from the divine world until cleansed of the effects of earthiness.

This underworld, of course, had its own population of demonic figures, corresponding to the angels of the heavenly order. The philosophically minded may have discounted them, but archaeological discoveries from Egypt to Mesopotamia attest to the attempts of Jews to use incantations and other ritual practices to prevent such demons from interfering in their fortunes—or to encourage them to interfere in the fortunes of enemies (see Chapter Five). Later rabbinic sages, we shall learn, knew quite a lot about them.

Some few souls, and we will return to them in Chapter Six, had mastered the mystery of liberating the soul from the body even in life. They could enjoy spectacular disembodied tours of the heavens. Philo, for example, describes one of his own such tours.[9] Others, divorced from philosophical circles but sharing some traditions with the rabbinic sages, claimed to do so themselves by invoking the aid of an angelic teacher, the Prince of the Torah. What made this cosmic structure part of a distinctly Judaic world vision was, of course, the place of the God of Israel at the top and, obviously, the significance of the Jews at the bottom.

For most Hellenistic geographers and ethnographers, the Jews were an exotic curiosity, and their land lay at the backwaters of civilization. Only Jews found a central role for Israel in the human order. But here we find an important point of geographical differentiation among the Jews. Most philosophically oriented Jewish works were written in the Greek-speaking Diaspora, while works more centrally in touch with Middle Eastern traditions were written in Hebrew or Aramaic by Palestinians. This perhaps explains why Palestinians tended to exceed Diaspora writers in according the Land of Israel a distinctive role in the structure of the world's space.

Philo of Alexandria, for example, routinely portrayed the people Israel as the philosophical nation par excellence, commissioned by its lawgiver, Moses, to embody the highest truths of wisdom through its loyalty to the specific laws of the Torah of Moses. Thus, Israel as a national group is of

---

The Satan as a Source of Cosmic Evil

The biblical canon knows of a mysterious figure, the Satan, who seems to inhabit the heavenly regions as a kind of adviser or messenger of God (e.g., Job 1:6, Zech 3:1–2). The name itself means "obstructor" or "adversary"; and in canonical settings, he seems to obstruct human designs. Throughout much of the history of early Judaism, however, the Satan's image grew to cosmic proportions, as he came to be perceived as a source of cosmic evil in opposition to God.

In the community that formed in the Dead Sea region of Qumran, it was clear that the Satan could have human allies on earth. The following text is from a document called "Curses of Satan and His Lot" (4Q286–7). It is probably part of a set of curses used by the Qumran community against its human adversaries. (The translation is from G. Vermes, *The Dead Sea Scrolls in English* [Penguin: New York, 1990], p. 61.)

> *Afterward they shall damn Satan and all his guilty lot. They shall answer and say, Cursed be Satan in his hostile design, and damned in his guilty dominion. Cursed be all the spirits of his lot in their wicked design, and damned in their thoughts of unclean impurity. For they are the lot of darkness and their visitation is for eternal destruction. Amen.*

---

central importance within the human order. It exemplifies and transmits the wisdom that lies at the very heart of all reality. But the Land of Israel for Philo tended to be shorn of concrete significance. To be sure, it served as a home for the temple, in which priestly philosophers offered sacrifices that drew attention to important philosophical principles. The land served as a vehicle for the expression of a variety of virtues, such as love for one's country. But the land had no broader cosmic significance. The entire cosmos was the text within which the divine thought expressed itself, and the Torah given to Israel offered the code for deciphering that text. The Land of Israel, however, was neutral—equal to other lands, surely, but no higher.[10]

In Palestinian traditions of wisdom, to the contrary, the Land of Israel in general, and Jerusalem and its temple in particular, figure prominently. A good example is the work of the Jerusalemite scribe Joshua ben Sira. Earlier we noted his concern to point out that the universal law of Torah makes its presence concretely known in Zion. Accordingly, the post-exilic history

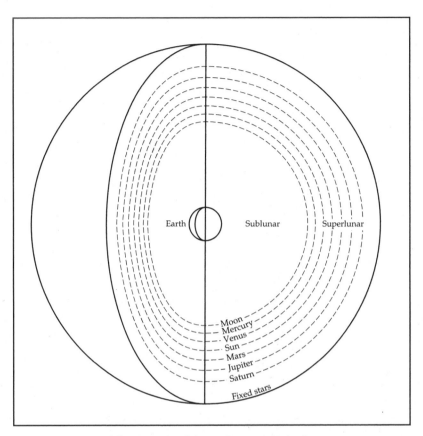

The Cosmos of Greco-Roman Antiquity

Jews, along with other members of Greco-Roman culture, conceived the Universe as a series of concentric spheres with the earth at the core and the ethereal sphere of the fixed stars at the periphery. Various categories of divine beings, conceived in early Judaism as angels, populated the realms between them. In the religious worlds of Hellenism, including Judaism, the spatial movement from the core to the periphery corresponds to a progressive refinement of being, from coarsest materiality to the most rarified spirituality.

Source: Luther H. Martin, *Hellenistic Religions: An Introduction*, fig.2, page 9. Copyright © 1987 by Oxford University Press, Inc. Used by permission of Oxford University Press, Inc.

of the land, which interested Philo hardly at all, was of great interest to ben Sira.

Ben Sira concluded his book by recounting all the heroes of Israel's past, beginning with Abraham and ending with the high priest of his pre-Hasmonean day. In each, he found a model of wisdom and piety capable of being emulated in the present. The most-loving attentions of the cosmic king, who rules the whole universe, were elicited by the lavish grandeur of the sacrificial service offered in the temple. That service culminated in a moment of union and communion between God and the temple assembly as, under the raised hands of the priest, Simon, "they bow in worship to receive the blessing from the Most High" (Sir 50:21). For all of the cosmic importance of wisdom, the most intense experience of the god of the universe remained available only in Jerusalem, the place of that god's choosing.

The worlds imagined within the wisdom traditions pay little explicit attention to the future-oriented historical concerns represented by ideas such as Exile or Messiah. These are absent almost entirely in Philo and reflect his larger disinterest in the Land of Israel as a geographical reality. But even Palestinian traditions of wisdom underplay orientations toward the future.

Joshua ben Sira's history of Israelite heroes, for example, shows little interest in the theme of Exile. His recollections of David, like those of Philo, offer no clue that in other Judaic worlds David could be imagined as a coming political leader who would preside over the end of exile. Rather, ben Sira's king dwells safely in the past among vanished heroes. He is an ancient embodiment of wisdom and piety, not a hope for the future. The messiah of interest to ben Sira, to the contrary, is the high priest of Jerusalem. Here, though, the messianic function is not political or historical, but liturgical. His sacrificial service and utterings of the priestly blessings, we have seen, establish and maintain the lines of communication that link Israel on earth to its god in heaven.

It is always the world of vertical space that engages the imagination of ben Sira and other proponents of this stream of the wisdom tradition. Even centuries later, after the Jews of Palestine and the Diaspora had risen in messianic wars against Rome, tractate *Avot* and the rest of Rabbi's Mishnah are almost entirely silent on the question of Exile and the role of the Messiah in bringing it to an end. For instruction on how the historical plane of experience could figure in the structure of Judaic worlds, therefore, we shall have to look elsewhere.

Worlds Constructed along the Horizontal Axis

Greek-speaking Jews, as well as those at home in Aramaic or Hebrew, inherited more than wisdom traditions. They inherited the visionary tradition of Israelite literature—a tradition rich in concern for the moral fabric of Israelite society and its prospects for the future. The most influential works in this tradition had been gathered in the canon of *Nevi'im*. They were attributed to poets and preachers known collectively as prophets, "spokespersons" for God.

The largest canonical collections of visionary prophecies were gathered in the names of Isaiah, Jeremiah, and Ezekiel. But tradition transmitted as scripture twelve comparatively small works in the names of other prophets as well, equally charged with visionary promises. These writings often present dialogues between the prophets and the God of Israel, in which the prophet is commissioned to proclaim how divine interventions would shape Israel's and the world's future in response to Israel's loyalty or disloyalty to God. In most of these writings, Exile—as a threat or an accomplished fact—is the fundamental issue; and the character of redemption from Exile, including the nature of the redeemer from Exile, is a prominent topic.[11]

The Redeemer in the Canon of Nevi'im

Works compiled and edited after the destruction of Yehudah in 587 BCE offer particularly rich explorations of the messianic theme. Here the redeemer of Israel is portrayed as a figure appointed by God. The diversity of these messianic conceptions is, in fact, extraordinary, especially in light of the exclusive focus of the later rabbinic and Christian traditions upon a messiah of the House of David.[12]

One post-exilic visionary poet, whose songs now appear in chapters 40–55 of the book of Isaiah, employs a remarkable array of non-Davidic images through which to imagine the redemptive plan of God for Israel. In the following passage, for example, he extends the notion of a divinely anointed king entirely beyond the Israelite framework. For him, God's Messiah is none other than the Persian emperor, Cyrus, who destroyed the Babylonian captors of Israel.

Note how the prophet interprets Cyrus' victories as the redemptive work of the God of Israel on behalf of his scattered people (Isa 45:1–6):

> Thus says the LORD to his Messiah, to Cyrus, whose right hand I have grasped to subdue the nations before him and strip kings of their robes…I will give you the treasures of darkness and riches hidden in secret places, so that you may know that it is I, the LORD, the God of Israel, who call

you by your name. For the sake of my servant Jacob, and Israel my chosen, I call you by your name, I surname you though you do not know me. I am the LORD, and there is no other; besides me there is no god. I arm you, though you do not know me, so that they may know, from the rising of the sun and from the west, that there is no one besides me; I am the LORD, and there is no other.

A Babylonian document from this period, the Cyrus Cylinder, suggests that the king credited his victories to the power of Marduk, the chief god of the Babylonian pantheon. In Cyrus' view, Marduk had invited Cyrus to punish Babylonian impiety. But the Hebrew prophet affirms that the new world order under Cyrus is nothing but the hand of Israel's god at work on behalf of a penitent community.

Cyrus is not the only figure upon whom this Isaiah focuses the lens of messianic interpretation. In other passages, which became very important for early Christian preaching regarding Jesus' messiahship, the prophet speaks of a servant of God who "was wounded for our transgressions, crushed for our iniquities; upon him was the punishment that made us whole, and by his bruises we are healed" (Isa 53:5).

Elsewhere in Isaiah's discussion of this servant, however, the redemptive sufferer seems to be Israel. Its suffering is borne in service of God's cosmic plan (Isa 49:1–7):

The Lord called me before I was born, while I was in my mother's womb he named me…And he said to me, "You are my servant, Israel, in whom I will be glorified."…He says, "It is too light a thing that you should be my servant to raise up the tribes of Jacob and to restore the survivors of Israel; I will give you as light to the nations, that my salvation may reach to the end of the earth." Thus says the LORD, the Redeemer of Israel and his Holy One, to one deeply despised, abhorred by the nations, the slave of rulers, "Kings shall see and stand up, princes, and they shall prostrate themselves, because of the LORD, who is faithful, the Holy One of Israel, who has chosen you."

The identity of this divine servant is, to be sure, given as "Israel," but the servant is also to "raise up the tribes of Jacob." Is Israel, then, its own redeemer? The prophet's text is never explicit.

In other post-exilic collections of visions, Israel's redeemer is never imagined as anyone but the God of Israel. An excellent example is the prophet whose visions are collected in chapters 9–14 of the book of Zechariah, who lived in the Jerusalem community of Persian Yehud. For him, Exile was a fact of life even in the homeland. But he looked forward to an auspicious end to Exile at the conclusion of a cataclysmic world war in which the God of Israel would emerge as the visible ruler of the Earth.

The following passages, probably from the late sixth century BCE, echo for centuries in later Jewish and Christian thinking about the end of history (Zech 14:1ff.):

> See, a day is coming for the LORD, when the plunder taken from you will be divided in your midst. For I will gather all the nations against Jerusalem to battle, and the city shall be taken and the houses looted and the women raped; half the city shall go into exile, but the rest of the people shall not be cut off from the city. Then the LORD will go forth and fight against those nations as when he fights on a day of battle. On that day his feet shall stand on the Mount of Olives, which lies before Jerusalem on the east; and the Mount of Olives shall be split in two from east to west by a very wide valley. ...Then the LORD my God will come, and all the holy ones with him. On that day there shall be neither cold nor frost. And there shall be continuous day...On that day living waters shall flow out from Jerusalem, half of them to the eastern sea and half of them to the western sea; it shall continue in summer as in winter. And the LORD will become king over all the earth; on that day the LORD will be one and his name one...Then all who survive of the nations that have come against Jerusalem shall go up year after year to worship the King, the LORD of hosts, and to keep the festival of Sukkot...

The end of Israel's Exile is, for this visionary, the end of all history as it has been known since the expulsion from the Garden. "Living waters" will spring up as in Eden and Jerusalem's temple will serve as the new Garden of humanity, where the God of Israel alone will be acknowledged by the entire world as its king.

A Diaspora Vision of Redemption

In addition to visions such as these, transmitted in the canonical works of prophecy, both Greek-speaking and Aramaic-speaking Jews were familiar with other works that described visions of the future communicated by God or angels to ancient seers. Greek culture, for example, had for some centuries preserved oracles concerning the future in the names of prophetesses known collectively as Sibyls. These oracles were communicated in Greek poetic forms and were represented as messages from various gods. Jews throughout the Greek-speaking world, and especially in Egypt, preserved their own collections of Sibylline Oracles, which used Greek poetic conventions to deliver messages of distinctly Judaic import.

Especially during the era of Roman domination in the first century CE, many such oracles expressed violent hatred of Roman rule and the conviction of imminent liberation at the hands of a divinely sent redeemer. The following example, from first century CE Egypt, is framed in the past tense, by way of anticipating the coming redemption (Syb Or 5:414–430):[13]

> For a blessed man came from the expanses of heaven with a scepter in his hands that God gave him, and he gained sway over all things well, and gave back the wealth to all the good, which previous men had taken. He destroyed every city from its foundations with much fire and burned nations of mortals who were formerly evildoers. And the city that God desired, this he made more brilliant than stars and sun and moon, and he provided ornaments and made a holy temple, exceedingly beautiful in its fair shrine, and he fashioned a great and immense tower over many stadia touching even the clouds and visible to all, so that all faithful and all righteous people could see the glory of eternal God, a form desired. For terrible things no longer happen to wretched mortals, no adulteries or illicit love of boys, no murder, or din of battle, but competition is fair among all. It is the last time of holy people when God, who thunders on high, founder of the greatest temple, accomplishes these things.

The "blessed man" of this passage has no messianic name, but he is clearly more than a human king, arriving as he does "from the expanses of heaven with a scepter in his hand." His victory is more than a political one, for it changes the very nature of time, inaugurating an era in which "terrible things no longer happen to wretched mortals." He reigns over a transformed human community as God's deputy.

Redemption in the Palestinian Apocalypses

While the Diaspora proved hospitable to the visions of Jewish Sybils, the real home of speculation about the end of history in early Judaism was the Land of Israel. Many surviving Hebrew and Aramaic texts, written from the late third century BCE until the close of the first century CE, used the rhetoric of scriptural prophecy to articulate ever more concretely imagined scenarios about a coming resolution to the catastrophe of Exile. These texts were invariably presented as the record of revelations to ancient visionaries. Contemporary scholars often classify them collectively as apocalyptic literature, from the Greek word for "revelation."[14]

Such apocalypses were normally mediated by angelic interpreters (not unlike the book of Jubilees). Sometimes, as in chapters 7–12 of the scriptural book of Daniel (written at the outbreak of the Maccabean wars), the narrator describes a perplexing vision on his bed, which an angel comes to explain. At other times these visions take the form of heavenly journeys guided by the interpreting angels.

The content of many such visions is a dramatic, highly imagistic portrayal of the end of time. Events of this cataclysm include the redemption of Israel from Exile, the punishment of those Jews and non-Jews deemed to have impeded God's plans for redemption, and the restoration to God of sovereignty over the world. In more than a few such writings, God's coming kingdom is presided over by a super-human messiah, often of Davidic origins. In others the messiah is just as likely to stem from a non-Davidic Israelite hero, e.g., a descendant of a royal figure like Joseph or of the priestly clan, Levi.

The heavenly journey of the visionary is so common in these writings that we should consider one example.[15] The following vision is preserved in a second century BCE work called the Book of the Watchers, which is now the first part of a larger collection called I Enoch. The narrator, Enoch, is a figure from antediluvian times who appears briefly in Genesis 5:25 as one who "walked with God."

Now we learn where he went. Dreaming on his bed one night, Enoch sees the heavens open up. Suddenly (I Enoch 14:8–25):[16]

> I saw the clouds: And they were calling me in a vision; and the fogs were calling me; and the course of the stars and the lightnings were rushing me and causing me to desire; and in the vision, the winds were causing me to fly and rushing me high up into heaven. And I kept coming into heaven until I approached a wall that was built of white marble and surrounded by tongues of fire; and it began to frighten me. And I came into the tongues of fire and drew near to a great house that was built of white marble, and the inner walls were like mosaics of white marble, the floor of crystal, the ceiling like the path of the stars and lightnings between which stood fiery cherubim and their heaven of water, and flaming fire surrounded the walls, and its gates were burning with fire. And I entered into the house, which was hot like fire and cold like ice, and there was nothing inside it; so fear covered me and trembling seized me. And as I shook and trembled, I fell upon my face and saw a vision... And I observed and saw inside a lofty throne—its appearance was like crystal and its wheels like the shining sun; and I heard the voice of cherubim; as from beneath the throne were issuing streams of fire. ...And the Great Glory was sitting upon it—as for his gown, which was shining more brightly than the sun, it was whiter than snow. None of the angels was able to come in and see the face of the Excellent and the Glorious One; and no one of the flesh can see him—the flaming fire was round about him, and a great fire stood before him. No one could come near unto him from among those that surrounded the tens of millions that stood before him...Until then I was prostrate with my face covered and trembling. And the LORD called me with his own mouth and said to me, "Come near to me, Enoch, and to my holy Word."

At the top of the cosmos, in the highest level of the universe, is the palace of God, surrounded by angels and bathed in a brilliant light emanating from the throne room. Upon the throne sits God himself, too brilliant to gaze upon, but speaking, nonetheless, in human language, to his loyal subject Enoch. What he explains in the discourse that follows this vision is the origin of human sin, which befouls the earth and causes the sufferings of history. It all began when the angelic giants of Genesis 6 descended to frolic with the daughters of men.

The Connection of Past, Present and Future

We have seen enough of early Judaism's redemptive vision to ask an obvious question: What distinguished visions like Enoch's from the larger conceptions of reality of Hebrew and Greek wisdom tradition? It was, in part, an insistence upon the relation of past and future. The past was no longer simply a static picture of various patterns of human virtue or vice. Rather, figures like Adam and Eve, or the giants, did things in the past that still shaped the present. For this reason, figures from the past could be represented as sources of urgent messages about the present and the immediate future.

Past and present were bound together in a unified movement toward a future that was about to culminate in the cataclysmic end of time itself. Ancient heroes were held to be important transmitters of these visions precisely because they lived when God still spoke directly to his prophets rather than through the written records transcribed in books. In the near future, however, it was often hoped that God would once again speak directly to his community still living in the End of Days. For the time being the study of the heroes' preserved words was important precisely because they contained the information needed in order to know the timing of the cataclysm and how to prepare for it.

Timetables became important. In Chapter Two, we discussed how the book of Jubilees developed a complex scheme of ancient chronology. Now the future as well was placed on schedule. When, in particular, would redemption come? Often the compilers of visionary writings described signs—wars, the reversal of natural processes, starvation—that would portend the coming time.

Many of these, revealed in response to the direct questions of Ezra the scribe, are listed in a first century CE work called IV Ezra (IV Ezra 6:21–24):

> Infants a year old shall speak with their voices, and women with child shall give birth to premature children at three or four months, and these shall live and dance. Sown places shall suddenly appear unsown, and full storehouses shall suddenly be found to be empty; and the trumpet shall sound

aloud, and when all hear it, they shall suddenly be terrified. At that time friends shall make war on friends like enemies, and the earth and those who inhabit it shall be terrified.[17]

But more important than the timing itself was knowledge about the details of the redemptive events. God's detailed response to Ezra's questions on this matter bears extensive repeating (IV Ezra 7:26ff.):

> For behold, the time will come when the signs that I have foretold to you will come to pass; the city that now is not seen shall appear, and the land that now is hidden shall be disclosed. And everyone who has been delivered from the evils that I have foretold shall see my wonders. For my son the Messiah shall be revealed with those who are with him, and those who remain shall rejoice four hundred years. And after these years my son the Messiah shall die, and all who draw human breath. And the world shall be turned back to primeval silence for seven days, as it was at the first beginnings; so that no one shall be left. And after seven days, the world, which is not yet awake, shall be roused, and that which is corruptible shall perish. And the earth shall give up those who are asleep in it; and the chambers shall give up the souls that have been committed to them. And the Most High shall be revealed upon the seat of judgment, and compassion shall pass away, and patience shall be withdrawn; but judgment alone shall remain, truth shall stand, and faithfulness shall grow strong....Then the pit of torment shall appear, and opposite it shall be the place of rest; and the furnace of Gehenna shall be disclosed, and opposite it the Paradise of delight. Then the Most High will say to the nations that have been raised from the dead, "Look now, and understand whom you have denied, whom you have not served, whose commandments you have despised!" ...thus he will speak to them on the day of judgment—a day that has no sun or moon or stars, or cloud or thunder or lightning or wind or water or air, or darkness or evening or morning, or summer or spring or heat or winter or frost or cold or hail or rain or dew, or noon or night, or dawn or shining or brightness or light, but only the splendor of the glory of the Most High, by which all shall see what has been determined for them. For it will last for about a week of years. This is my judgment and its prescribed order; and to you alone have I shown these things.

Note that in Ezra's conception, the Messiah is a curiously amorphous figure. On the one hand, as God's "son," he is a kind of angel. But, unlike an angel, he is to die; like Moses, he is not to preside over the final redemption. His kingdom of four hundred years is the first stage of a final dissolution of all reality, a return to the state of pre-creation. The important moments follow only thereafter, the resurrection and judgment of the dead, and the inauguration of a new world order under the direct rule of God, the Most High. Only then is the world at rest, a rest reproducing the peace of the Garden, prior to the hopeless rebellion that inaugurated human history.

The Vertical and Horizontal Axes in Tension

You have seen enough of the visionary literature of our period to grasp its essential thrust. The space of the cosmos was vast and imposing. But everything in it found its place between the heaven of God and the earth upon which Israel served God. Even what was beneath the earth had its meaning in terms of what God and Israel did above. Thus far, the vertical emphases of the wisdom traditions and the horizontal emphases of the visionary traditions share much. At issue was the conception of time in these worlds.

Where the spacial axis represented in the symbols of God-Torah-Israel dominated, Judaic imagination focused upon the place of the soul in the cosmic order and the means by which knowledge of Torah ensured restoration to God's domain at life's end. The past showed Israel how to live for immortality; its future was confined to the future of the soul after the body's death.

Where, by contrast, Exile and Messiah governed the symbolic imagination of Jews, all time was colored by the fundamental fact of human alienation from God represented by the rebellious assertion of human self-determination. The destiny of the individual soul was bound up with the collective destiny of Israel in history. Humanity was in Exile from God, a fact that resulted in the story of suffering and death that is human history. Israel was likewise in Exile.

All time gained meaning, therefore, both in terms of its origins and in terms of where it was headed. Originating in creation and the Garden, it was headed toward a final goal that would reproduce its origins in a new form. Torah, in this vision of reality, was a source of guidance from the past that helped individuals and the entire community to prepare itself for the coming future reconstruction of the world.

For many, time was moving toward the moment when Israel and humanity would be reconciled to each other and God in an all-embracing kingdom. In other scenarios, only righteous Israelites would survive to enjoy the new Eden. But in either case, history, the great disrupter of stability and atemporal order, would be overcome in a new and final reorientation of all reality. In some views, that new reorientation would restore to the world direct rule by God. In others, his Messiah, Davidic or otherwise, served as the regent of God's dominion. But on any terms, it was a world that could not come without a radical transformation of space as well. A fundamentally new heaven and earth would witness the perfection of time.

Messianic Movements in Early Judaism

The vivid messianic longings expressed in apocalyptic writings seem to have been paralleled in a number of anti-Roman social movements in Palestine during the first and second centuries CE. These messianic movements, which attracted primarily a peasant following, all centered on a leader claiming the right to rule Israel as king. Accordingly, the movements were actively suppressed by Roman authorities. The messiahs either died fighting or were executed as political criminals.

Judas b. Ezekias, 6 CE
Simon, 6
Athronges, 6
Jesus of Nazareth, 30–32
Menachem b. Judas, 66
Simon b. Giora, ca. 68–70
Shimon b. Kosiba, 132–135

With the exception of the movements surrounding Jesus of Nazareth and Shimon bar Kosiba, we know about most of them only from sketchy portraits in the writings of the first-century Jewish historian Josephus, who found them distinctly distasteful. Among the messiahs, only Jesus seems to have attracted the claim to descend from the House of David. His is, as well, the only movement to have survived and thrived after the messiah's death.

Source: Richard A. Horsely with John S. Hanson, *Bandits, Prophets, and Messiahs: Popular Movements at the Time of Jesus* (San Francisco: Harper & Row, 1985), pp. 88–134.

Horizontal and Vertical in the Rabbinic World

Predictions of the world's imminent transformation, of course, proved to be premature. In the history of early Judaic worlds, even the devastating historical wars of 66–73, 115–117 and 132–135 proved more a disruption than an absolute end. Surely, the Judaic worlds that began to emerge throughout the Roman Empire by the fourth century were increasingly modeled by rabbinic architects and builders. But they salvaged bricks liberally from the structures of imagination that preceded them and built their world on the old foundation: the spacial order of reality imagined through the symbolic axis of God-Torah-Israel and the future-oriented world of history captured in the axis of Exile-Messiah. By 650 CE they had built a world that, with various expansions, renovations, and rewirings, would serve as home for a millennium.

The Cosmic Torah of the Master of the Universe

That world, especially in its rich reflection upon the vertical axes of God-Torah-Israel, preserved much of the scribal and philosophical temperament of earlier Judaic worlds. Among the sages, as among earlier Jewish scribes and philosophers, Torah and wisdom were equivalent terms, transcendent cosmic realities that linked God to Israel in a timeless relationship. This perception is fundamental to the earliest homiletic collections of rabbinic literature, such as tractate Avot, and receives elaboration in the midrashic and talmudic compilations of the fourth to sixth centuries.[18]

In the first century CE, Philo had compared God's creation of the world to the work of an architect (On Creation: 4). Now we find a similar image with a striking change: Torah is portrayed as the very blueprint for reality. The idea appears in Genesis Rabbah, a fourth-fifth century Palestinian midrash on the book of Genesis. The rabbinic comment is inspired by Proverbs 8:30–31, which portrays wisdom as a child frolicking before God prior to creation (Gen Rab 1:1):

> The word "child" (*amon*) sounds like the word for "craftsman" (*oman*). The Torah says: "I was the Blessed Holy One's crafting tool." In everyday experience, when a human king builds a palace he doesn't build it out of his own imagination. Rather, he hires a craftsman. And the craftsman doesn't build it out of his own imagination either. Rather, he has designs and diagrams to help him plan the rooms and doorways. So, too, the Blessed Holy One looked into the Torah and created the world.

Indeed, the passage goes on to recommend a remarkable interpretation of the first sentence of the Torah of Moses. The plain meaning is: "In the beginning God created the heavens and earth" (Gen 1:1). Underlying this rendering, however, midrash finds a deeper significance: "Through the Torah God created the heavens and the earth."

If anything, the rabbinic conception of Torah as a cosmic principle was perhaps more comprehensive than earlier conceptions, for it colored the concrete meaning of all terms with which it was connected. As we saw in the last chapter, sages viewed Torah as first of all a written text. This Written Torah provided authoritative instruction in the history of Israel and in God's will for Israel. But Torah was also, as it proceeded from the mouth of the sage into the ears of the disciple, a medium by which God spoke through a specific human relationship. The knowledge the sage transmitted through his behavior and teaching was Oral Torah, a model of a life perfected in communication with God. Thus, in intellectual and moral training, Torah served as both a world-structuring principle and a means of perfecting human beings.[19]

The disciple's task in this life, accordingly, was to labor in the study of Torah at the feet of rabbinic sages, to perform deeds of Torah. Mishnah Avot 2:8 transmits the following advice in the name of Rabban Yohanan b. Zakkai: "If you have learned much Torah, don't think so highly of yourself—what were you created for?" To study Torah, then, was to fulfill the purpose of one's creation.

In this sense, the reward of a life lived in Torah was, to a degree, a worldly one. It drew one close to the sage and, through him, to the God of Israel on a daily basis. But, apprenticeship to a sage in earthly life was merely preparation for eternal discipleship as a student of Torah before God. This is part of what sages termed the life of the world-to-come, an inheritance of the soul beyond death where it returns to heaven with the souls of the righteous. Included, of course, are those of departed sages. Thus, in aggadic homilies of the later midrashic and talmudic compilations, the soul can be imagined as studying Torah in heaven with God and Moses.

As in pre-rabbinic traditions of Judaic wisdom, God remained for sages a cosmic king. He is routinely referred to in rabbinic writings as *ribbono shel ha'olam* ("Master of the Universe"). Rabbinic parables are particularly rich in imagining him in his royal role. The divine king who looks into the blueprint of the Torah is just one of numerous examples.[20]

But earlier wisdom traditions produced no image of God as heavenly scribe or philosopher. Their reticence stands in sharp contrast to the rabbinic willingness to portray God—for the purposes of aggadic rhetoric, at least— as an assiduous master of Torah, as a dutiful copyist of the Torah's text, or as the headmaster of the Heavenly Torah Academy (*yeshivah shel ma'alah*) who intervenes in the halakhic debates of earthly sages (and can be overruled by them if he holds a minority opinion!). Rabbinic descriptions of the meaning of Torah and the cosmic lordship of God, then, draw freely from earlier Judaic wisdom traditions. But everything borrowed is transmuted in terms of the sages' particular concerns and perceptions.

The People and Land of Israel in the Cosmic Order

This pattern of borrowing and transmutation continues as other details of earlier Judaic worlds are also incorporated into the rabbinic cosmology. The rabbinic cosmos is the same seven-tiered structure known to earlier Judaic worlds, replete with its entire complement of angels and demons. What makes this a rabbinic cosmos is the way the symbol of Torah organizes the relations of the vast cosmic spaces. Rabbinic sages and their most special disciples used what they called "the secrets of Torah" to facilitate the heavenly journeys that earlier Jews might have attempted through philosophical contemplation or prophetic vision (see Chapter Six). As masters of Torah, moreover, sages knew how to use its secrets to avert the harmful effects of demonic activity.[21]

The Babylonian Talmud is particularly rich in depicting the demonic surroundings of everyday life. Demons (*shedim*) congregated in isolated places, ruins, and outhouses. They inhabited the moon shadows of stone walls and the stumps of palm trees. They might even surround one's bed at night. But sages could offer diagnoses of and protection from demonic activities, as suggested by the following (BT Ber 6a):

> Said Rava: "…One who wishes to know where demons are takes ashes and sprinkles them around the bed. In the morning, he will see something like a rooster's footprints. One who wishes to see them must take the afterbirth of a black cat, and its offspring—the firstborn of the firstborn. Roast it in fire and grind it to powder. When he puts the ashes in his eye, he'll see them…" Rav Bibi bar Abayye did this and saw them. But he was stricken. Rabbis prayed for mercy for him, and he was healed.

The sages' prayers, a function of their Torah mastery, enabled them to avert the consequences when a colleague had mismanaged his powers. All the more so did their Torah empower them to manage other relations at all levels of the cosmos—the human, the angelic, and the divine.

Like all worlds built upon the symbolic triad of God-Torah-Israel, that of the sages accorded special cosmic significance to the People Israel as well. Among this people, after all, the eternal Torah had come to rest in the world of time. Israel embodied within the world God's original plan for the entire human order—to incorporate all life under the canopy of the divine will as expressed in Torah. Where the Israel of the sages differed most from that of earlier wisdom traditions, however, is in the second aspect of the term's meaning—the Land of Israel itself.

Philo's lack of interest in the geographical space of the Jewish homeland is entirely foreign to the sages. Rather, much more in the manner of Palestinian wisdom traditions, the Land of Israel is for sages a special preoccupation. But its symbolic importance exceeds anything we know from the wisdom traditions of Palestine. For Joshua ben Sira, we have seen, the land was important because of the temple that stood upon it. Rabbinic sages, however, lived in a world without a temple. Nevertheless, in their view, the land retained a holiness in its very soil that distinguished it from any other spot on earth.

The Mishnah, for example, expresses this viewpoint in a complex body of rules governing the tithing of food. As we saw in Chapter Two, these attracted the attention of the Gospels' authors. Farmers were to offer tithes to priests, Levites, and the poor. From the Mishnah's perspective, however, these rules had more than a charitable function. They offered a procedure for respecting the holiness present in the Land of Israel by treating its produce as a sanctified object. For this reason, priestly and levitical tithes needed to be separated even though, with the temple gone, priests and Levites could no longer eat the offerings.[22]

Sages expressed their views about the uniqueness of the Land of Israel in other ways as well. They regarded all foreign lands—the lands of "the worshippers of stars and constellations"—as intrinsically unclean, polluting the bodies of the Jews who lived in them. In contrast, the Land of Israel needed to be preserved from uncleanliness so as to respect its intrinsic holiness.[23] A large part of the Mishnah's earliest ritual and legal traditions, therefore, is concerned about maintaining the ritual purity of the Jewish body and the Jewish household in the Land of Israel. Scriptural sources, naturally, are combed for guidance in maintaining such purity. Sages ignored, however, the fact that the Torah of Moses imposes the need for purification only upon one entering the Sanctuary. For sages, at least in legal theory, such purity was incumbent upon all Jews in the Land of Israel who wished to eat a simple meal at the level of holiness appropriate to a disciple of the sages.[24]

It is as if, with the destruction of the physical temple, the land and people of Israel had themselves absorbed the invisible essence that constituted its holiness. Laws that once protected the holiness and purity of the temple and its personnel were now applied to the territory and the people that the temple had sanctified. So, in this aspect of the vertical triad as well—the role of the land and people of Israel in the spatial structure of reality—the rabbinic world must be distinguished from the scribal and philosophical traditions upon which it drew. Constructed well after the temple had passed into the images of legend, the rabbinic world embodied the temple's sanctity in the surviving realities of the land and people of Israel.

Torah and Messiah in the Redemption of Israel

The rabbinic world embodied in the Mishnah was the only Judaic world of the first millennium for which the temple was never a physical presence or even a recent memory. It was the one Judaic world, therefore, in which the implications of Exile, in both geographic and cosmological dimensions, were most fully explored. And, as we have seen, once the symbol of Exile began to resonate, the early Judaic imagination was almost reflexively drawn to construct scenarios for its end.

Thus, as rabbinic teaching reached increasing definition from the third through seventh centuries, sages' understanding of the spatial order of reality—structured by the symbols of God-Torah-Israel—became ever more hospitable to a future-oriented perspective. Sages living in Palestine and Babylonia were equally displaced in space. The corrective had to be found in time, in a future in which Israel would be restored to its proper land, the temple to its ancient mountain, and the world to its proper course. The question of Messiah had to be squarely addressed.

In their conceptions of Israel's ultimate redemption from exile, sages drew upon images and ideas from the entire scriptural and apocalyptic traditions at their disposal.[25] But they filtered these images and ideas through their own overriding commitment to the central, and richly complex, symbol of Torah.

A sample from a Babylonian collection of traditions about messianic times gives some idea of the range of speculation on this matter and evokes our earlier discussions of the books of Zechariah, Jubilees, IV Ezra and I Enoch in particular (BT San 97a–b):

> Said Rav Katina: The world will exist for 6000 years and be destroyed for 1000, as it is said in Scripture: "And the LORD alone shall be raised up on that day" (Isa 2:11). Abayye said: It will be desolate for two thousand years, as it is said: "After two days he will restore us, on the third day he will raise us and we shall live before him" (Hos 6:2).
>
> Traditional teaching supports the view of Rav Katina as follows: Just as the law of the Sabbatical Year requires that fields lie fallow one of every seven years, so too the world will lie fallow for 1000 years of 7000, as it is said: "And the LORD alone shall be raised up on that day"...and it says: "A thousand years in your eyes are like a day that has passed" (Ps 90:4).
>
> A tradition-reciter from the school of Elijah reports: The world will last for 6000 years. Chaos will reign for 2000. Torah will reign for 2000. The Days of Messiah will last for 2000. But because of our numerous sins, those years have been taken away.
>
> Said Elijah the Prophet to Rav Judah, the brother of Rav Sala the Pious: The world will last at least eighty-five jubilees. And in the last jubilee the Son of David will come. Rav Judah replied: In the first part or the latter part? Elijah said: I don't know. Rav Judah asked: Will the entire time pass before he comes or not? Elijah replied: I don't know. Rav Ashi commented: This is what he meant—until then, don't expect him; from then on, expect him.

There are familiar themes from earlier apocalyptic tradition. But the passage also illustrates why the rabbinic world must be distinguished from the apocalyptic world.

Principally, the compilers of the apocalypses had imagined the timing of the End as a hidden divine mystery, already foreordained. The secret could be disclosed only to ancient visionaries in highly coded riddles. Rabbinic sages differ from this view. First, we note their skepticism regarding attempts to discover a foreordained moment of Messianic deliverance. Elijah the Prophet is uncertain, and some rabbinic authorities are even more emphatic: "Said Rabbi Jonathan: Let their bones explode, those calculators of the End! For people might say: 'Since he has not come, perhaps he isn't coming?'" (BT San 97b).

But more importantly, sages incorporated Torah itself into the Messianic design. Between the return to chaos and the ultimate reign of Messiah, the world is prepared by a reign of pure Torah, as we saw above. Moreover, their conception of Torah made it possible for sages to argue that Messiah could come at any moment. As they imagined it, the conditions for his coming were intimately tied to Israel's own behavior. The same section from Sanhedrin contains the following story in which Elijah is again the protagonist:

> Rabbi Joshua ben Levi found Elijah standing at the entrance of the tomb of Rabbi Shimon ben Yohai....He said to him: When is Messiah coming? Elijah replied: Go ask him yourself! He asked: Where does he live? Elijah replied: At the gate of the city. He asked: What are his distinguishing features? Elijah replied: He is sitting among the diseased poor. All of them untie and tie their bandages together, but he unties them one by one, thinking, "Should I be summoned, I don't want to delay."
>
> Rabbi Joshua ben Levi went to Messiah and said: Peace to you, my Master and Teacher! Messiah replied: Peace to you, ben Levi! ...He asked: When is Master coming? Messiah replied: Today! Rabbi Joshua ben Levi returned to Elijah, who said: What did he say to you? Rabbi Joshua ben Levi replied: ...He lied to me, for he said: "I am coming today"—but he did not come! Elijah replied: He was referring to this verse, "Today, if you will obey his voice" (Ps 95:7).

This story assumes an intimate connection between the coming of Messiah and the condition of Torah among Israel. True, Torah was a cosmic principle with its mysteries. But it was expressed in a form that humans could comprehend without prophetic powers—the Written and Oral traditions of the sages. Messiah would come when Israel perfected its knowledge of and loyalty to Torah. Not prophets, but Israel led by sages could bring Messiah.

And who would Messiah be? The Talmud uses the title "Son of David," which expresses the dominant rabbinic view that Messiah would be a descendant of the ancient royal house of Israel. But sages were reticent to focus upon any living figure as Messiah. Early Jewish followers of Jesus of Nazareth, of course, had seen in him the fulfillment of messianic promises. But he had died a criminal's death and left the world in Exile entirely as it had been, tales of his resurrection notwithstanding.

The second-century hero of Israel's war against Rome, Shimon bar Kosiba, seems to have won the approval of some sages as Messiah. Yet his failure made him, and those who supported his Messianic candidacy, the butt of rabbinic jokes: "When Rabbi Akiva saw Bar Kosiba he said: This is King Messiah! Rabbi Yohanan ben Torta said to him: Akiva, grass will grow through your cheek bones and the Son of David will still not have come!" (PT Ta'an 68d).

In rabbinic opinion, Messiah would surely be a warrior, defeating oppressive nations in battle, as many apocalyptic visions had imagined. And, of course, he would also be a king, ruling over the kingdom established by God, as God himself had promised to prophets such as Ezekiel. But of crucial importance was that he be a sage, a master and teacher of Torah. These assumptions, perhaps, explain the rabbinic tendency to focus messianic attention upon the figure of David. Of all the figures known to scriptural tradition, or who enjoyed messianic status in the apocalyptic traditions, David most plausibly combined in a single figure all the criteria of messiahship. As warrior he had created the largest Israelite empire in history. And everyone knew he had been God's most beloved and loyal king. But most crucially, the reputed author of the book of Psalms could be imagined as both prophet and sage, a master of Torah. A story about David's miraculous alarm clock makes the point: "Rav Shimon the Pious said: David had a harp hanging over his bed. When midnight came, the north wind would blow on the strings, and the harp would play by itself. David would immediately arise and engage in Torah study till dawn" (BT Ber 3b).

So the Son of David, descendant of a king who had studied Torah from midnight to daybreak, would come to redeem Israel from Exile. He would rebuild the "Fallen Tabernacle of David" (Amos 9:11) just as the last survivors of the Babylonian Exile had rebuilt Solomon's temple. And it was he who would preside over the events promised by generations of apocalyptic visionaries: the resurrection of the dead to judgment and God's transformation of the universe back to its original harmony. But the day of his arrival depended entirely upon Israel. As we have seen, he could come even today—but only if Israel listened to God's voice as heard in the Torah of the sage.

In this sense, the rabbinic world achieved a balance between its vertical and horizontal axes that seems to have been rare in other worlds of early Judaism. Within it, reflection upon the vertical axis of cosmic space drew one's attention inevitably to the horizontal axis of unredeemed time. Meticulous absorption in charting and embodying the fullness of Torah served to heighten anticipation of that time when, under the shadow of the restored temple, all the world would stream to rebuilt Jerusalem to bask in the fullness of the Divine Presence. Messiah would redeem the Exiles and hasten the day when God, Torah, and Israel would be One.

Conclusion

This chapter has brought you through a complex body of ideas and images. But the point has been a simple one. We have tried to show how Judaic worlds of antiquity imagined the structure of reality, how people came to arrange their knowledge of the world. We have seen that such knowledge was structured by five fundamental symbols arranged along vertical and horizontal axes. Along the vertical axis the symbolic triad of God-Torah-Israel served as the structuring elements by which Jews arranged whatever they held to be true about the created order and the ancient past. Along the horizontal axis of Exile-Messiah, they plotted the meaning of the past, the possibilities of the present, and the promise of the future.

In order to illustrate this we focused upon three model worlds. The first, represented by the wisdom traditions of ancient Judaism, portrayed a world deeply committed to the symbols of the vertical axis, one that ignored or at least underplayed the symbolic meaning of Exile and Messiah. The second, represented by various prophetic and visionary writings within and beyond the scriptural canon, stressed the horizontal axis. It retained the cosmological structure known to wisdom traditions. But it used that structure as a backdrop to its own distinctive drama—the coming transformation of the world under messianic circumstances. Finally, we reviewed the rabbinic world structure, which for centuries embodied a rather precarious, but normally successful, attempt to balance and integrate both symbolic axes. It inherited much from preceding Judaic worlds but altered everything in light of its own distinctive emphasis upon the crucial symbol of Torah.

Notes

1. The concepts of "symbol" and "symbolic vocabulary" used in this chapter are quite close to the more detailed discussion of Robert S. Ellwood, *Introducing Religion: From Inside and Outside*, 3rd ed. (Englewood Cliffs, N.J.: Prentice Hall Inc., 1993), pp. 65–89.

2. For a somewhat different scheme of core symbols than those pursued here, see Seth Schwartz, *Imperialism and Jewish Society, 200 BCE–640 CE* (Princeton, N.J.: Princeton University Press, 2001), pp. 49–87. Isolation of what is central to Jewish or any other religious discourse is often dependent upon the larger questions that shape our research.

3. James Kugel and Rowan A. Greer, *Early Biblical Interpretation* (Philadelphia: The Westminster Press, 1988), pp. 40–51, have a very thoughtful discussion of how Jews comprehended their past during the Persian and Hellenistic periods. See also John J. Collins, *Between Athens and Jerusalem* (New York: Crossroad, 1983), pp. 25–59 and Erich S. Gruen, *Heritage and Hellenism: The Reinvention of Jewish Tradition* (Berkeley: University of California Press, 1998), pp. 110–136.

4. For an orientation to the Israelite tradition of wisdom, see James L. Crenshaw, *Old Testament Wisdom: An Introduction* (Atlanta: John Knox Press, 1981). On the figure of the sage, see Joseph Blenkinsopp, *Sage, Priest, Prophet: Religious and Intellectual Leadership in Ancient Israel* (Louisville, Ky.: Westminster John Knox Press, 1995), pp. 9–65.

5. See Collins, *Between Athens and Jerusalem*, pp. 137–194 for a fine overview of the Judaic forms of the Hellenistic philosophical tradition. A dated, though still useful, introduction to Philo of Alexandria as a Judaic thinker is that of Samuel Sandmel, *Philo of Alexandria: An Introduction* (New York and Oxford: Oxford University Press, 1979).

6. Elias J. Bickerman, one of the great modern students of Greek-speaking Judaism, offers a useful chapter on the translation techniques of the Septuagint in his *The Jews in the Greek Age* (Cambridge, Mass. and London: Harvard University Press, 1988), pp. 101–116.

7. For the migrations of "do unto others" in particular, see Raymond F. Collins, "The Golden Rule," *The Anchor Bible Dictionary*, Volume II (New York: Doubleday, 1992), pp. 1070–1071.

8. As you might imagine, discussion of ancient Judaic angelology is a rather esoteric academic discipline. A good place to go for an introduction is the multi-authored article "Angels and Angelology" in *The Encyclopaedia Judaica* (1972), vol. 2, 956–978.

9. See *The Special Laws* III:1 in F.H. Colson, trans., *Philo VII* (Cambridge, Mass. and London: Harvard University Press and Heinemann, 1937), pp. 475–477 and On the Creation, 23 in F.H. Colson and G.H. Whitaker, trans., *Philo I* (Cambridge, Mass. and London: Harvard University Press and Heinemann, 1929), pp. 55–57.

10. Philo's disinterest in the Jewish political past in the Land of Israel or its messianic future is discussed in Sandmel, *Philo*, pp. 102–110.

11. For a social description of Israelite prophecy, see J. Blenkinsopp, *Sage, Priest, Prophet*, pp. 115–165.

12. A common expectation among Jews of a messianic redeemer of Davidic descent did not emerge until the first century BCE. An excellent recent study of the question is that of Kenneth E. Pomykala, *The Davidic Dynasty Tradition in Early Judaism: Its History and Significance for Messianism* (Atlanta: Scholars Press, 1995).

13. I quote from the translation of John J. Collins, "The Sybilline Oracles," in James H. Charlesworth, *The Old Testament Pseudepigrapha*, I (Garden City, N.Y.: Doubleday & Company, 1983). See his introduction in that volume, pp. 317–324.

14. An ambitious and illuminating study of the diverse apocalyptic tradition in Judaism is that of John J. Collins, *Seers, Sibyls and Sages in Hellenistic-Roman Judaism* (Boston and Leiden: Brill Academic Publishers, 2001).

15. For comparative studies of these journey motifs, see Martha Himmelfarb, *Ascent to Heaven in Jewish & Christian Apocalypses* (New York and Oxford: Oxford University Press, 1993).

16. I quote the translation of Ephraim Isaac, in J. Charlesworth, *The Old Testament Pseudepigrapha*, I, 20–21.

17. This quote and the one to follow are from the translation of Bruce M. Metzger, in J. Charlesworth, *The Old Testament Pseudepigrapha*, I, 535, 537–538.

18. The most comprehensive survey of rabbinic ideas of Torah, which tracks as well the development of these ideas in different rabbinic texts, is that of Jacob Neusner, *Torah: From Scroll to Symbol in Formative Judaism* (Philadelphia: Fortress Press, 1985).

19. This point is made with great effect in Jonathan Schofer, *The Making of a Sage: A Study in Rabbinic Ethics* (Madison, Wisc.: University of Wisconsin Press, 2005).

20. A fine study of the image of God in rabbinic parables is that of David Stern, *Parables in Midrash: Narrative and Exegesis in Rabbinic Literature* (Cambridge, Mass. and London: Oxford University Press, 1991).

21. For the role of magical practices in rabbinic cultures, see Michael D. Swartz, *Scholastic Magic: Ritual and Revelation in Early Jewish Mysticism* (Princeton, N.J.: Princeton University Press, 1996), pp. 33–54.

22. The laws of tithing and uncleanness are highly complex. A good introduction to the tithing system is Alan J. Avery-Peck, *Mishnah's Division of Agriculture: A History and Theology of Seder Zeraim* (Chico, Calif.: Scholars Press, 1985), pp. 13–32.

23. For the conceptual background of rabbinic conceptions of cleanliness and uncleanliness, including the relation of these concepts to moral conditions,

see Jonathan Klawans, *Impurity and Sin in Ancient Judaism* (Oxford and New York: Oxford University Press, 2000) and Christine E. Hayes, *Gentile Impurities and Jewish Identities: Intermarriage and Conversion from the Bible to the Talmud* (Oxford and New York: Oxford University Press, 2005).

24. The ritual rinsing of hands prior to eating is one important link between the Pharisees and the later sages. See J. Poirier, "Why Did the Pharisees Wash Their Hands?" *Journal of Jewish Studies* 47 (1996), pp. 219–233.

25. A fine collection of essays on the various messianic traditions of ancient Judaism and their bearing upon rabbinic messianic ideas is found in Jacob Neusner, William S. Green, Ernest Frerichs, eds., *Judaisms and Their Messiahs at the Turn of the Christian Era* (Cambridge: Cambridge University Press, 1987). For the development of rabbinic messianic ideas between the second and the sixth centuries, see Jacob Neusner, *Messiah in Context: Israel's History and Destiny in Formative Judaism* (Philadelphia: Fortress Press, 1984).

CHAPTER 4

Social Foundations of Early Judaic Worlds

THE SCATTERED Mediterranean and Levantine communities descended from exiled Judeans had shared neither a spoken language nor a single territory since the early sixth century BCE. Yet, throughout the first Judaic millennium, most recognized among themselves enough common traits to regard themselves as a distinct people within the larger, multi-ethnic environment of the Greco-Roman and Sasanian empires. Their self-perception coincided with the way their neighbors perceived them.[1]

A key element in this common perception was the understanding that Jews lived in accord with customs that distinguished them rather markedly from most other nations. It was, after all, the common customs of the descendants of Judean exiles that earned them the Greek name *ioudaioi* and their way of life the title *ioudaismos*, "Judaism." What, then, was this *ioudaismos* that caught the notice of Hellenistic observers from the fish markets of Alexandria to the hill country of Jerusalem and on to the rich farmlands of Mesopotamia?[2]

As we shall see in this chapter, it was not one, but many things. We will begin our survey by sketching the broadest outlines of agreement among ancient Jews about what constituted the distinctive traits of the Jewish nation. There were, indeed, broad areas of agreement as to how Jews were distinguished from non-Jews. But this consensus also led to sharp debates about the ways in which Jewish life should reflect Jewish national identity. In Second Temple Palestine, where the historical evidence is most plentiful, the very existence of an international consensus about Judaism created the conditions for sharp sectarian social divisions among Jews. These distinctions were at one and the same time social, ethnic, and religious in character, and most were routinely linked to interpretations of the common Judaic symbolic vocabulary.

The result was a plurality of Judaic religious worlds, each with distinctive types of religious leadership, unique patterns of communal discipline, and varying kinds of social possibilities for men and women. Most Jewish communities were relatively accommodating to the participation of non-Jewish outsiders in various dimensions of the communal life. Others could be nearly closed even to Jewish outsiders. An underlying theme of this chapter, accordingly, is precisely how diverse Judaic communities viewed Jewish and non-Jewish outsiders. We'll see that some of these outsiders became insiders, "converts," either to Judaism or to a form of Judaism other than the one they were born into. Such converts routinely expressed their new self-understanding by taking up a new kind of Judaic life among other like-minded people. To convert was to enter a new social group with its own intensely experienced world.

Judaism as National Custom

Many striking impressions about early Judaism are preserved in the Greek and Latin writings of non-Jewish historians, ethnographers, philosophers, poets, and geographers of the Hellenistic world. Some of these authors observed Jews at first hand in their own city or during travels to Judea, Syria or points east. Other impressions were passed on as common knowledge, what "everyone" knew about the Jews. As with most amateur anthropology, much of this literature tells us more about the interests of the observers than the lives of the observed. Some comments are flattering, presenting Jews as a barbarian ("stuttering," i.e., non-Greek-speaking) people whom even Greeks might do well to emulate; some are mean-spirited. Some observers regard the Jews as a race of philosophers; others, noting their tendency toward communal self-segregation, regard them as unsociable misanthropes, "haters of humanity." In any case, what drew the attention of most writers were exotic oddities.[3]

Some Jewish Curiosities

The Roman historian Dio Cassius (160–230 CE) expressed himself in a way typical of many others, adopting a tone of detached, slightly amused condescension. In the course of describing the events leading to Rome's conquest of Jerusalem in 63 BCE, Dio Cassius offered his Greek readers the following observations on the Judean natives (*Roman History*, 37:16–17):[4]

> The country has been named Judea, and the people themselves Jews. I do not know how this title came to be given them, but it applies also to all the rest of mankind, although of alien race, who affect their customs. This class exists even among the Romans....They are distinguished from the rest of mankind in practically every detail of life, and especially by the fact that they do not honour any of the usual gods, but show extreme reverence

for one particular divinity. They never had any statue of him even in Jerusalem itself, but believing him to be unnameable and invisible, they worship
him in the most extravagant fashion on earth....They dedicate to him the
day called the day of Saturn, on which, among many other most peculiar
observances, they undertake no serious occupation.

Dio Cassius begins by pointing out that there are many, "of alien race," even
Romans, who follow Jewish customs and are called Jews. We'll return to
this point later. For now we focus on what interests him: the Jews' exclusive
worship of an invisible god and their odd reverence for Saturday, a day on
which they do none of the normal work of the world.

The Jews were widely known as monotheists who, contrary to normal
practice, tolerated no images of their divinity. While many Hellenistic writers praised Judaic monotheism as a philosophically sound idea, the Jews' failure to respect the One God with a properly impressive figurative statue
perplexed many. Had these anthropologists read the Septuagint's many in-
junctions against depicting the God of Israel in an image (e.g., Exodus 20),
they might have remained perplexed; but they would have at least understood the source of the Jews' stubbornness on the matter.

Dio is correct as well in his notion that Jews refrained from working on
the Sabbath (Hebrew: *shabbat*) as a way of dedicating themselves to the God
of Israel (see Exod 20:8–11). His reference to the "peculiar observances"
associated with the Sabbath is vague. Perhaps it points toward patterns of
communal worship or Torah study mentioned by first-century CE Jewish
writers such as Philo and the Jewish historian Flavius Josephus.

Many Greek and Latin writers noticed an oddity in Jewish dietary habits.
Plutarch (ca. 40–120 CE) composed an entertaining depiction of cultivated
men engaging, in good Roman style, in thoughtful reflection at a meal. As
the wine flows conversation wanders to the arcane. Quite naturally, the
topic of the Jews arises. Perhaps because of the culinary setting, attention
turns to their well-known aversion to the meat of pigs and other delicacies
treasured by civilized peoples. It is asked: Do they, perhaps, hate the pig or,
to the contrary, hold the pig in some sort of reverence? (*Dinner Conversations*, 5:2–3):[5]

> "My impression," said Callistratus, "is that the beast enjoys a certain
> respect among that folk;...according to the story, it was the first to cut
> the soil with its projecting snout, thus producing a furrow and teaching
> man the function of a plowshare....So I think the Jews would kill pigs if
> they hated them, as the Magi (i.e., Persians) kill water mice; but in fact it
> is as unlawful for Jews to destroy pigs as to eat them. Perhaps it is consistent
> that they should revere the pig who taught them sowing and plowing,
> inasmuch as they honour the ass who first led them to a spring of water.

Otherwise, so help me, someone will say that the Jews abstain from the hare because they can't stomach anything so filthy and unclean."

"No indeed," countered Lamprias, "they abstain from the hare because of its very close resemblance to the ass, which they prize so highly....The Jews apparently abominate pork because barbarians especially abhor skin diseases like lepra and white scale, and believe that human beings are ravaged by such maladies through contagion."

From here, the conversation passes on to other oddities about the Jews, including the possibility that their famous invisible deity is really Bacchus or Dionysis.

Plutarch's explanations of the Jews' dietary aversions are no more convincing than many posed before and since. But he clearly knew something: pigs, hares, and asses are among the many animals of field, water, and air that are regarded in Leviticus 11:1–46 and Deuteronomy 14:3–21 as "unclean," and forbidden to Jews as food.

Jews as They Explained Themselves

Jews, of course, could always point to scripture (usually in Greek) to explain the origins of some of their most striking customs. But they were often unclear about how to defend those customs in terms that cultivated Hellenists might grasp. From the second century BCE until the first CE, Jews writing in Greek expended much energy explaining the beneficial effects of such rules on Jewish moral and physical well-being. A pioneer in this vein was the anonymous Egyptian Jewish writer of the *Letter of Aristeas to Philocrates* (ca. 150 BCE). The letter describes the circumstances that led to the translation of the Torah into Greek. But in the course of things, the author demonstrates the rational grounds of some Jewish customs that drew ridicule from Greek observers *(Letter of Aristeas* 142–155):[6]

> To prevent our being perverted by contact with others or by mixing with bad influences, Moses hedged us in on all sides with strict observances connected with meat and drink and touch and hearing and sight, after the manner of the Law (*nomos:* "Torah")....Do not take the contemptible view that Moses enacted this legislation because of an excessive preoccupation with mice and weasels or suchlike creatures....
>
> Everything pertaining to conduct permitted us toward these creatures and toward beasts has been set out symbolically. Thus the cloven hoof (e.g., Lev 11:3), that is the separation of the claws of the hoof, is a sign of setting apart each of our actions for good, because the strength of the whole body with its action rests upon the shoulders and the legs. The symbolism conveyed by these things compels us to make a distinction in the performance of our acts, with righteousness as our aim....

The man with whom the aforesaid manner of disposition is concerned is the man on whom the legislator has also stamped that of memory. For example, all cloven-footed creatures and ruminants quite clearly express, to those who perceive it, the phenomenon of memory. Rumination is nothing but the recalling of the creature's life and constitution, life being usually constituted by nourishment. So we are exhorted through scripture also by the one who says thus: "Thou shalt remember the Lord, who did great and wonderful deeds in thee."

The point, one supposes, is that you are what you eat. Consumption of hoof-parting cud-chewers encourages the ability to distinguish between right and wrong, just as it will enhance memory, the central faculty in the mastery of wisdom. Had Plutarch's diners only read the *Letter of Aristeas*, they could have spared themselves a good deal of idle speculation about the motives of at least some Jews who refrained from pork!

The Jews, among a host of other barbarian types from urban society, were a favorite target for the Roman satirists. The first century CE Persius, lampooning the sights and smells of the Sabbath in Rome's Jewish neighborhood, adds one other commonly noticed detail (*Satires* 5:180–184):[7]

> But when the day of Herod comes round, when the lamps wreathed with violets and ranged round the greasy window-sills have spat forth their thick clouds of smoke, when the floppy tuna's tails are curled round the dishes of red ware, and the white jars are swollen out with wine, you silently twitch your lips, turning pale at the Sabbath of the circumcised.

Persius is the first to observe a common Sabbath custom among Jews: eating fish and drinking wine. But he interests us in the present context because of his reference to circumcision—the surgical removal of the foreskin.

Many peoples (then and now) practiced circumcision as part of a boy's passage into manhood. But the Jews of antiquity (and now) were commonly thought to be unique in imposing circumcision on infants. Greeks and Romans saw it as a sign of extreme crudity—marring the beauty of the human form. Jewish men, for their part, believed it to be the mark of their descent from, Abraham, who, at the age of ninety-nine, had circumcised himself as well as all the males of his household at God's command (Gen 17:9–27).[8]

One of the ablest interpreters of circumcision in early Judaism was Philo of Alexandria. His massive explanation of the laws of the Torah, entitled *The Special Laws*, begins auspiciously with a vigorous defense of circumcision on a variety of grounds (*Special Laws* I, I):[9]

> I will begin with that which is an object of ridicule among many people,…namely the circumcision of the genital organs. It is very zealously

observed by many other nations, particularly by the Egyptians, a race regarded as preeminent for its populousness, its antiquity, and its attachment to philosophy. And, therefore, it would be well for the detractors to desist from childish mockery and to inquire in a wiser and more serious spirit into the causes of which the persistence of this custom is due.

Philo's first line of defense is to point out that the Egyptians, universally held to be a wise nation, are themselves fond of circumcision. The Jews, by implication, are not fools. He then proceeds to list four arguments for circumcision. These are grounded in hygienic explanations "handed down to us from the old-time studies of divinely gifted men who made deep research into the writings of Moses" (*Special Laws* I: II). But appeals to tradition are rarely enough for Philo. His final defense of circumcision, as we should expect, is philosophical:

> I consider circumcision to be a symbol of two things most necessary to our well-being. One is the excision of pleasures that bewitch the mind. For since among the love-lures of pleasure the palm is held by the mating of man and woman, the legislators thought good to dock the organ that ministers to such intercourse, thus making circumcision the figure of the excision of excessive and superfluous pleasures signified by one, the most imperious.
>
> The other reason is that a man should know himself and banish from the soul the grievous malady of conceit. For there are some who have prided themselves on their power of fashioning as with a sculptor's cunning the fairest of creatures, man, and in their braggart pride assumed godship, closing their eyes to the Cause of all that come into being.... The evil belief, therefore, needs to be excised from the mind with any others that are not loyal to God.

Circumcision, for Philo, is an outward sign that continually reminds its bearer of an inner truth: that pleasure is fleeting and that God alone is truly the creator of life. We cannot, of course, know who might have been convinced by Philo's argument. But that he felt obliged to make it indicates the centrality that he and other Jews ascribed to it in the domain of Jewish custom.

Together, then, with religious loyalty to an invisible god, the preservation of Saturn's day as a day of rest, and the avoidance of perfectly good foods, circumcision was one of the distinguishing traits of the Jews. The earliest writings that describe Jews as willing to fight and die in defense of their national customs are all associated with these same traits. Compelling descriptions are preserved in a Jewish work, written in Hebrew late in the second century BCE, entitled II Maccabees. It is preserved in Greek translation in many Old Testament canons.

Most of the book describes the rise of the Hasmonean kingdom, beginning in the revolt of the Maccabees against attempts to suppress distinctive Jewish customs. This suppression is vividly portrayed (*II Macc* 5:8–20):[10]

> At the suggestion of the people of Ptolemais a decree was issued to the neighboring Greek cities that they should…make the Jews partake of the sacrifices (to Zeus, the High God), and should kill those who did not choose to change over to Greek customs. One could see, therefore, the misery that had come upon them. For example, two women were brought in for having circumcised their children. They publicly paraded them around the city, with their babies hanging at their breasts, and then hurled them down headlong from the wall. Others, who had assembled in the caves nearby, in order to observe the seventh day (i.e., the Sabbath) secretly, were betrayed…and were all burned together, because their piety kept them from defending themselves, in view of their regard for that most holy day.…Eleazar, one of the scribes in high position, a man now advanced in age, was being forced to open his mouth to eat swine's flesh. But he, welcoming death with honor rather than life with pollution, went up to the rack of his own accord, spitting out the flesh, as all ought to go who have the courage to refuse things that are not right to taste, even for the natural love of life.

Described here are more than customs. Refusal to violate the Sabbath, eat pork, worship foreign gods, or spare their sons circumcision were principles of behavior for which some Jews would rather die than betray.

It is quite possible, of course, that Jewish writers focused upon aspects of Jewish custom that were the most visible to foreigners. In light of silence about less controversial customs, these may appear to stand out as particularly central. Nevertheless, the broad agreement across centuries and languages suggests that the traits we have isolated were, indeed, crucial markers of membership in the Jewish nation.

Conversion to Judaism

It is surprising that these customs seem to have proved attractive to many non-Jews. Dio Cassius is only one of a number of writers who, from the first century CE onward, pointed out that Jewish communities included people of non-Jewish birth. You'll recall that he knew of Romans who were called Jews after accepting Jewish customs.[11] Moreover, women—usually of relatively high social standing and independent means—comprised a highly visible segment of those attracted to Jewish communities. Perhaps the most famous such convert was one Queen Helene of Adiabene, who, according to Flavius Josephus, brought her entire country with her into the fold.[12] Other writers speak of God Fearers (*theosebeis*)—non-Jewish women and uncircumcised men—who congregated at Jewish prayer gatherings, celebrated the Sabbath, and otherwise participated in Jewish national customs. Archaeological inscriptions, moreover, reveal that at least some non-Jews—including at least one female philanthropist—might contribute to the construction or repair of Jewish communal buildings as gifts to the Jewish community in whose life they shared.[13]

Since no writing from a self-professed God Fearer or convert has survived, it is difficult to know what motivated such men and women to attach themselves to the nation of Israel or what their experience in it was like. It is also difficult to know how the Jews they joined interpreted the converts' motives.[14] Greek and Latin writers who comment on the phenomenon of non-Jewish participation in Judaism seem to regard it as bizarre in the way that contemporary journalists understand the "cult phenomenon." And, to a degree, this may be part of the truth.

The Roman Empire knew a rich array of religious communities that served needs unmet by the ceremonial, essentially patriotic, worship of the Roman emperor. In addition to ancestral or national religions, there were many private religious associations that were multi-ethnic in character. Mithraism, for example, was composed primarily of soldiers in the Roman army, without regard for national origins. And, of course, Christianity grew increasingly popular after the first century as a multi-ethnic religious community. Members of such associations shared initiatory rituals, worshipful allegiance to a protective god or goddess, and celebration of communal meals. All this bound people of diverse backgrounds into a single fellowship offering loving companionship in this life and the next.[15]

God Fearers probably regarded the Judaism they encountered as just such a private religious association. Its ancient origins in redemptive acts of God were well known. Members, moreover, enjoyed a richly evocative release from worldly concerns on the Sabbath. They observed subtle mysteries symbolized by prohibited and permitted foods and held an international membership, promising a meal and shelter wherever one travelled. And, for men at least, circumcision into the covenant of Abraham offered an appropriately heroic initiation procedure.

The Basic Markers of Judaic Social Identity

Let us now summarize our survey of the basic markers or outward signs of Jewish social identity in the middle centuries of our millennium. *Ioudaismos* included those born into the nation—the vast majority—and those who circulated within it as what might be called "associates." It was open in principle to those from outside on condition of accepting the nation's collective discipline. Presupposed was exclusive loyalty to a single god, the God of Israel, as the sole object of religious veneration (precisely how, we shall discuss in Chapter Five).

Bound up with exclusive loyalty to the God of Israel were a number of associated observances that together and individually combined to create important barriers between the free mixing of Jews and non-Jews. One was the day of rest, the Sabbath. Although no universal norms seem to have governed its celebration, it was clearly honored as a day free of labor, an opportunity to gather together to affirm loyalty to the God of Israel and membership in the community of Israel. While the world went on its course, the Jews separated from it to be among each other.

The dietary restrictions also served as an important marker of Jewish social separation. At the very least, those who followed dietary rules could not share entirely in the meals of their non-Jewish neighbors. In light of the attention this attracted among non-Jews, it seems certain that Jews were often not subtle about this, but used the custom as a way of limiting even permissible socializing with non-Jews over food.

Circumcision, too, conveyed an important social meaning, for physical nakedness was important in the public expression of Hellenistic civic identity. In the education of young men, as well as in city-wide cycles of public celebrations, athletic training and competition played a key role. Such competition was conducted by unclothed contestants. Their nakedness placed on display the perfection of the human form at the height of its skills. Participants in such sport, like athletic heroes of our own day, were perceived to embody and celebrate the Hellenistic cultural heritage.

On such occasions, the "mutilated" Jewish male would clearly constitute a reminder of the ethnic boundaries that separated him (and his barbaric nation) from the rest of the world. Such separation only began with a man's body. Symbolically, however, it extended all along the spacial, vertical axis of reality. From the body it reached upward into the highest summits of the cosmos, pointing toward a god different from all others; from his body its implications spread outward throughout the human community, marking off "a people dwelling alone, and not counting itself among the nations" (Num 23:9).

Natural and Intentional Judaic Communities

The customs that distinguished Jews from the non-Jewish world served also to distinguish Jews from one another. As we have seen, early Judaism had no central institution empowered to define a single pattern of living for all Jews. Rather, on the basis of certain core customs and a relatively shared symbolic vocabulary, Jews everywhere formed a variety of communities. Each community preserved its own traditions of Judaic expression. Out of these grew several quite discrete Judaic worlds.

Modern students of early Judaism commonly refer to the diversity of Judaism in the Greco-Roman period as an example of religious sectarianism. The term "sect," however, tends to carry connotations of conflict over the interpretation of creeds or theology. Moreover, as the term "sect" has been used by students of early Judaism, it often applies to groups that were not social separatists at all, such as the Zadokite priestly families, who constituted more of a clan or an estate than a self-defined religious community. The character of Jewish diversity in ancient times is better grasped by thinking of various communities as settings for the pursuit of distinct styles of life rather than the search for a common set of beliefs. Many Jews chose from a range of possible communal paths that promised a more intensive engagement with the world of the divine than was possible in their communities of birth.

These communities were societies of like-minded people who made a self-conscious decision to join a group that offered a form of Judaic life superior to others. These were, so to speak, "intentional" communities, groups formed of individuals who made conscious decisions to leave one life path for another. Such intentional communities can be contrasted with "natural" Judaic communities. The latter, surely incorporating the vast majority of Jews throughout the Greco-Roman world, perceived Jewish ethnic bonds as the primary basis of communal boundaries.

These ethnic bonds were cemented through the national customs we discussed in the first part of this chapter. Jews in natural communities shared certain common customs and recognized certain basic symbols as their own. But they were rather tolerant of wide ranges of behavior within the broad limits of Jewish social custom, and recognized few official interpretations of the common symbolic vocabulary as binding upon individual belief. They also seem to have been rather tolerant as well of God Fearers and other well-meaning non-Jews participating in communal life.

Members of intentional communities, by contrast, cultivated more careful rules for observing common Judaic customs, especially the Sabbath or the dietary rules. Similarly, insiders tended to have a clearly defined understanding of "right" and "wrong" interpretations of Judaic scriptures and symbolic vocabulary. Often, such rules and interpretations were taken as signs of special loyalty to God, and thus entitled members of the community to an enhanced status as the "remnant" or "elect" of Israel. Sometimes such communities could be very strict in requiring new Jewish members to abandon old ways of living. Presumably, it would be very difficult for non-Jewish God Fearers to feel welcome in such settings.

But these are only generalizations. We will begin our survey of specific communities with the Samaritans, who survive even today as a separate ethnic-religious group in the State of Israel. Their example will help us clarify how it is that a religious world can be "Judaic," yet, at the same time, be regarded by itself and others as outside the community of Judaism. From the Samaritans our attention will turn to vigorous intentional communities. All of them made clear demands that initiates undertake radically new ways of living in conjunction with deeply changed self-understandings. These are the members of the Dead Sea community at Qumran (ca. 150 BCE–68 CE), the Therapeutae of Egypt (first century CE), and the early Jewish communities committed to the messiahship of Jesus of Nazareth (ca. 32 CE–200 CE). We will conclude our survey with the emerging communities of rabbinic disciples (ca. 80 CE–250 CE).

The Samaritans: Israel but Not Jews

Those raised in cultures shaped by Christian traditions are used to thinking of the word "Samaritan" as a synonym for one who performs an unusual act of humanitarianism. The image, of course, comes from the famous parable of the "Good Samaritan" in the Gospel of Luke 10:29–37. A look at this parable will prove useful here. To Jesus' reminder to "love your neighbor as yourself" (quoted from Lev 19:18), an obtuse lawyer responds, "Who is my neighbor?" Jesus replies:

> "A man was going down from Jerusalem to Jericho, and fell into the hands of robbers, who stripped him, beat him, and went away, leaving him half dead. Now by chance a priest was going down that road; and when he saw him, he passed by on the other side. So likewise a Levite, when he came to the place and saw him, passed by on the other side. But a Samaritan while traveling came near him; and when he saw him, he was moved to pity. He went to him and bandaged his wounds, having poured oil and wine on them. Then he put him on his own animal, brought him to an inn, and took care of him. The next day he took out two *denarii* (coins), gave them to the innkeeper, and said, 'Take care of him; and when I come back, I will repay you whatever more you spend.' Which of these three, do you think, was a neighbor of the man who fell into the hands of the robbers?" He (the lawyer) said, "The one who showed him mercy." Jesus said to him, "Go and do likewise."

To understand the power of the parable, you have to know that Samaritans were regarded with great contempt by many Jews of that time. The "good

Samaritan" of this parable is a figure chosen to shame people with pretensions to being righteous before God. The parable is intended to surprise its audience: even a Samaritan, a member of a despised minority, could fulfill a simple commandment of the Torah in a way that the powerful and privileged might well emulate.

Who were these Samaritans and why did the Gospel writer take for granted that Jews had contempt for them?[16] To describe the "who" will help answer the "why." The term "Samaritan," like the term "Jew," links a distinct people to a particular place—the district of Roman Palestine called Samaria (Hebrew: *shomron*), bordered by Judea to the south and the Galilee to the north. Samaritans claimed to be descendants of the ancient northern kingdom of Yisrael. It's first king, Jeroboam, had broken away from Solomon's Yehudah-based empire in 920 BCE. Under numerous subsequent dynasties, Yisrael pursued its own cultural and political life until it was destroyed by Assyria in 722 BCE. Its capital city, Samaria, lent its name to the remnant that still populated the area.

It was not the Samaritans' location that attracted unpleasant attention to them. Rather, it was their claim to be the only authentic survivors of the exiled Israelite nation. From their homeland, which divided Roman Palestine between Judea and the Galilee, they denied the historical authenticity of the political and religious institutions of Jerusalem. This conflict between the Samaritans and the Judeans had persisted throughout the Hellenistic period. Its focus was the temple.

Contrary to the long-standing tradition of most Diaspora and Palestinian Jews, the Samaritans insisted that Mt. Gerizim in Samaria was the place that God had long ago chosen as the sole place from which to offer sacrifice. They had built a temple there and refused to acknowledge the legitimacy of the temple in Jerusalem. The final break between the Samaritan and the Judean communities probably came during the Hasmonean period. The Hasmonean king, John Hyrcanus, for motives that might have been both practical and theological, destroyed the Mt. Gerizim temple in 128 BCE. It was never rebuilt.

No doubt many who had worshipped there later blended into the larger Jewish population of Palestine and turned their loyalties to Jerusalem. But many others continued to refuse submission to the centrality of Jerusalem, its temple, priesthood, and royal dynasty. They were the creators of a distinctive Samaritan identity over against that of other Jews of Judea or the Galilee. They continued to offer sacrifices on Mt. Gerizim—a rite conducted by Samaritan priests up till the present—and developed their own complex social and religious traditions.

The crucial literary expression of this Samaritan identity was produced within a century of the destruction of the sanctuary on Mt. Gerizim. It was a distinctively Samaritan scripture, a version of the Torah of Moses. This Torah differed from the Torah preserved in rabbinic tradition in many minor ways, a trait it shares with other ancient versions of the Torah of Moses. But what distinguished it from all other Jewish or Christian versions was its preoccupation with Mt. Gerizim as a divinely appointed sacrificial site.

We can look at its rendition of the Ten Commandments of Exod 20:1–17. In the Samaritan version, the following comment is added to verse 17:[17]

> And it shall be, when the LORD your God brings you up to the Land of the Canaanites that you are about to inherit, you shall set up for yourselves great stones. Coat them with lime and write upon them all the words of this Torah. And when you cross the Jordan, set up these stones, concerning which I command you this day, on Mt. Gerizim. And build there an altar to the LORD your God, an altar of stones,…and offer up upon it burnt offerings to the LORD your God, and sacrifice peace offerings. And you shall eat and rejoice there before the LORD your God on that mountain, across the Jordan, toward the setting sun, in the Land of the Canaanite, who dwells in the Arevah, opposite Gilgal, near Elon Moreh, opposite Shechem.

These lines are composed of verses found elsewhere in the Torah (e.g., Deut 11:29, 27:2–7, 11:30), but you will not find them after Exodus 20:17 in any Jewish or Christian Bible, ancient or modern.

Like all the versions of the Mosaic Torah we discussed in Chapter Two, the Samaritan Torah constitutes a community's judgment regarding the true revelation of God to Moses. In this case, that judgment was capable of surviving even after the rabbinic version of the Torah suppressed all its earlier competitors. Indeed, the Samaritan Torah is the basis of a rich body of Samaritan interpretive tradition that began in antiquity and reached great heights during the Middle Ages.

The Samaritan case offers one example of how far we can stretch the concept of a Judaic world. In many respects, the Samaritans were much like Jews. Like Jews, Samaritans were monotheists who revered the God of Israel. They honored the Sabbath as well, sharing many Sabbath customs with other Palestinian Jews. They circumcised their male children and avoided forbidden foods like the Jews. But, at the same time, they distinguished themselves from Jews. Their social relations with Jews were kept to a minimum. Moreover, they worshiped at their own sites and celebrated biblical festivals in their own fashion, in accord with their own calendrical system. Most important, while Jews and Samaritans would identify them-

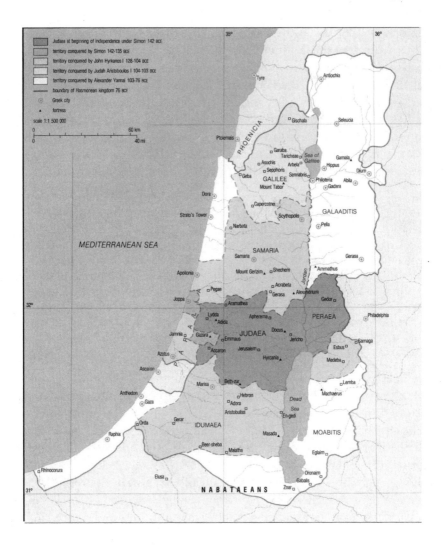

Samaria: Between Judea and Galilee

Source: Based on Nicholas De Lange, *Atlas of the Jewish World*
(Oxford: Equinox, 1984), p. 24.

selves as ethnic "Israelites," the Samaritans would deny they were also "Jews." Samaritans regarded Jews as a foreign people, and so did the Jews regard them. Samaritan customs and the Samaritan conception of Israel's past served to define a Judaic religious world over against that of the dominant religious worlds of the Jews. Both communities shared key symbolic elements such as the vertical triad of God-Torah-Israel. And at least one

Samaritan group, the first-century CE Dositheans, developed as well a powerful messianic movement based upon a redeemer of Mosaic rather than Davidic ancestry.[18]

These parallels and contrasts lead us to an unavoidable conclusion. The Samaritans' religious world is an example of a Judaic world that, in its own view as well as in the eyes of Jews—is not part of Judaism. Neither the Samaritans nor the Jews regarded the religious world of the Samaritans as continuous with Judaism, yet the historian of religion must surely include the Samaritan world in any discussion of the worlds of early Judaism.

The Yakhad: The Converts of Israel in Damascus

As natural as Jewish identity in antiquity might have seemed to the Jews and those who wrote about them, there were many Jews who perceived their precise way of expressing Jewish customs as a self-conscious decision. What distinguished different Judaic communities was, among other things, the degree to which the decision to live in a certain kind of communal discipline was valued as a turning point in a person's devotion to the God of Israel.

One intentional Jewish community that stressed the need for an active choice of a new Judaic way of life seems, appropriately, to have called itself the *yakhad* (Community). An important settlement from this group flourished in the Judean Desert south of Jerusalem, in a barren region called Wadi Qumran, near the shore of the Dead Sea. For this reason, the group is often referred to as the Dead Sea Sect or the Qumran Sect, even though it seems clear that the settlement at Qumran was one of perhaps several locations settled by the community. While most scholars have agreed for some decades that the group was founded early in the Hasmonean dynasty, there is vigorous debate about nearly every other important question about the community.[19]

Some of the Yakhad's own writings seem to have been preserved among the other literary works now widely known as the Dead Sea Scrolls. In scrolls such as the Damascus Rule, the Community Rule, and others, we find numerous references to the Yakhad's leadership, initiation procedures, and other illuminating information. What emerges is a very vivid picture of a community clearly committed to an ideal of total life reorientation—conversion—as the only way to be truly part of Israel's covenant relationship with the God of Israel.[20]

The circumstances of the group's origins are unclear. Most historians suspect that the Yakhad originated in a group of Jerusalem priestly families claiming descent from Zadok. Reputed to have been a descendant of Aaron, Zadok had been appointed high priest by King Solomon (I Kings 2:35). His descendants dominated the Jerusalem temple throughout much of the history of ancient Yehudah and, it appears, were installed in the high priesthood during the Persian and Hellenistic periods as well. This changed in the wake of the Maccabean wars. By 152 BCE the high priesthood was filled by members of the non-Zadokite Hasmonean family (see Chapter One). The founders of the Yakhad, it is argued, may have been demoted or deprived of their due by the new order.

Since the discovery of the community's writings and communal buildings, many historians have tried to link the Yakhad to one of the Jewish groups mentioned in the writings of Flavius Josephus, Philo, and other ancient writers. Most contemporary historians believe that the Yakhad was part of a community known in ancient Greek-language sources as the Essenes, a monastic group reported to have lived in the Dead Sea area. This is likely, but the Qumran texts do not yield any obvious Hebrew equivalents of the name "Essene." Moreover, there are many ways in which ancient descriptions of the Essenes do not match the profile of the literature at Qumran.[21]

A more recent proposal links the Yakhad to yet another group that figured prominently in the temple bureaucracy of the Hasmonean and Herodian administrations. This group is known in Greek writings as the Sadducees and in rabbinic texts as the Zadokites (Hebrew: *tzaduqim*). They appear to have been in routine conflict with the early Pharisees about numerous legal and theological points. Until recently, these disputes were reported only second-hand in Josephus' writings and those of the rabbis. The publication of a fragmentary text called the "Halakhic Letter" (Hebrew: *miqtzat ma'aseh torah*) from among the Qumran scrolls, however, reveals that the writer of this letter held some legal views ascribed in the Mishnah to the Sadducees. The letter appears to have been written by a member of the Yakhad to a Hasmonean priest-king. It describes certain points of dispute between the writer's community and the official teachings emanating from Jerusalem. Since the Yakhad seems also to have been hostile to the Pharisees, it is indeed possible that the Yakhad and the Sadducees had some traditions in common.[22]

There is one major difficulty, however, in linking the Yakhad's self-designation as Zadokites too firmly to the Sadducees. The latter are said by Josephus and the writers of the Gospels to have enjoyed great power in the Jerusalem temple in the Hasmonean and Herodian times—precisely when the founders of the Yakhad seem to have been deprived of their Zadokite prerogatives. Perhaps before us is the record of two distinct priestly groups each claiming authentic Zadokite lineage. One dominated, the other went

Zadokite Law in the Halakhic Letter and the Mishnah

The anonymous author of the Halakhic Letter found at Qumran Cave 4 sought to summarize for an unnamed Hasmonean king some areas of halakhic dispute that divided his own community from other Jews. His discussion raises some fascinating historical questions. Included in his list of disagreements is the following observation:

> *And concerning liquid streams* (mutzakot): *we are of the opinion that they are not pure, and these streams do not act as a separative between impure and pure (liquids). For the liquid of streams and (that) of (the vessel) which receives them are alike, (being) a single liquid.* (MMT: B 55–58; translation cited from E. Qimron and J. Strugnell, eds., *Discoveries in the Judaean Desert. X. Qumran Cave 4. V. Miqsat Ma'ase Ha-Torah* [Oxford: Clarendon Press, 1994], p. 53).

The problem is a technical matter involving the transmission of ritual uncleanness from one pitcher to another. I have a clean pitcher full of clean water. What happens if I pour the water into an unclean pitcher? According to our author, the uncleanness of the empty pitcher will climb, as it were, "upstream" via the stream of water descending into it from the clean pitcher. The water and both pitchers are now unclean.

See now the opinion recorded in M. Makhshirin 5:9: *Any liquid stream* (nitzok) *is pure.* The Mishnah holds the very opposite view on the case described in MMT. The uncleanness of the lower pitcher does not travel up the spout into the clean pitcher.

Another mishnaic passage, M. Yadaim 4:7, sheds fascinating light upon the identities of both the Qumranian group and those whose opinion the Mishnah records:

> *The Zadokites say: We challenge you, Pharisees! For you declare the liquid stream pure!*

Remarkably, the Halakhic Letter and M. Yadaim 4:6–8 offer catalogs of legal disputes in which the Zadokite figures of the Mishnah represent the view of the author of MMT, while the Mishnah's Pharisees represent the views of MMT's author.

Does this prove that the Qumran community was of Sadduceean origin? Does it prove that the Pharisaic *halakhah* of the second century BCE was identical to that of the Hasmonean state?

into exile in the Judean wilderness. In any event, closer identification of the Yakhad with the Sadducees, Essenes, or any other group must await further historical research.

It is obvious, however, that the nature of the Yakhad as a religious community was bound up with its principled opposition to the official Jewish administration controlling the temple. It's calendrical system, for example, was a solar calendar similar to that of the book of Jubilees, and thus contradicted the calendar by which the timing of Jerusalem's festivals was calculated. The Yakhad's opposition began shortly after the Hasmonean victory over the Seleucids. Some of their writings recall the rise to power of a "Wicked Priest" who, after a brief period of favorable rule, "forsook God and betrayed the precepts for the sake of riches."[23] In response, the founders of the Yakhad and other sympathizers seem to have left (or were forced to leave) Jerusalem. They created their own priestly communities throughout southern Judea. The site at Qumran is perhaps one of them.

Claiming priestly descent through Zadok, the Yakhad's founders interpreted their separation from Jerusalem as a self-exile of the pure and holy genuine priests from the impure political appointees who had gained control of the temple. Unlike most worlds associated with priestly groups, however, theirs was deeply marked by the horizontal or historical axes of Judaic symbols. They awaited a time in the near future when God himself would restore the true descendants of Zadok to the temple service in a cosmic battle. This war, between the Children of Light (the Yakhad) and the Children of Darkness (other Jews and their imperial supporters), would usher in the end of time and the direct rule of God.[24]

The Yakhad's communal discipline must be interpreted against this background. Although its writings are not in total agreement about all aspects of the Yakhad's structure and government, there is enough agreement to permit some useful generalizations. It is clear, to begin with, that the Yakhad's view of the priesthood was complex. On the one hand, in accord with universally held assumptions, it was inherited through one's family. On the other, one could assume certain priestly prerogatives through a transformation of one's moral life. This is reflected in the social composition of the group. The leaders seem to have been priests by family lineage, but many members were clearly not of priestly families. Their priestly status, rather, was acquired by their commitment to living in accord with a rigorous communal discipline.

We quote from the Damascus Rule's interpretation of a verse from the canonical book of Ezekiel (Damascus, 3–4):[25]

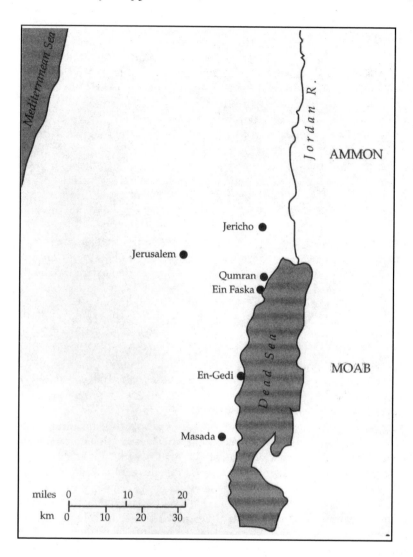

The Dead Sea Wilderness Region

Source: Based on H. Shanks et el., *The Dead Sea Scrolls after Forty Years*
(Washington, D.C.: Biblical Archaeology Society, 1991, 1992), p. x.

Archaeological Remains of the Yakhad

The ruins on the far left seem to have housed a communal dining room. The function of many of the rooms remains unclear. The ruins sit on a prominent bluff (center) overlooking a wadi, or dried riverbed (on the right).

Source: Sonia Halliday Photographs

"The Priests, the Levites, and the sons of Zadok who kept the charge of my sanctuary when the children of Israel strayed from me, they shall offer me fat and blood" (Ezek 44:15). The "Priests" are the converts of Israel who departed from the land of Judah, and the "Levites" are those who joined them. The "sons of Zadok" are the elect of Israel, the men called by name who shall stand at the end of days.

This statement contains the Yakhad's self-understanding in a nutshell. Ezekiel's references to various orders of inherited priesthood are systematically expanded to include non-priests who have taken up the community's life.

The Hebrew phrase, *shavei yisrael* literally means, the "returners of Israel," the elect who have separated themselves from the rest of Israel, and, in preparation for the end of days, have returned to the true service of God.

With the Jerusalem temple polluted, the members of the Yakhad saw their own communal life as a pure sacrificial offering that alone brought atonement and purification from the increasingly heavy weight of Israel's sinfulness.

According to the Damascus Rule, returners were viewed as having entered a "New Covenant in the land of Damascus" (that is, Exile—Qumran).[26] The commitment to this New Covenant was total, involving one's entire personhood and possessions. Thus, the Community Rule (Community, 1):[27]

> All those who freely devote themselves to [God's] truth shall bring all their knowledge, powers, and possessions into the Community of God, that they may purify their knowledge in the truth of God's precepts and order their powers according to His ways of perfection, and all their possessions according to His righteous counsel.

In order to prepare for this total commitment, returners served a period of training at the fringes of the community and learned how to follow its specific interpretations of the rules of the Torah. Both the Damascus Rule and the Community Rule list scores of such rules that govern all areas of personal life, interpersonal relations, hierarchies of communal authority, and ritual matters.

According to the Community Rule, individuals had to demonstrate over a period of two years their suitability to join the community. During this testing period, prospective members were denied full participation in the community's ritual meals. Finally, after passing an examination before a council composed of communal leaders, "if it be his destiny...then he shall be inscribed among his brethren in the order of his rank for the Torah, and for justice, and for the pure meal; his property shall be merged and he shall offer his counsel and judgment to the community."[28]

The borders of the Yakhad, obviously, were not easy to cross. One was required to become cleansed physically and spiritually so as not to pollute the common life that constituted the Yakhad's sacrificial offering. Converts could move from outside the group to the inside only by becoming a disciple, learning in a period of initiation the distinctive life-style that distinguished the wise and pious from the ignorant and wicked. It is difficult to imagine that those born of non-Jewish parents (by any definition of Jewishness) could have been considered as initiates. This was a community of "Israel" open only to those born into the Jewish nation willing to commit to the true path of covenantal life.

What was communal life like? Despite rigid hierarchies based upon priestly birth and knowledge of scripture, it was characterized by an overall sense of powerful community. Thus, the Community Rule: "These are the ways in which all of them shall walk, each man with his companion, wherever they dwell. The man of lesser rank shall obey the greater in matters of work and money. They shall eat in common and pray in common and deliberate in common."[29] A focus of communal life was a communal meal presided over by hereditary priests. These meals also seem to have served as teaching occasions at which "there shall never lack a man among them who shall study the Torah continually, day and night, concerning the right conduct of man with his companion."[30]

Some writings of the Yakhad speak of a mysterious Teacher of Righteousness (*moreh tzedeq*), an inspired leader raised by God, who disclosed to the original members of the Yakhad important mysteries contained in scripture. It is unclear how his authority was inherited or transmitted in later generations. What seems beyond doubt, however, is that scriptural study at Qumran, under a series of figures who held the title of Interpreter of the Torah (*doresh hatorah*), was regarded as a kind of revelatory experience.

Gathered around the Interpreter, members felt in the presence of prophecy, as the Torah's "hidden things" (Deut 29:28) became manifest to all. This was especially so, perhaps, in the teaching of new initiates. "When they have been confirmed for two years in perfection...they shall be set apart as holy.... And the Interpreter shall not conceal from them, out of fear of the spirit of apostasy, any of those things hidden from Israel that have been discovered by him."[31]

Let us make a few observations at this point. Before us is a small, cohesive society viewing itself as the "true" Israel. Unlike the Samaritan example, however, this claim was not historical or ethnic in focus. Rather it was entirely moral. "Israel," to be sure, is an historical people for the Yakhad. But the true Israel is the community of Jews who penitently returned to the service of the God of Israel. Whereas the Samaritan communities might have regarded themselves as the *original* Israelite people, the members of the Yakhad seem to have viewed themselves as the *last* Israelite people.

The members of the Yakhad, as an expression of their conversion to the New Covenant, had separated themselves from the rest of Israel. Their identity as Israel was grounded in this conversion, a moral transformation of each individual member. Those Jews who remained loyal to the corrupt regime of Jerusalem—and their non-Jewish imperial allies—were doomed to destruction in the coming war in which the forces of Light would overwhelm those of Darkness. The morally transformed would prevail.

The Yakhad's communal style of life was entirely centered around the act of conversion, which brought one into the community of Light. Elab-

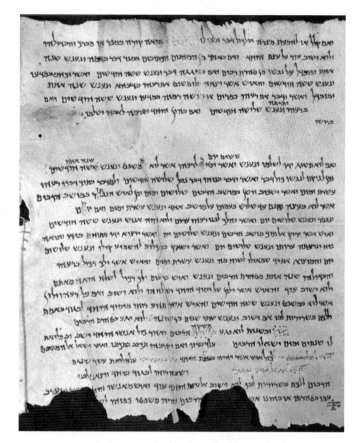

The Community Rule of the Yakhad

This photograph shows column 7 of the Community Rule, which spells out behavior expected of initiates into the Yakhad. The paragraph at the top of the column begins as follows:

> If any man has uttered the Venerable Name even though frivolously, or as a result of shock, or for any other reason whatever, while reading the Book or praying, he shall be dismissed and shall return to the Council of the Community no more. If he has spoken in anger against one of the Priests inscribed in the Book, he shall do penance for one year and shall be excluded for his soul's sake from the pure Meal of the Congregation. But if he has spoken unwittingly, he shall do penance for six months. Whoever has deliberately lied shall do penance for six months. Whoever has deliberately insulted his companion unjustly shall do penance for one year and shall be excluded.

Source: Photograph by John C. Trever. Courtesy of the School of Theology at Claremont, Ancient Biblical Manuscript Center.

orate initiation disciplines filtered out those whose original conversion
proved insincere. Once fully incorporated into the community, however,
the initiate enjoyed an intense life structured around obedience to detailed
rules for living and submission to the teachings of charismatic leaders gifted
with prophetic powers.

What did the Yakhad share with other Judaic communities? Not much,
if we use as our standard the relatively open-bordered "natural" Jewish
communities described by Hellenistic writers. The Yakhad maintained a
detailed body of rules that governed their observance of Jewish custom. This
discipline served as a way to exclude other Jews who might have, for example, revered the Sabbath or avoided forbidden meats, but observed such
customs in ways rejected by the Yakhad as too lenient or without prophetic
authority. In addition to establishing a social distance from other Jews, the
discipline surely served to limit interactions with non-Jews.

Most important, the Yakhad understood its way of life as a conscious
rejection of a person's own past. Entering the community was the beginning
of a new, redeemed life, a life free of earlier sins and untainted by others who
continued to sin. In the new community one found fellow travellers upon
a road that would lead to the coming redemption. Redemption would
confirm that the choice made in conversion was the only choice to be made.

The Therapeutae: An Israel for Women

The decision to leave one form of life and, through moral transformation,
enter another more intensely lived community is a common pattern among
Jewish groups in antiquity. The freedom to make such a decision for oneself
and for one's immediate family seems to have been largely a prerogative
enjoyed by men. With the exception of some women at the very pinnacles
of the social and economic ladder, most women of the Greco-Roman
world, Jewish or otherwise, were economically and legally subordinated to
their husbands or fathers (if unmarried).[32] In the case of intentional Jewish
communities, such as the Yakhad, it is probable that a married man's entry
into the community would automatically include his wife and children. But
could a married woman, regarded as part of her husband's household, make
a decision on behalf of her husband and children? This is highly unlikely.
Similarly, there is no reason to believe that an unmarried woman could take
up life in the Yakhad or in one of its outlying communities independently
of a male sponsor, such as a brother or father.

In one community, however, it is certain that women freely undertook
the project of personal transformation within a communal Jewish setting.
It was possible, however, only for women whose personal circumstances

had freed them from family obligations. The community in question thrived in first-century CE Egypt, and was known in Greek as Therapeutae, which seems to mean "healers" or, perhaps, "worshippers." They practiced a life of prayer, ascetic discipline and study on the outskirts of Alexandria. Among them, men and women joined equally of their own free will and pursued a common discipline in sexually segregated societies.

All our information about the Therapeutae comes from Philo of Alexandria, who discusses them in detail in his book *On the Contemplative Life*.[33] They serve him as a model of what it means to live in pursuit of philosophical knowledge and the loving service of God. Since Philo is our only source of information—and so clearly uses the Therapeutae to model his own ideas of virtue and piety—it is hard to be sure that his picture is any more accurate than those of Greek and Latin writers on the Jews. On the other hand, Philo had a generally dismal view of women, regarding them as lustful and unsuited to intellectual pursuits, making it is hard to imagine him inventing a group of women philosophers. By reading his account carefully, we can draw some cautious conclusions.

In Philo's view Therapeutic men and women (the latter are called by the feminine form, Therapeutrides) pursued an identical discipline in their separate communities. They passed their days living alone in simple huts, undisturbed by the needs of children or the tempests of sexual relationships. Let Philo describe their way of life in his own words (*Life* 25–28):[34]

> In each house there is a consecrated room that is called a sanctuary or monastery and closeted in this they are initiated into the mysteries of the sanctified life. They take nothing into it, either food or drink or any other of the things necessary for the needs of the body, but laws and oracles delivered through the mouth of prophets, and psalms, and anything else that fosters and perfects knowledge and piety. They keep the memory of God alive and never forget it, so that even in their dreams the picture is nothing else but the loveliness of divine excellences and powers.
>
> Twice every day they pray, at dawn and at evening; at sunrise they pray for a fine bright day…in the true sense of the heavenly daylight, which they pray may fill their minds. At sunset they ask that the soul may be wholly relieved from the press of the senses and the objects of sense and, sitting where she is consistory and council chamber, to herself pursue the quest of truth. The interval between early morning and evening is spent entirely in spiritual exercise. They read the holy scriptures and seek wisdom from their ancestral philosophy by taking scripture as an allegory, since they think that the words of the literal text are symbols of something whose hidden nature is revealed by studying the underlying meaning.

Philo here describes the ideal of philosophical existence in terms distinctive to Jews.

Although contemplation of God is the object that these Jews share with Greco-Roman philosophers, the source of philosophical study is not Plato, Aristotle, or the writings of the Stoic teachers, but the Torah of Moses and the writings of the prophets, as filtered through the interpretive lens of philosophical allegory. Through it, these men and women are initiated into the ultimate mysteries of holy living. Philo, we sense, would feel very much at home among them.

Men and women mingled only in celebration of the Sabbath and the late spring festival of Shavuot. Philo depicts the Sabbath celebration as a philosophical discourse offered by a senior male member of the community in a house set aside for communal functions. Here men and women sat separately, divided by a partition that, according to Philo, served two purposes: "the modesty becoming to the female sex is preserved, while the women sitting within ear-shot can easily follow what is said, since there is nothing to obstruct the voice of the speaker" (*Life*, 33).[35] After the discourse, members shared a simple communal meal of bread and salt seasoned with herbs.

The Shavuot celebration seems also to have taken the form of a philosophical discourse and common meal, but with an added feature—communal song. Philo interprets these hymns as commemorative in nature, re-enactments of the songs sung by Israelite men and women upon their redemptive passage through the waters of the Red Sea after the liberation from Egypt (Exodus 15).

His admiration of the participants shines through his description of their song (*Life*, 88–89):[36]

> It is on this model above all that the choir of the Therapeutae of either sex, note in response to note and voice to voice, the treble of the women blending with the bass of the men, create a harmonious concert, music in the truest sense.... Thus they continue till dawn, drunk with this drunkenness in which there is no shame, then not with heavy heads or drowsy eyes but more alert and wakeful than when they came to the banquet, they stand with their faces and whole body turned to the east and when they see the sun rising they stretch their hands up to heaven and pray for bright days and knowledge of the truth and the power of keen-sighted thinking. And after the prayers they depart each to his private sanctuary once more to ply the trade and till the field of their philosophy.

In this song the purest mingling of male and female takes place, the mingling of ethereal voices divorced from physical desire and passion. Male and female transcend each other in that most Hellenistic of liberations, liberation from the limitations of the corrupt, mortal body.

Philo's description of the women attending the Shavuot celebration offers insight into the women attracted to this sort of community and a clue into what it offered them as women in particular. He (*Life*, 68) describes them, on the whole as:[37]

> aged virgins, who have kept their chastity not under compulsion, like some of the Greek priestesses, but of their own free will in their ardent yearning for wisdom. Eager to have her (Wisdom) for their life mate they have spurned the pleasures of the body and desire no mortal offspring but those immortal children that only the soul that is dear to God can bring to the birth unaided, because the Father has sown in her spiritual rays enabling her to behold the verities of wisdom.

Let us reflect on this in light of other things we have learned about the Therapeutae.

In order to have engaged in the strenuous Therapeutic discipline of textual and philosophical study, women would have had to be highly educated. In Philo's Egypt, this would have been the privilege of very few men, not to mention women. This suggests, therefore, that the Therapeutae in general came from a rather exclusive sector of Egyptian Jewry. The Therapeutrides must have been well born as well.

These women are described as older "virgins" (Greek: *parthenoi*). In the Greek of Philo's day, this term could refer either to a young woman without a legitimate sexual partner, a woman who had never had sexual relations, or one who had ceased to have them. This suggests that these women were either unmarried throughout their lives or, if married at one time, were now freed of that relationship by the death of their husbands or, perhaps, divorce. What made it possible to become a Therapeutride, therefore, was a combination of social privilege and freedom from the responsibility to care for a husband and family. The only children they cared for, as Philo puts it, were the immortal conceptions of the mind, impregnated there by the seeds of God's own Word.

The Therapeutrides, then, were a community of single women who separated from families and social obligations to pursue a life of disciplined study and reflection upon Wisdom (that is, Torah and philosophy). It would be exciting to find a text produced by a Therapeutride who reflected upon her experience in this women's Israel. Unfortunately we can draw inferences only from Philo.

Women within this community enjoyed two kinds of freedom. On the one hand, they were inducted into the essential mysteries of God and constituted a spiritual elite within the larger community of Israel. The freedom from ignorance offered by knowledge of Torah was fully theirs in a way few

Jews of that day, men or women, would ever enjoy. On the other hand, this initiation also freed them from their culturally defined roles as caregivers and childbearers. Husbandless and childless, they became free to create themselves anew as souls who, responsible to no one but God, were no longer defined by common expectations of what women might do or be. This choice of community, of course, had broad implications. It was a choice not only against other styles of life available in the Egyptian Jewish community, but against the dominant Hellenistic conceptions of what a woman could hope for and become.[38]

The Jesus Communities: An Israel for Jews and the Nations

Another communal setting that proved particularly attractive to a wide range of the Greco-Roman population were the numerous communities of born-Jews and non-Jews who gathered together for common meals and ritual celebrations in the name of the Messiah (in Greek: *Christos*), Jesus of Nazareth *(Iesou* is the Greek form of the Hebrew name *Yeshua)*. The designation of these groups as "Christian" was coined in Syria in the second century CE, a century after Jesus' death. But, like "Judaism" itself, a broad term like "Christianity" hardly does justice to the diversity of these communities, either in first century CE Palestine or throughout the Mediterranean and Middle East for some centuries thereafter. Here we can only hint at the details of what, from the perspective of those beyond the Jewish nation, became the most important intentional community ever created within Judaism.[39]

Christian leaders of the second to fourth centuries commonly noted the survival of various sorts of Jewish Christians, who constituted a curious or even threatening minority presence within the emerging universal Church. Some of these were understood to be communities of ethnic Jews who celebrated Jesus' messiahship, while others seem to have been, at least in part, ethnically non-Jewish. What troubled bishops about such groups was their tendency to observe some or all of the common Jewish customs.[40]

Circumcision and a persistence in celebrating Jewish Sabbaths and festivals seem to have been fairly common. In some groups, women were said to use their menstrual periods, in accord with Mosaic law (Lev 15:19ff.), as an excuse to abstain from sexual relations.[41] Groups like the Nazoreans and the Ebionites were believed even to preserve their own gospel traditions in Hebrew or Aramaic, in addition to (or instead of) the Greek Gospels used by most Christian communities.

We do not know which, if any, of these communities preserved any real continuity with Jesus' original disciples, the Jewish founders of what had become Christianity. For that matter, the lives and beliefs of the original disciples of Jesus are difficult to reconstruct from the Gospel traditions recorded near the end of the first century CE. Historians are usually very cautious in claiming to know what Christianity was like before it began to claim an identity distinct from Judaism. It is likely, however, that most Jewish devotees of Jesus in the mid-first century CE would have been surprised to hear that their communities were anything but an expression of Judaism.[42]

Rather, they had chosen to pursue a particularly intense form of Judaic communal life. This life, with its own discipline, brought them into routine relation with the God of Israel, through his chosen Messiah. Jesus, to be sure, had not conquered Rome in a victorious battle; rather, he had been executed for political crimes against the Roman state. But Jesus' disciples claimed that his death had been followed by a miraculous resurrection. This miracle threw a surprising light on all the messianic hopes of the Jewish people as preserved in the canonical scriptures.

The Messiah would, indeed, transform all of the world and preside as Davidic heir over God's kingdom. But his primary redemptive act was first experienced by individuals in their own lives. By conquering death on the Cross, Jesus was believed to have exercised a role previously reserved for God. He had conquered the power of death over those who accepted his self-sacrifice on their behalf. To place one's faith in Jesus' messianic self-sacrifice was to be reborn into a this-worldly immortality and placed in a new relationship to God. In hymns, prayers, and other forms of veneration, those redeemed from death by the Messiah commonly celebrated him as a heavenly being, hardly distinguishable from the God who had sent him.[43]

Like the Yakhad, the communities gathered in Jesus' name were grounded in personal conversions expressed by taking up a new way of life. Converts embarked upon the new life of immortality through a purifying baptism. They reconfirmed its power in a celebratory ritual meal (Greek: *eucharist*) in which members became part of the "Body of Christ" by symbolically consuming Jesus' body and blood in the form of bread and wine. They expressed it morally by living within the communities of those redeemed in Jesus.

There is little in the communities we have described that is not congruent with the symbolic vocabulary we have found in early Judaic worlds. Jews of the first century CE knew of heavenly beings who, like Jesus, were close to God and served as his agents. Some also preserved traditions that a messianic figure would die prior to the redemptive drama. True, the symbolic eating of the Messiah would have struck many as extremely puzzling.

But, for all that, Jewish communities founded in Jesus' name prior to 100 CE probably shared a good deal with most "natural" communities of Jews. Certainly they were no more idiosyncratic than, for example, the Samaritans (who portrayed themselves, we recall, as Israelites who were not "Jews"), the Yakhad (who regarded the temple priesthood as a kind of government of occupation), or the Therapeutae (who considered themselves a spiritual elite). By contrast, Jewish followers of Jesus regarded themselves as part of the Jewish people, offered temple sacrifices alongside other Jews at the appropriate festivals, and, like other Jews, eagerly anticipated the transformation of the world in the messianic age.

Indeed, the Jesus communities seem to have achieved a balance between "insiders" and "outsiders" rare within early Judaic communities. They represented an openness of boundaries similar to natural Jewish communities, even while cultivating an intense communal life characteristic of intentional communities. In terms of overall patterns of custom, for example, these communities would have appeared typically Jewish—preserving Sabbath rest, dietary restrictions, and circumcision. Like many natural Jewish communities (and unlike the Yakhad, for example), both Jews and non-Jewish God Fearers were welcome among them, even if they did not fully share the discipline of the group.

For initiates, rigid hierarchies based on social rank and wealth were relatively lax—more so, for example, than at Qumran. Women, too, seem to have enjoyed degrees of authority as prophets or teachers. It is difficult to find evidence of women in such positions in other Jewish communities of the period. Even the Therapeutrides, you'll recall, listened through a screen while men offered philosophical teaching. Women and men, finally, could become members on their own, without giving up families who remained outside the fold.[44]

These messianic communities seem, then, to have been well integrated into the spectrum of Judaic communities of the mid-first century CE. Yet, by the end of that century, it had become clear to many that the Jesus-communities were not "Judaism" but something else. What had happened?

What happened, in essence, is that the message of Jesus' redemptive conquest of death had become more attractive beyond the communities of Judaism than within them. Increasing numbers of non-Jews had associated themselves with the Jesus-communities. In some cases, non-Jewish members were required, as part of their conversion, to accept the patterns of circumcision, Sabbath observance, and dietary customs common to most natural Jewish communities. In others, however, the issue was raised as to whether participation in the redemptive common life require a convert to accept Jewish social customs.

The most important responses to this question were offered by Paul of Tarsus (died, ca. 62 CE), a brilliant interpreter of early traditions about Jesus. A Greek-speaking Jew from Asia Minor, Paul had not known Jesus personally. But shortly after learning of Jesus' career, he became convinced that Jesus' death and resurrection had a unique significance. Paul had accepted a fundamental tradition that Jesus had risen to heaven upon his resurrection and would soon return as God's messianic agent to preside over the resurrection of the dead, the judgment of humanity, and the perfection of human history. To this, Paul added his own distinctive insight: Jesus' resurrection as Messiah was the first act of a redemptive drama that would incorporate Israel and the non-Jewish nations into a single body of humanity redeemed from sin and death. Messiah had come to redeem not only Israel, but all humans who trusted in the power of his self-sacrifice.[45]

Paul, a man of intense energy, possessed remarkable rhetorical skills. He became one of the most successful of many messengers of the redemptive good news (*euangelion*; "Gospel") then traversing the Roman Empire. The New Testament's book of Acts offers a description of his evangelizing practice as it was recalled by Gentile Christian tradition a generation after his death. Entering a city, he would set up teaching in a Jewish community in which God Fearers were numerous. There he would try to prove that various verses from the canonical scriptures contained predictions of Jesus' redemptive death.

Sometimes, as in Lystra in southern Turkey, he made himself a disruptive presence and was beaten and expelled (Acts 14:19–20). Often enough, as Acts relates matters, both Jews and God Fearers would find his proofs and teaching convincing. Under his guidance they would create a special community (*ekklesia,* "church") in which to pursue a new form of life "in Christ." Initiation into such a life began with baptism, which purified the soul from sin and enabled its rebirth into a new life. It was lived in light of retellings of the stories of Jesus' miracles and teachings designed to evoke his presence. It often reached peaks of ecstatic experience, interpreted as prophetic inspiration.

All this involved, as you might guess, a radical reinterpretation of fundamental elements in the symbolic vocabulary of Judaism. One of Paul's principle messages was that in the community of those redeemed in Christ, ethnic distinctions between "Jew and Greek" were meaningless. "Israel," that is, acquired a new meaning in Paul's symbolic vocabulary. It defined

Adoration of Jesus as Messiah and God as Ruler: A Striking Liturgical Theme in Early Judaism

The prominent role of Jesus as an angelic or divine figure for early Christians should not obscure the deep roots of such devotion in the traditions of early Judaism. Below is a case in which a liturgical tradition of Christian prayer surfaced centuries later among non-Christian Jews.

This passage from an early Christian hymn is quoted by the apostle Paul in his letter to a community he founded at Philippi in Macedonia (Philippians 2:5–11). The letter was probably written around 60 CE and testifies to a very early form of worshipful adoration of Jesus as divinely appointed Messiah:

> Therefore God also highly exalted him and gave him the name that is above every name, so *that at the name of Jesus every knee should bend, in heaven and on earth and under the earth, and every tongue should confess* that Jesus Christ is Lord, *to the glory of God the Father.*

Compare the images of this passage with the one that follows. This hymn first appears in the literature of heavenly ascent that circulated at the fringes of rabbinic communities in the last centuries of our period. By the early Middle Ages, the hymn became part of the rabbinic New Year liturgy. In more recent centuries, it has come to be sung at the conclusion of every daily worship service.

> Therefore, we hope for you, our God, quickly to see the splendor of your power to banish idols from the earth and that the false gods be cut down; to perfect the world under the reign of the Almighty, and that all flesh and blood call upon your name that all the wicked of the earth turn to you. May all who dwell on Earth recognize and know *that to you every knee must bend and every tongue must swear,* and before you every living thing must kneel and prostrate; *to the glory of your name* they must give honor.

Most probably, the Pauline text reflects the way an earlier Jewish hymn to God was adapted to refer to Messiah Jesus. Were it not for this Pauline passage, our earliest reference to the hymn would come from the centuries-later version cited in the second passage.

Sources: Philippians quoted from *HarperCollins Study Bible* (New York: HarperCollins, 1993); Maaseh Merkavah revised from the translation of M. Swartz, *Mystical Prayer in Ancient Judaism* (Tübingen: Mohr [Paul Siebeek], 1992).

a fundamentally new human possibility, as explained in a letter to his community in Rome (Rom 9:6–8):

> For not all Israelites truly belong to Israel, and not all of Abraham's descendants; but "It is through Isaac that descendants shall be named for you" (Gen 21:12). This means that it is not the children of the flesh who are the children of God, but the children of the promise are counted as descendants.

As Paul's earliest interpreters phrased it, in distinction to Fleshly Israel (the Jews) stood Spiritual Israel (the Church). Members of the Yakhad, of course, had long ago made a similar distinction between true Israel, Children of Light, and those who merely claimed the name Israel, Children of Darkness. But this spiritual Israel, Children of the Promise, defined an unprecedented community of both Jews and gentiles. All nations were entitled to the redemption offered by Christ's conquest of death and sin.

Paul's reinterpretation of the meaning of Israel is, in fact, part of a much more fundamental restructuring of the received Judaic symbolic vocabulary. As a sign of the universality of the redeemed life, Paul cautioned non-Jewish members of the Church from adopting the customs that had distinguished Jews from non-Jews. Where Jews might commonly view circumcision or dietary laws as signs of Israel's special relation to God, Paul regarded them as mere signs of confusion about the truer meaning of redemption.

In other words, Paul subordinated the symbol of Torah, which represented the body of Jewish covenantal customs, to the symbol of Messiah. Messiah, not Torah, now constituted the link between God and the Spiritual Israel. Accordingly, works of the Law (*nomos* or Torah), such as circumcision, would never help non-Jews establish a proper relation with God. This was possible only through works of faith (*pistis*) in the redemption offered by Christ to Jew and Greek (Rom 9:30–32):

> What then are we to say? Gentiles, who did not strive for righteousness, have attained it, that is, righteousness through faith; but Israel, who did strive for the righteousness that is based on the law, did not succeed in fulfilling that law. Why not? Because they did not strive for it on the basis of faith, but as if it were based on works. They have stumbled over the stumbling stone....

It is, perhaps, Paul's subordination of Torah to Messiah, his collapsing of the vertical and horizontal axes of Jewish symbolic thought into one another, which most clearly distinguishes his religious world from other early Judaic worlds.

To be sure, Paul had vigorous opponents among other early Jewish apostles. Many saw little harm in the preservation of Jewish customs in the churches. But his general approach prevailed and ultimately entered the canonical tradition of Christianity. A result of his success was that churches became dominated by non-Jewish converts for whom Jewish customs would have no particular meaning. Jewish converts to the community of Christ, by contrast, may have been much more comfortable retaining their customs within exclusively Jewish churches, even if they acknowledged that this was not a norm for all members of the Body of Christ. Such churches became marginal, however, once the link of Christian identity to Jewish national custom had been severed in most communities by the devaluation of the place of Torah in the new life.

In the meantime, most Jews outside the Jesus communities refused Jewish fellowship to uncircumcised Romans, Galatians, and others who ate pork and violated the Sabbath, yet who insisted that the Messiah had made them the True Israel. Churches, therefore, grew increasingly estranged from even the most loosely defined Judaic communities. What had begun as yet another intentional Jewish community was becoming a new kind of world altogether, built on an entirely new pool of converts.

But the parting of these worlds would take some time to solidify. By the late fourth century CE, most Christians had lost any sense of ethnic connection to Jews. Yet, the sermons of Christian bishops, like John Chrysostom of Syria, sought to identify the Christian "Judaizers" of their own day with the original Jewish opponents of Jesus. Thus, while the Gospels portray various Jewish groups engaging intensely in debate over Jesus' teaching, Christians of later centuries would perceive this debate as one between a fully formed "Christianity" and a fully corrupted "Judaism." Similarly, later rabbinic sages, seeking to defend themselves from a newly empowered State Christianity, would imagine Christianity as the invention of Jesus, designed to seduce Israel into magic, superstition, and disobedience to the Torah.[46]

The Rabbinic Communities: An Israel of Discipleship

The history of Christianity, we have seen, begins in one sort of Judaic intentional community. The character of Judaism, for the past fifteen hundred years, has been deeply stamped by another. We speak, of course, of that form of community in which the rabbinic sage played the complex role of moral guide, legal authority, and model of human perfection. For virtually the entire period covered in this book, rabbinic Judaism constituted a relatively bounded intentional community of sages and disciples, working at the margin of Jewish society in the cities and villages of the Galilee and Mesopotamia. The transformation of rabbinic Judaism into a religion that transcended the master-disciple circles and incorporated within itself most of the world's Jewish population is a story properly set in the period after the rise of Islam. But the ground for the spread of rabbinic Judaism was certainly prepared by the sages of the Land of Israel and Babylonia during the third to seventh centuries CE.

Classical rabbinic literature—the Mishnah, the Talmuds, and the various midrashic sources discussed in Chapter Two—preserves two distinct but related images of the formative rabbinic societies of the first and second centuries CE. One model recalls the sages as a kind of voluntary association grounded in particularly stringent standards surrounding the production, sale, and consumption of food.[47] Members of such communities called one another "Associates" (*khaverim*). One could join the Khavurah (Association) only after prolonged instruction in the community's food practices, which included efforts to eat daily food in a state of ritual purity normally expected only of priests performing temple service. Novices were admitted into the Khavurah by the administration of oaths that obliged members to discipline themselves along the following lines (Tosefta Demai 2:2):[48]

> He who accepts upon himself four matters, they receive him as an Associate:
>
> 1. Not to give priestly offerings and tithes to [a priest who is an] ignoramus [and might eat these offerings while impure].
> 2. Not to prepare food requiring ritual purity near an ignoramus [who might render them unclean through his ignorance].
> 3. To eat common food in a state of ritual purity [even though this is not required by the Torah for non-priests].
> 4. To tithe what he eats, and what he sells, and what he buys. And he does not accept the hospitality of an ignoramus.

Clearly, the Khavurah's rules recall aspects of the Yakhad that we have already observed. This is particularly evident in the Khavurah's apparent hostility toward Jews beyond the circle of its own membership. Such Jews are characterized in this and many other rabbinic texts as *ammei ha-aretz*, literally "people of the land," but in texts concerning the Khavurah in particular it has the connotation of "ignoramus." And so have I translated it here. Such ignoramuses were not merely ignorant. They were regarded also as hostile to members of the Khavurah and, in many cases, morally indecent (e.g., BT Pes 49b).

The other, and more common, model of early rabbinic sociability recalls sages as a community grounded in the study of scripture and associated oral traditions that were collectively called Torah. By the third century CE, however, rabbinic societies generally referred to themselves collectively as *khakhamim* (sages) or, more humbly, *talmidei khakhamim* (disciples of sages). The model represented by the Khavurah had ceased to exist as an active social reality. Tithing and purity of food were still studied, but few within the society of sages distinguished themselves from other students of rabbinic tradition as Khaverim. The effective form of rabbinic society was the circle of masters and disciples grounded in the study and transmission of traditions of Torah. While these circles recognized clear distinctions between sages and other Jews, they did not harbor profound hostility toward those regarded as *ammei ha-aretz*. Indeed, the *ammei ha-aretz* were regarded as potential recruits to rabbinic discipleship.[49]

While the wives and daughters of these communities of sages conducted their lives in accordance with rabbinic traditions, they were, in fact, peripheral to the main focus of communal life—the institution of discipleship. All known sages were male, and they chose their students exclusively from their sons, extended male relations, and even from the sons of Jews who were not born into the rabbinic communal orbit. Some rabbinic sources do recall the existence of women—usually the daughters or wives of great sages—who had sophisticated knowledge of rabbinic traditions. But it is clear that the moral and religious opportunities opened up by intimate fellowship to sages were reserved for men.[50]

The distinctiveness of rabbinic communities lay in their rather complex body of rules for performing the customs common to all Jews of antiquity. These included not only particular rabbinic traditions for observing the Sabbath, dietary restrictions, and other nearly universal markers of Jewish ethnicity in the ancient world, but also a host of practices, customs, and traditions that many non-rabbinic Jews would have regarded as thoroughly unfamiliar. These were summarized in the Mishnah by 220 CE and would become the subject of complex developments in subsequent centuries.

The Mishnah already represents the stringencies of the Association as merely of historical interest. Nevertheless, it contains many rules governing the production of food, preparations for its consumption, and even table etiquette, that seem designed to limit the range of Jews with whom rabbinic families might eat common meals. Nearly all Jews, for example, refused to eat certain meats. But rabbinic communities would only eat meat that had been slaughtered and examined in accordance with complex rabbinic procedures. Moreover, they interpreted a scriptural prohibition against boiling a goat in its mother's milk (e.g., Exod 23:19) as a prohibition against cooking meat and dairy foods together. Such rules, apparently unknown in other Jewish communities, prevented Jews who observed them from eating in the homes of Jews who did not.[51]

Other important rules regulated the celebration of the Sabbath and the festivals. These could have important social implications. Consider, for example, the rabbinic institution of a mixed domain (Hebrew: *eruv*) for the Sabbath. Rabbinic custom was to place a dish of food in a courtyard shared by several homes on Friday afternoon before the Sabbath. This food, placed in the name of all the residents, had the effect of turning the houses and the courtyard into a single "home." Legally defined as inhabitants of a single household, the several families were now free to share food and other household items with all their neighbors on the Sabbath. If, however, even one household refused to acknowledge the *eruv*, none of them could be joined together. Accordingly, outsiders to the rabbinic communities found themselves forced to either reject the *eruv*, and thus incur the displeasure of their neighbors, or to accept it and become, to a degree, participants in the Sabbath rhythms of the rabbinic community.[52]

Much rabbinic custom concerned marriage, that most important means of establishing social bonds. In the ancient world in general, marriage was not viewed primarily as a means of joining lovers together into a legitimate relationship. Rather, as much as anything else, it was a financial relationship between extended families. In a world of very rigid social hierarchies, marriage enabled families to move up (or down!) the social ladder on the backs of their marriageable children.

To these concerns, which all Jewish families might have shared in contemplating a marital match, rabbinic families added others. They would marry off their sons and daughters only to families who accepted rabbinic rules for contracting and solemnifying marriages. Terms for dowries, maintenance, and settlements in the case of divorce would be set by rabbinic guidelines. Divorced men and women could remarry a member of a rabbinic community only if the divorce had been governed by rabbinic regulations. Such laws ensured that new families would be drawn into the rabbinic communities on terms that those communities had the power to define.[53]

All these rules, in addition to a host of others covering all aspects of life, were regarded in rabbinic communities as *halakhah*. You'll recall from Chapter Two that *halakhah* was understood as tradition that had been transmitted by an unbroken line of prophets and sages from the most ancient of times and providentially preserved only by the rabbis. By the third century halakhic norms were regarded as nothing less than part of Revelation itself, the Oral Torah that God had transmitted to Moses on Sinai.

The sages' possession of Oral Torah explains the character of the most important human relationship within rabbinic communities. This, we have already observed, was the relationship between the sage *(khakham)*, the Master of Torah, and his exclusively male disciples *(talmidei khakhamim)*. The term "rabbi" originated as a form of address to any social superior. It means "My Master." In rabbinic communities, however, it was a title conferred upon a disciple by a sage. The title granted its holder the right to expound Torah in public settings, such as schools or other gatherings, to independently establish halakhic norms for other Jews, and to sit on rabbinic courts of law.

In addition to these teaching and legal privileges, however, the rabbinic sage enjoyed another kind of authority. It was grounded in his complete mastery of scripture and his ability to recall, analyze, and apply to life traditions of rabbinic learning known as Mishnah, "Repeated Tradition" (see Chapter Two). The sage's power to shape the lives and consciences of his disciples lay in great measure in their perception of him. He represented a living embodiment of what Torah could mean in human life. The Written and Oral Torah were at his total command; they flowed from his mouth as life-giving waters from a fountain.

While discoursing on Torah, the sage formed sentences and thoughts not in the Aramaic and Greek dialects of other Jews, but in the classic Hebrew phrases of the scriptures and the traditions of ancient sages going back to Moses himself. His teaching, moreover, was not confined to his public discourses. Even his most common actions—the way he blessed his bread, uttered his prayers, purchased his vegetables, or even cleaned himself in the latrine—could become sources of halakhah, disciplines by which disciples might pursue their own self-perfection. As an embodiment of Torah, the sage had insight into each disciple's character; his rebuke was devastating, while his advice and praise could set a disciple on his own path to perfecting the discipline of Torah.[54]

Rabbinic communities most probably began as collections of households in which the male heads were disciples of one or another sage. Such households would have conducted their affairs in light of the sage's teaching, as mediated through the householders, his disciples. Prior to the third century CE, it is possible that communities formed around a specific sage might have had antagonistic relations with communities formed around others. Reports about conflict between the first-century disciples of Shammai and Hillel may preserve memories of such social as well as legal conflict.

The Mishnah (Shabbat 1:5; elaborated in PT Shabbat 1:7, 3c), for example, recalls a day on which the disciples of Shammai "packed" a study session to ensure the suppression of the views of the disciples of Hillel. In another case, a sage is told that he "deserved to forfeit his life" for following a prayer practice of the disciples of Shammai (M Ber 1:3).[55] But from the time of Rabbi Judah the Patriarch's ascendancy in the late second century, the rabbinic communities seem to have displayed tolerance for the minority traditions among them.

At any event, minority viewpoints were carefully preserved, becoming part of the legal tradition awaiting the disciple's mastery. Rabbi's Mishnah is rich in reports of sages' disputes regarding details of halakhic practice as well as in views regarded as superseded. Indeed, it is largely composed of such disagreements. The mishnaic tractate Eduyot 1:5 contains an important justification for preserving them:

> Now why do they record the opinion of an individual in addition to that of the majority, since the *halakhah* accords with the majority opinion? So that when a court prefers the minority opinion it may rely upon it.

In other words, minority positions were carefully preserved so that, through judicial creativity, they might one day reenter tradition and have new life. The value of such views was stressed, a few centuries after the compilation of the Mishnah, in a famous passage of the Babylonian Talmud. In response to a dispute between the disciples of Hillel and Shammai, a heavenly voice is said to have rung out, declaring: "Both opinions express the views of the Living God—but the *halakhah* conforms to the view of the disciples of Hillel!" (BT Eruvin 13b).

From the third century on, then, halakhic disputes appear to define legitimate ranges of difference within a community rather than the norms of mutually exclusive societies. The Babylonian Talmud portrays on nearly every page the diversity of rabbinic custom as practiced by different teachers until well into the sixth and seventh centuries. At any rate, the differences rabbinic groups preserved among themselves were insignificant in comparison to the differences between rabbinic communities on the whole and non-rabbinic Jewish communities. To enter a rabbinic community was to undergo a kind of conversion; not to Judaism, but to the Torah tradition embodied by a particular sage. He and his disciples would become the guide of a new household into the orbit of halakhic discipline.

This rabbinic model of an intentional Judaic community was obviously distinct from the exclusivism cultivated at Qumran or the monasticism of the Therapeutae. In contrast, it sought to include the entire community of Israel in the practice of rabbinic tradition. Not every Jewish male had the intellectual gifts or moral strength to become a formal disciple of the sages. But every Jewish man and woman had, as the sages taught, an obligation to conduct his or her personal and public life in accord with rabbinic traditions of Torah interpretation. The rabbis were apostles of Torah in the same way that early Jewish followers of Jesus had been apostles of the Messiah. Historians still debate the degree of rabbinic enthusiasm for non-Jewish converts.[56] But there is no doubt that the sages' primary interest was focused upon a fundamental social goal within ethnically Jewish communities. They wanted to govern Jewish society beyond the circle of immediate disciples, on the basis of rabbinic legal tradition as contained in the Oral Torah as a whole. Thus, as we saw in Chapter One, they sought and readily gained permission from Roman and Mesopotamian authorities to establish themselves as the justices of local Jewish courts and as civic leaders of Jewish communities.

For the sages, therefore, it was not enough to be a personal guide over a disciple's private quest. Seeking through moral suasion and personal example to convert Jewish individuals to the halakhic path, they also sought the political power to assert the authority of halakhic tradition as Jewish public law. As a religious style of life, halakhic tradition sought an inner transformation of natural Jews into a holy people. As a social policy, however, *halakhah* sought to shape the public dimension of Jewish society according to rabbinic traditions, regardless of the inner feelings of the larger community.

If Jewish farmers in the Land of Israel could be made to harvest their crops in accord with halakhic norms, if Jewish merchants in Tiberias or Antioch could be required to employ rabbinically regulated weights and measures, if Jewish litigants in Rome or Ktesiphon could be required to accept rabbinic mediation, then the transformation of the inner life of Israel would follow. All of Israel could become an intentional community of disciples inwardly as well as a natural community pursuing Jewish national customs in accord with rabbinic dictates.

Conclusions

This chapter has shown how a single religion can gain expression in a multiplicity of communal and social forms. The large masses of those calling themselves Jews certainly shared many common practices that distinguished and separated them from their neighbors wherever they lived. But of greater interest to us here are the many ways in which Jews, specifically those in relatively self-selecting "intentional" communities, were even more eager to mark themselves off from other Jews. If you want to imagine early Judaism as a single religious world, you need to account for the very different sorts of communities Jews created within that world. Our study suggests that it is better to imagine the various intentional communities as discrete Judaic worlds, societies with clear views regarding who was inside, who was outside, and why the distinction was crucial.

As we have seen, all certainly acknowledged a body of national custom that defined natural or ethnic membership in the Jewish people. But even such obvious social facts could be controversial, as the case of the Samaritanism, "Israelites" who refused to be "Jews," has shown. Often, national custom was only the point of departure for a more crucial journey: the attempt to embody the national tradition in a communal form demanding intense personal reorientation. The communities we have studied shared the view that Jewish life required a kind of conversion, a transformation of the person. That transformation was conceived as more than therapy for unhappy personalities. The healing was achieved by reorienting people to reality itself, a reality that included, as its principle foundation, the God of Israel. Life in these communities was conceived as the continuous pursuit of such reorientation. By the end of our period and the dawn of the Christian and Islamic Middle Ages, rabbinic Judaism would gather all these themes of personal transformation into its own Judaic world. Expanding from an intentional community of masters and disciples, it would become the natural community of most Jews. But its diverse movements of religious renewal, from Kabbalah to Hasidism, would continue to represent the goal of Jewish life as radical transformation of the self in relation to God.

Notes

1. The question of how ancient Jews understood their relationship to Jewish and non-Jewish "others" or outsiders has recently received enormous attention. See the pioneering collection of essays in Jacob Neusner and Ernest S. Frerichs, eds., *"To See Ourselves as Others See Us": Christians, Jews, "Others" in Late Antiquity* (Chico, Calif.: Scholars Press, 1985). Important recent contributions include: Robert Goldenberg, *The Nations that Know Thee Not: Ancient Jewish Attitudes towards Other Religions* (New York: New York University Press, 1998); Sacha Stern, *Jewish Identity in Early Rabbinic Writings* (Leiden, et al.: E.J. Brill, 1994); Sian Jones and Sarah Pearce, eds., *Jewish Local Patriotism and Self-Identification in the Graeco-Roman Period* (Sheffield: Sheffield Academic Press, 1998); Shaye J.D. Cohen, *The Beginnings of Jewishness: Boundaries, Varieties, Uncertainties* (Berkeley, et al.: University of California Press, 1999); and Isaiah M. Gafni, *Land, Center and Diaspora: Jewish Constructs in Late Antiquity* (Sheffield: Sheffield Academic Press, 1997).

2. For the century immediately surrounding the emergence of Christianity, the most comprehensive source of information on the diversity of Judaism is E.P. Sanders, *Judaism: Practice & Belief, 63 BCE–66 CE* (London and Philadelphia: SCM Press and Trinity Press International, 1992). Compare Seth Schwartz, *Imperialism and Jewish Society, 200 BCE–640 CE* (Princeton, N.J.: Princeton University Press, 2001), pp. 49–99.

3. Many scholars have noticed the highly derogatory stereotypes about Jews that circulated throughout the Greco-Roman world from the second century BCE onward, and have sought to trace modern anti-Semitism to these ancient prejudices. Some scholars, such as Peter Schaefer, *Judeophobia: Attitudes toward the Jews in the Ancient World* (Cambridge, Mass. and London: Harvard University Press, 1997), find a genuinely anti-Semitic tradition infecting the pre-Christian, non-Jewish world from the early centuries BCE. Others, such as Rosemary R. Reuther, *Faith and Fratricide: The Theological Roots of Antisemitism* (New York: Seabury Press, 1974), find Christianity guilty of the creation and perpetuation of anti-Semitism. For a well-considered critique of her position, see John G. Gager, *The Origins of Antisemitism: Attitudes toward Judaism in Pagan and Christian Antiquity* (Oxford and New York: Oxford University Press, 1985). Finally, others scholars, such as Louis H. Feldman, *Jew and Gentile in the Ancient World: Attitudes and Interactions from Alexander to Justinian* (Princeton, N.J.: Princeton University Press, 1993), stress the existence of highly flattering conceptions of Jews in antiquity. For an excellent survey of the primary sources, see Louis H. Feldman and Meyer Reinhold, eds., *Jewish Life and Thought among Greeks and Romans* (Minneapolis: Fortress Press, 1996), pp. 77–122.

4. The translation is adapted from Menahem Stern, ed. and trans., *Greek and Latin Authors on Jews and Judaism. II: From Tacitus to Simplicius* (Jerusalem: Israel Academy of Sciences and Humanities, 1980), p. 351.

5. The translation is adapted from Menahem Stern, ed. and trans., *Greek and Latin Authors on Jews and Judaism. I: From Herodotus to Plutarch* (Jerusalem: Israel Academy of Sciences and Humanities, 1976), p. 555.

6. The translation is adapted from R.J.H. Shutt, "Letter of Aristeas," in James H. Charlesworth, *The Old Testament Pseudepigrapha,* II (Garden City, N.Y.: Doubleday & Company), pp. 22–23.

7. The translation is from Stern, *Greek and Latin Authors,* I, p. 436.

8. An excellent study of the origins of Jewish circumcision, the developing understandings of its significance, and its role in modeling gender constructions in the history of Judaism is that of Lawrence A. Hoffman, *Covenant of Blood: Circumcision and Gender in Rabbinic Judaism* (Chicago: University of Chicago Press, 1996). We will discuss the rabbinic form of circumcision in Chapter Five.

9. The translation of this and the following passage is from F.H. Colson, trans., *Philo VII* (Cambridge, Mass. and London: Harvard University Press and Heinemann, 1934), pp. 101–105.

10. The translation is from Wayne A. Meeks, ed., *The HarperCollins Study Bible: New Revised Standard Version with the Apocryphal/Deuterocanonical Books* (New York: HarperCollins, 1993), pp. 1703–1704.

11. A clear effort to identify the kinds of non-Jews who became attracted to Judaism is available in Martin Goodman, "Jewish Proselytizing in the First Century," in J. Lieu, J. North, and T. Rajak, *Jews among Pagans and Christians*

(London and New York: Routledge, 1994), pp. 53–78.

12. Josephus discusses the event in his *Jewish Antiquities* 20.2.1–5, translated by Louis H. Feldman, *Josephus: Jewish Antiquities. Books 18–20.* Volume 9 (Cambridge, Mass. and London: Harvard University Press and Heinemann, 1969), pp. 399–419. For discussion of other prominent women reported to have joined Jewish communities in the Second Temple period, see Tal Ilan, *Jewish Women in Greco-Roman Palestine* (Peabody, Mass.: Hendreckson Publishers, 1996), pp. 211–214; T. Ilan, *Integrating Women into Second Temple History* (Tübingen: Mohr Siebeck, 1999), pp. 11–42; and Shelly Matthews, *First Converts: Rich Pagan Women and the Rhetoric of Mission in Early Judaism and Christianity* (Stanford: Stanford University Press, 2001).

13. See Tessa Rajak, "The Jewish Community and Its Boundaries," in J. Lieu, et al., *Jews among Pagans and Christians*, pp. 22–24; and Ross Shepard Kraemer, *Women's Religions in the Greco-Roman World: A Sourcebook*, 2nd ed. (Oxford: Oxford University Press, 2004), p. 163.

14. For some suggestive comments, see R. Goldenberg, *The Nations that Know Thee Not*, pp. 56–62.

15. The relevance of Greco-Roman voluntary associations to the historical interpretation of early Judaism has been explored by Albert I. Baumgarten, "Greco-Roman Voluntary Associations and Ancient Jewish Sects," in Martin Goodman, ed., *The Jews in a Graeco-Roman World* (Oxford and New York: Oxford University Press, 1998), pp. 93–111.

16. Scholarship on the Samaritans is highly specialized and esoteric. For a useful introduction, see Robert T. Anderson, "Samaritans," in *Anchor Bible Dictionary*, V, pp. 940–947. A recent study is offered by Ingrid Hjelm, *The Samaritans and Early Judaism: A Literary Analysis* (Sheffield: Sheffield University Press, 2000).

17. I translate the text of August Freiherr von Gall, ed., *Der Hebräische Pentateuch der Samaritaner* (Giessen: Topelmann, 1918), p. 158.

18. The ancient sources regarding the Dosithean movement are all analyzed in Stanley J. Isser, *The Dositheans: A Samaritan Sect in Late Antiquity* (Leiden: E.J. Brill, 1976).

19. Among the questions still "on the table" among scholars are such apparently basic matters as: Who founded and led the community? What role did the settlement at Qumran play in the larger community? Were Qumran's residents responsible for creating or hiding the scrolls? Did the Qumran community represent a powerful and popular form of Judaism or an esoteric minority view? Was the group destroyed in the war of 66–73 or, by contrast, in a late first-century CE natural disaster? To appreciate the full range of competing views on the origins and nature of the Yakhad, it is best to compare the recent works of five excellent scholars who differ widely on many fundamental issues: James C. VanderKam, *The Dead Sea Scrolls Today* (Grand Rapids, Mich.: Eerdmans Publishing Co., 1994); Lawrence H. Schiffman, *Reclaiming the Dead Sea Scrolls* (Philadelphia: Jewish Publication Society,

1994); Norman Golb, *Who Wrote the Dead Sea Scrolls?: The Search for the Secret of Qumran* (New York, et al.: Scribner, 1995); Gabriele Boccaccini, *Beyond the Essene Hypothesis: The Parting of the Ways between Qumran and Enochic Judaism* (Grand Rapids, Mich.: Eerdmans, 1998); and Jodi Magness, *The Archeology of Qumran and the Dead Sea Scrolls* (Grand Rapids, Mich.: Eerdmans, 2002).

20. A very useful overview of the religious world emerging from the Yakhad's writings can be found in Johann Maier, "The Judaic System of the Dead Sea Scrolls," in Jacob Neusner, ed., *Judaism in Late Antiquity,* 2, pp. 84–108.

21. See J. VanderKam, *The Dead Sea Scrolls Today,* pp. 71–92.

22. See L. Schiffman, *Reclaiming the Dead Sea Scrolls,* pp. 83–95.

23. I quote from the Commentary on Habakkuk, translated in G. Vermes ed. and trans., *Dead Sea Scrolls in English,* 4th ed. (London: Penguin Books, 1995), p. 344. Other excellent and up-to-date translations include Florentino Garcia Martinez, *The Dead Sea Scrolls Translated: The Qumran Texts in English,* trans., Wilfred G.E. Watson (Leiden: E.J. Brill, 1994) and Michael Wise, Martin Abegg, Jr., and Edward Cook, *The Dead Sea Scrolls: A New Translation* (San Francisco: Harper San Francisco, 1996).

24. This battle is described in the War Rule. See Vermes, *Dead Sea Scrolls,* pp. 123–145.

25. Translated by Vermes, *Dead Sea Scrolls,* p. 99.

26. Vermes, *Dead Sea Scrolls,* p. 105.

27. Vermes, *Dead Sea Scrolls,* p. 70.

28. Vermes, *Dead Sea Scrolls,* p. 78

29. Vermes, *Dead Sea Scrolls,* p. 77.

30. Vermes, *Dead Sea Scrolls,* p. 77.

31. Community Rule, 8. In Vermes, *Dead Sea Scrolls,* p. 81.

32. Ross S. Kraemer, "Jewish Mothers and Daughters in the Greco-Roman World," in Shaye J.D. Cohen, ed., *The Jewish Family in Antiquity* (Atlanta: Scholars Press, 1993), pp. 89–112; Tal Ilan, *Jewish Women in Greco-Roman Palestine,* pp. 44–96; Michael L. Satlow, *Jewish Marriage in Antiquity* (Princeton, N.J.: Princeton University Press, 2001), pp. 93–100, 199–224.

33. My discussion of the Therapeutae is based upon the pioneering article of Ross S. Kraemer, "Monastic Jewish Women in Greco-Roman Egypt: Philo Judaeus on the Therapeutrides," *Signs* 14 (1989), pp. 342–370. This has been incorporated into a more general chapter on "Jewish Women's Religious Lives and Offices in the Greco-Roman Diaspora" in Ross Shepard Kraemer, *Her Share of the Blessings: Women's Religions among Pagans, Jews, and Christians in the Greco-Roman World* (New York: Oxford University Press, 1992), pp. 106–127.

34. Translated by F.H. Colson, *Philo IX* (Cambridge, Mass. and London: Harvard University Press and Heinemann, 1917), pp. 127–128.

35. Colson, *Philo IX,* p. 133.

36. Colson, *Philo IX*, pp. 167–169.

37. Colson, *Philo IX*, p. 155.

38. See R. Kraemer, *Women's Religions in the Greco-Roman World* for a comprehensive presentation of sources for the piety of women in the Greco-Roman period and their roles within various religious traditions. Much of the material is analyzed from a sociological perspective in her companion volume, *Her Share of the Blessings*, cited above.

39. The question of Christian origins within early Judaism has generated a massive body of scholarship, and that on the nature of "Jewish Christianity" is, in addition, very technical. For basic orientation, consult: Gottfried Schille, "Early Jewish Christianity," in *Anchor Bible Dictionary*, I, pp. 935–938 and Stephen G. Wilson, "Jewish-Christian Relations, 70–170 CE," *Anchor Bible Dictionary*, III, pp. 834–839. A recent and very useful guide is Bart D. Ehrman, *Lost Christianities: The Battle for Scripture and the Faiths We Never Knew* (Oxford and New York: Oxford University Press, 2003).

40. See J. Gager, *The Origins of Anti-Semitism*, pp. 117–133.

41. Charlotte Fonrobert, *Menstrual Purity: Rabbinic and Christian Reconstructions of Biblical Gender* (Stanford: Stanford University Press, 2000), pp. 160–187.

42. An increasingly influential body of scholarship has begun to insist that the definitive period of Jewish and Christian self-definition as distinct and competing religious communities is to be located in the fourth and fifth centuries CE rather than the first and the second. Important versions of this argument are: Jacob Neusner, *Judaism and Christianity in the Age of Constantine* (Chicago and London: University of Chicago Press, 1987); Daniel Boyarin, *Dying for God: Martyrdom and the Making of Christianity and Judaism* (Stanford: Stanford University Press, 1999); D. Boyarin, *Border Lines: The Partition of Judaeo-Christianity* (Philadelphia: University of Pennsylvania Press, 2004); S. Schwartz, *Imperialism and Jewish Society* (Princeton, N.J.: Princeton University Press, 2001); Azzan Yadin, *Scripture as Logos: Rabbi Ishmael and the Origins of Midrash* (Philadelphia: University of Pennsylvania Press, 2004), esp. pp. 168–175.

43. An illuminating discussion of how early Christians applied to Jesus forms of veneration that other Jews reserved for angelic figures or God is found in Larry Hurtado, *One God One Lord: Early Christian Devotion and Ancient Jewish Monotheism*, 2nd edition (New York: Continuum, 2003).

44. Kraemer, *Her Share of the Blessings*, pp. 128–156 offers a lucid description of women in Christian communities of the first century after Jesus' death.

45. A perceptive account of the psychology of Paul's conversion as reflected in his thought is offered by Alan Segal, *Paul the Convert* (New Haven: Yale University Press, 1990), pp. 96–116. Lloyd Gaston, *Paul and the Torah* (Vancouver: University of British Columbia Press, 1987) is a fine place to start a study of Paul's conceptions of Israel and Torah.

46. There is an enormous literature on the inter-religious polemics of Judaism and Christianity in antiquity. The scholarly foundation of the most recent

discussions is laid by Marcel Simon, *Verus Israel: A Study of the Relations between Christians and Jews in the Roman Empire AD 135–425*, trans. H. Mc-Keating (London: Littman Library, 1996). See in particular, pp. 156–201.

47. See the pioneering study of the Association by Jacob Neusner, "The Fellowship (*hbwrh*) in the Second Jewish Commonwealth," in *Harvard Theological Review* 53 (1960), pp. 125–142.

48. I have edited this citation slightly in light of some textual irregularities. Rich rabbinic discussions of the Association are found in Mishnah Demai 2:2 and Tosefta Demai 2:2–22, with parallels in PT Demai 2: 2, 22d and BT Bekhorot 30a–b. These materials are discussed at length by Richard S. Sarason, *A History of the Mishnaic Law of Agriculture: A Study of Tractate Dema'i*, 2nd edition, (Leiden: E.J. Brill, 2005).

49. A nuanced discussion of the rabbinic material on the *ammei ha-aretz* may be consulted in S. Stern, *Jewish Identity in Early Rabbinic Writings*, pp. 114–123. A somewhat more technical, but highly illuminating, discussion has just become available in Stuart S. Miller, *Sages and Commoners in Late Antique 'Erez Israel: A Philological Inquiry into Local Traditions in Talmud Yerushalmi* (Tübingen: Mohr-Siebeck, 2004). See in particular, the chapter, "Local Jewish Commoners and the 'Ammei Ha-'Arez: One and the Same?"

50. See the detailed study of early rabbinic social structure in C. Hezser, *The Social Structure of the Rabbinic Movement in Roman Palestine* (Tübingen: J.C.B. Mohr [Paul Siebeck], 1997). On the roles assigned to women at the peripheries of rabbinic discipleship communities, see T. Ilan, *Jewish Women in Greco-Roman Palestine*, pp. 190–204; and Miriam B. Peskowitz, *Spinning Fantasies: Rabbis, Gender, and History* (Berkeley: University of California Press, 1997), pp. 72–76.

51. For a taste of the rabbinic dietary rules, consult the mishnaic tractate Hullin ("Common Food") in Jacob Neusner, ed. and trans., *The Mishnah: A New Translation* (New Haven: Yale University Press, 1988), pp. 765–786.

52. The rules for the courtyard *eruv* are in the mishnaic tractate Eruvin, chapters 6–7, in Neusner, *The Mishnah*, pp. 218–223.A fresh approach to the social significance of the rabbinic *eruv* is now available from Charlotte Fonrobert, "From Separatism to Urbanism: The Dead Sea Scrolls and the Origins of the Rabbinic Eruv," in *Dead Sea Discoveries* 11:1 (2004), pp. 43–71.

53. A full picture of the theory and practice of marriage in early Judaism, with great attention to the rabbinic evidence, is that of Michael Satlow, *Jewish Marriage in Antiquity* (Princeton, N.J.: Princeton University Press, 2001).

54. For aspects of rabbinic discipleship, see M. Jaffee, "A Rabbinic Ontology of the Written and Spoken Word," in *Journal of the American Academy of Religion* 65 (1997), pp. 525–549.

55. These and other traditions about these two famous bodies of disciples have been collected and studied from the perspective of legal history by Jacob Neusner, *The Rabbinic Traditions about the Pharisees before 70. Part II. The Houses* (Leiden, E.J. Brill, 1971).

56. The pros and cons are fully explored in Martin Goodman, *Mission and Conversion* (Oxford: Oxford University Press, 1994); and Gary Porton, *The Stranger within Your Gates: Converts and Conversion in Rabbinic Literature* (Chicago: University of Chicago Press, 1994).

CHAPTER 5

Ritual Space and Performance in Early Judaism

THE RELIGIOUS WORLDS OF EARLY JUDAISM emerged in civilizations that had, for millennia, been grounded in the sacrificial pageantry associated with temples and their priesthoods.[1] From North Africa to Mesopotamia, the ritual systems of the great temples were, in part, solemnifications of political allegiance in which sacrificial offerings were slain and burnt on altars in return for the security of the royal state. Temple sacrificial rites also had the role of awakening and channeling the fertilizing powers of the cosmos, embodied in the divine personalities who brought the rains and floods that nourished the regenerative capacity of the fields and flocks. The ancient Israelite temple shared in this venerable tradition. And, as we have seen, this tradition of priestly sacrificial ceremony inevitably shaped the foundational patterns of early Judaism in the restored Persian Yehud. The Torah that governed Judean life in the temple-state focused much of its attention on the concerns of the priestly administrators who conducted the temple's cultic life in accord with a sacred calendar of festivals and appropriate rites. Thus, the earliest form of early Judaism was a ritual system of priestly sacrifice that linked the political and social authority of the Judean temple to the will of the God of Israel.

The first half (450 BCE–70 CE) of the first millennium of the history of early Judaism closed with the destruction of the temple's sacrificial system—one of the many catastrophic results of the Jewish-Roman war of 66–73 CE. The remainder witnessed the emergence, over several centuries, of two crucial ritual spaces that would appropriate the functions of the temple system and reconfigure Jewish practices of collective worship. These ritual spaces were the synagogue, as a center of communal Torah study and public prayer, and the home, as a center of family-oriented ritual practices. The present chapter, accordingly, will focus on some important continuities and discontinuities that may be noticed in the ritual patterns that emerged in the Jerusalem temple and, in transfigured ways, survived it in rabbinic liturgical customs.

The study of religion is rich in theories of the function and meaning of religious ritual.[2] Recent work among scholars of ritual, however, has suggested that it is hasty to posit a single function of ritual in the social order or to provide a single theory of ritual activities that applies universally.[3] Moreover, it is perilous to claim knowledge of the meanings that rituals held for their participants. Anthropological theories of ritual are usually built upon close observation of ritual societies in the fullness of social life. This is clearly impossible for students of ancient ritual communities. Our ritual actors lived in the distant past and cannot share with us their views about the meaning of their actions. Moreover, we cannot directly observe their rituals. Rather, we must attempt to reconstruct them on the basis of partial archaeological remains and texts produced by priestly elites, whose own views may have represented a small stratum of the larger ritual community. So we can offer an estimate of the meaning of the public ceremonies of the ancient Jewish temple, synagogue, and home only with the greatest caution.

This chapter will explore a variety of rituals that can be at least partially reconstructed form the evidence of texts and archaeological remains. Most of them will be rituals of the liturgical type—rituals of communal worship— for these are among the most richly documented in the sources of early Judaism.[4] We shall also attempt to convey how the construction and design of three distinct ritual spaces accommodated the specific rituals that took place within them and enhanced their evocative power. To those familiar with the cultural code of ritual spaces, they conveyed and reinforced conceptions of the structure of the visible cosmos, as well as ways in which that cosmos may be permeable, at various points, to powers conceived as angelic or divine. So, at various points, we will offer some suggestions regarding how specific combinations of ritual spaces and associated actions—whether in temple, synagogue, or home—communicated conceptions of the cosmos "as it really was" in the domain of mortals and immortals.

In examining these rituals we will be forced to devote most of our attention to the male ritual performances of the priestly temple service and the rabbinic halakhic tradition. Of the Jewish literatures of antiquity, priestly and rabbinic writings offer the clearest examples of how ritual performance related to the worlds of those who produced ritual texts. But they do not tell us all we would like to know. Feminist scholars of religion have successfully argued, for example, that these sources are androcentric.[5] That is, they unself-consciously represent the world from a perspective that accepts as natural and inevitable male domination of social institutions. For this reason, androcentric religious texts offer skewed images of the religious past. First, as literatures written by men for a male audience, the biblical and rabbinic literatures report primarily on rituals performed by men. Second, where they report on women's activities, these are mostly rituals prescribed for women by men.

We know from rabbinic ritual texts what male rabbinic sages may have thought women should have done by way of ritual acts. But it is not obvious that this is precisely what women did. Nor were rabbinic sages particularly interested in areas of women's ritual lives that may have been well known to women but of no particular interest to the rabbinic halakhic system. Accordingly, the ritual world of early Judaism is available to us largely through male eyes. Scholars have for several years attempted to filter old evidence and discover new evidence for the ritual lives of women in Judaism. But the picture remains too incomplete to interpret in an introductory study such as this one.[6]

The Jerusalem Temple as a Ritual Center

The Jerusalem temple stood at the center of the political and religious life of the Judeans from 515 BCE until 70 CE, providing the most widely recognized "official" ritual setting in ancient Judaism.[7] Most surviving information about the Second Temple concerns the massively renovated structure begun under Herod. The work started about 20 BCE and was completed less than a decade before the temple's destruction in 70 CE, by which time it covered over 169,000 square yards. Like its Solomonic, Persian, and Hasmonean predecessors, Herod's was housed on a low hill adjoining the eastern wall of Jerusalem, facing the Mount of Olives. The temple included a main sanctuary, a courtyard for sacrificial rites, and adjoining courtyards for visitors and worshippers. It stood at the center of an enormous, roughly rectangular terrace running to the north and south of the city wall. If Jewish writers of the time, such as Josephus, are to be believed, it was one of the truly marvelous national temples of the ancient world.[8]

The Ritual Setting

In addition to its physical magnificence, Herod's temple inherited the aura of sanctity enjoyed by its predecessors in Israel's historical memory. The temple of Solomon, which stood for some three and a half centuries prior to 587 BCE, had preserved the holiness of the desert Tent of Meeting, the first shrine established by Moses as a dwelling place for the God of Israel. The Second Temple, rebuilt by 515 BCE, was seen as the smaller, but still holy, embodiment of God's promise to dwell among his people. Herod's temple, for its part, was a far grander structure than its Persian or Hasmonean prede-

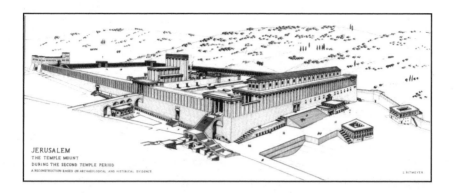

Herod's Temple Viewed from the Southwest

Source: Reproduced by permission of the artist, Leen Ritmeyer, and Hershel Shanks,
Editor, Biblical Archaeology Society.

cessors. Its very grandeur added to the international prestige of the god and people whom it represented and the land it protected.

The temple linked Jews to the world of heaven as well as serving as a visible link to the Jewish national past. Many regarded the temple as the earthly manifestation of an ethereal palace that existed in God's domain. Moses was said to have seen the model on Sinai (Exod 25:9, 40), and Ezekiel had been given a tour (Ezek 40–48) by an angel. Some apocalyptic visionaries, like those of the Enoch tradition (Chapter Three), described journeys of other ancient prophets to the throne of God in a heavenly temple.

In addition to its capacity to evoke speculation about its heavenly counterpart, the temple was also viewed as a visual representation of the cosmos itself. Josephus, historian and priest, offers an example of such conceptions. He wrote that certain furnishings of the temple served as reminders of cosmic realities. The embroidered curtain that covered the entrance to the main sanctuary represented to him the four elements of creation: earth, air, fire, and water. Similarly, some of its inner furnishings recalled the cosmic order of the zodiac and the four corners of the sea and earth.[9]

For most, to see the temple on earth was to come as close as they would to heaven. Precisely because it was perceived to be an earthly version of a heavenly prototype, the temple was a powerful symbol of the unity of all elements of God's cosmic design. Within its boundaries, the heavenly, earthly, and social realms were all joined together into a seamless whole. Israelite priestly tradition, we saw in Chapter Three, tended to imagine the earth's surface as divided between the clean land of Israel and the unclean lands of the nations, the holiness of the land and the commonness of all other space. The groundplan of the Herodian temple mirrored this conception of things.

The Gentile's Court. We may begin with the temple's outer reaches. The main entrance and exits to the compound were the two Huldah Gates on the southern perimeter. Visitors entering from this direction found themselves under beautifully columned porticoes that opened into an enormous plaza. Opposite stood the sanctuary—a massive stone structure covered in marble, polished granite, and gold—surrounded by its own wall, running east and west across the central plaza. This plaza could be populated by any visitor to the temple. But it was set aside especially for non-Jews who, out of courtesy or a sense of admiration for the God of Israel, might wish to make a sacrificial gift at his shrine. They could purchase a small goat or lamb from a merchant in the porticoed area and have it conveyed to a priest to be offered in their name.

But they could not penetrate any further than this outer plaza. As non-Jews, the more holy precincts of the temple area were closed to them. Signs in Greek and Latin made the point clearly: "No foreigner is to enter within the forecourt and the balustrade around the sanctuary. Whoever is caught will have himself to blame for his subsequent death."[10] In view of the extreme concentration of holiness within the temple itself, a non-Israelite presence would be a violation of its sanctity and a defilement of its purity.

Courts of Women and Israelites. Not even Jews could enter the temple at will. Those who wished to present offerings or witness the sacrificial service had to purify themselves, prior to entry, of any contact with death, bodily discharges, or other substances deemed to convey pollution to humans.[11] Only those who had immersed in water and were prepared for the sacrificial conclusion of their purification procedure could enter the temple area. They would enter through a separate eastern entrance.

On the inside, a series of inner courts, separated by ascending steps and gates, guided a successively more exclusive group of visitors westward and upward, toward the sanctuary itself. A square outer court at the eastern end of the temple, roughly 245 feet on each side, was designated the Women's Court. Jews of both sexes might gather there, but women normally could get no closer to the sacrificial service than the Nikanor Gate. It was centrally placed in a wall that divided the Women's Court from a second, smaller space called the Israelite Court. Unless women had the obligation to be involved in a purification sacrifice, they had to view the sacrificial acts from a balcony in their court. Men, however, could ascend the fifteen semi-circular steps through the Nikanor Gate into the Israelite Court, a narrow rectangular area 245 feet long and 20 feet wide.

The Heavenly Model of the Sanctuary:
Revelations to Moses and Ezekiel

The theme of the heavenly, eternal model of the physical temple is richly represented in the literature of the Second Temple period. It echoes in the canonical Scriptures as well. The first selection is set in the context of the revelation at Sinai, where Moses receives specific instructions from God regarding the construction of the wilderness Tent of Meeting. The second is part of a detailed description of the tour of the exiled prophet, Ezekiel, through the heavenly temple.

> The LORD spoke to Moses, saying: Tell the Israelite people to bring Me gifts; you shall accept gifts from Me from every person whose heart so moves him....And let them make Me a sanctuary that I may dwell among them. Exactly as I show you—the pattern of the Tabernacle and the pattern of all its furnishings—so shall you make it (Exod 25:1–9).

> Now you, O mortal, describe the temple to the House of Israel, and let them measure its design. But let them be ashamed of their iniquities: When they are ashamed of all they have done, make known to them the plan of the temple, and its layout, its exits and entrances—its entire plan, and all the laws and instructions, pertaining to its entire plan. Write it down before their eyes, that they may faithfully follow its entire plan and all its laws (Ezek 43:10–11).

> (Translation: *Tanakh* [Jewish Publication Society, 1988])

The Priests' Court. The Israelite Court was bounded by a stone wall about a yard high. Jewish men of non-levitical, non-priestly descent could pass no further unless they were obliged to engage in a purification sacrifice or other rite. But they had a clear view of the priestly activity, for before them lay the Priests' Court. Here, in a large space 245 feet long and 340 feet wide, the actual sacrificial rituals were performed by the priests to the musical accompaniment of the Levites' songs, cymbals, flutes, horns, and stringed instruments.

This court was dominated by the implements of the sacrificial rituals. On the northern end, cattle were slaughtered and butchered by priestly workers. In the center, toward the south, stood the altar, 58 feet long on each side and almost 30 feet high. Priests would ascend a ramp to place on its fires the

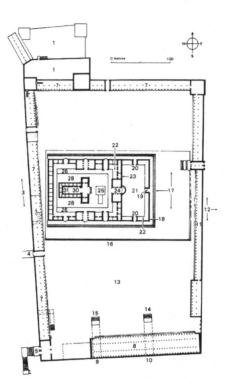

Floor Plan of the Herodian Temple

KEY: 9–10: Huldah Gates; 13: Gentile Court; 21: Women's Court; 24: Nikanor Gate; 25: Outer Altar; 26: Israelite Court; 28: Priests' Court; 30: First
Chamber of Sanctuary; 31: Holy of Holies.

Source: Th. Busink, *Der Tempel von Jerusalem* (Leiden: E. J. Brill, 1970, 1980), p. 1179.
Reproduced by permission.

carcasses of slaughtered animals and to smear its corners with sacrificial
blood. To the east of the altar stood a large basin that provided fresh water
for priestly ablutions.

The Sanctuary. Dominating the Priests' Court, at its easternmost end, was
the sanctuary. Its façade of pure white marble and gold plating stood about
182 feet high and was equally broad. While Levites served within the Priests'
Court, only priests, the holiest of the Israelite tribes, could walk up the 12
steps that led through enormous golden doors into the eastern part of the
sanctuary. They entered a long, rectangular room (about 73 × 36 feet) illu-
minated by a seven-branched, golden candelabrum (*menorah*). At the eastern end stood a golden altar for incense and a golden table that held twelve

loaves of bread, in accordance with the requirements of Exod 25:23–30. Priests would daily clean and kindle the *menorah,* offer incense and, on Sabbath Eve, change the loaves. But even they could penetrate no further than this antechamber.

The Holy of Holies. At the extreme western end of the sanctuary, behind an embroidered curtain, was the holiest, purest spot on earth, the Holy of Holies. It was a perfectly square room, about 36 feet on each side and equally as high. No one but the high priest could enter it; and even then, he could do so only on the Day of Absolution (*Yom haKippurim*). This was the holiest day of the year, for on it the people of Israel and the land itself were purged of the year's accumulation of sin.

In the wilderness Tent of Meeting and, later, in Solomon's temple, this space had been the resting place of a large chest, the Ark of the Covenant, reputed to contain the Mosaic tablets from Sinai. The Holy of Holies also had once contained a throne of solid gold models of heavenly beings, cherubim, whose wings sheltered the Ark and provided a throne for the hovering Glory (Hebrew: *kavod*) of God. From above the Cherubim, the scripture reported, God's voice had rung out to command Moses, Aaron, and generations of high priests after them.

But these holy objects had been lost by 587 BCE. What remained, according to later rabbinic tradition, was a flat stone called the Foundation Stone. Upon it, some rabbinic sages insisted, the world had been created. Their insistence upon this point highlights the cosmic function of the Holy of Holies itself. This room served as the meeting of heaven and earth, where all the forces of creation were present in their most intense form. At the center of the temple's rings of holiness, therefore, was nothing at all, an emptiness filled with the potential of infinite presence. God's Glory or Presence (Hebrew: *shekhinah*), that part of his being capable of worldly embodiment, could descend through it from the heavenly throne at any instant.

A Model of the Cosmos. This sketch of the temple complex suggests how it modeled the relations of all dimensions of the world—the cosmic, the geographical, and the social. The Holy of Holies assured access to the upper reaches of heaven, drawing from them a flow of holiness that descended in progressively broader waves toward the lower regions. Because of its holiness, the Holy of Holies required extreme protection from pollution. Accordingly, all the world's geographical and social space was mapped out in relation to the Holy of Holies in terms of various levels of purity.

The non-Jewish nations, represented in the farthest outer court, stood at the borders of the world; at the center, within the walls of the temple, was the domain of Israel. Thus, holy and common lands were represented in the world of the temple complex and separated from each other as well. Moreover, within the confines of purity there were also divisions and grades. Jews were divided into classes, each finding a place in the temple world matching its potential for holiness. Within this anthropology of holiness, men approached the holiest space more closely than women, priests and Levites more closely than male commoners, priests more closely than Levites, and the high priest more closely than other priests.

In the hierarchy of heaven and earth, then, the high priest, costumed in special vestments symbolizing celestial mysteries, stood more closely than any human to the world of heaven. He and his priestly kinsmen served as the human community that established and maintained connection between the various orders of being. Their labor in the temple preserved all other orders of being from collapse. Upon them, the people of Israel, the Land of Israel, and, ultimately, the entire cosmos and its population all depended.

Ritual Activities

The ritual activities taking place in the temple had an impact far beyond the boundaries of the temple complex and the experience of its priestly officiants. As a ritual representation of the cosmos, it helped to define for Jews the nature of all space surrounding it as well. If the temple was the hub or center of the world, everything else could be viewed as finding a place on a spoke emanating from that center toward the periphery of space. Thus, the outer reaches of the Jewish Diaspora could establish connections to the temple despite huge distances. We can appreciate the temple's capacity to transform the world around it by focusing on some typical activities.

THE *TAMID*-OFFERING

The most frequently repeated sacrificial ritual was the twice-daily Perpetual Offering (Hebrew: *tamid*). At dawn and dusk, a yearling lamb was slaughtered in the Priests' Court. To the accompaniment of fried wheat cakes and wine, its body was wholly burnt up on the altar's fires. These offerings were seen as the means to establish proper connection between the Earth and the power that created and sustained it. Sacrifices returned a portion of the bounty of the Land of Israel—its meat, grain, wine, and oil—to its heavenly Lord. Satisfying the divine claim upon the Land of Israel, the priests cleared a path for divine blessing to pulse into the world through the altar. Such blessing protected the Land of Israel from blight and drought and enabled the world to remain firm on the foundations originally created by God.[12]

The ritual of sacrifice, upon which the life of the world depended, was itself dependent upon the taking of life. Called *avodah* in Hebrew or "service," the sacrificial process was an arduous act of killing normally performed by a priest, acting as a holy executioner. Struggling, bleating victims had to be bound, slaughtered, disemboweled, dismembered and their parts disposed of in carefully prescribed ways. As sacrificial blood spurted from the throats of slaughtered lambs, an attending priest collected it in bowls, stirring the hot blood to prevent coagulation until the officiating priest was free to sprinkle it on the horns of the altar and the carcass was placed upon the fire.

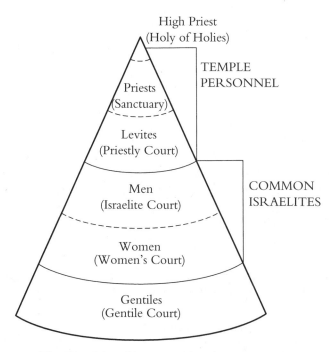

The Hierarchy of Human Holiness/Purity

The geographical space of the temple buffers the Holy of Holies from penetration by sources of uncleanness. Holiness and cleanness are correlated values. This correlation can be represented graphically as a cone. At the base are those visitors to the temple who are by nature beyond the continuum of holiness and cleanness. They are confined to the Court of the Gentiles. At the pinnacle is the high priest of Israel, who enters the Holy of Holies itself in a state of absolute holiness and purity. Between are various gradations of Israelites, who can penetrate successively more exclusive temple areas.

The culmination of the *tamid*-offering was the pouring of wine upon the altar and the conferring of a priestly blessing upon the assembled community. A pre-Hasmonean writer, Joshua ben Sira, described it as follows in around 180 BCE (Sir 50:16–21):

> Then the sons of Aaron shouted; they blew their trumpets of hammered metal; they sounded a mighty fanfare as a reminder before the Most High. Then all the people together quickly fell to the ground on their faces to worship their Lord, the Almighty, God Most High. Then the (Levite) singers praised him with their voices in sweet and full-toned melody. And the people of the LORD Most High offered their prayers before the Merciful One, until the order of worship of the LORD was ended, and they completed his ritual. Then Simon (the high priest) came down and raised his hands over the whole congregation of Israelites, to pronounce the blessing of the LORD with his lips, and to glory in his name; and they bowed down in worship a second time, to receive the blessing from the Most High.

When the spectacle of the victim's death and physical destruction was completed, the entire community in the temple court acknowledged the priest's success in bringing the power of life anew into the world. The worshippers sent their own adorations of God skyward with the aromatic smoke of the sacrificial victims whose deaths they had witnessed.

Although the priests did the work, the participatory witness of a communal audience was a crucial part of the temple's ritual life. The presence of witnesses, indeed, transformed the service from a private priestly rite into a public event that served as a tutorial in priestly conceptions of the world. These were made immediately tangible to the non-priestly majority through the powerful media of massive architectural presence and ritual pageantry. Indeed, the experience of the temple, rather than literary formulations of law and theology, where the primary means by which common Israelites would have identified with the biblical description of Israel as "a kingdom of priests and a holy nation" (Exod 19:6).

PILGRIMAGE FESTIVALS AND THE SPACE OF THE DIASPORA

In addition to daily offerings and the supplementary offerings of Sabbaths and New Moons, the temple calendar provided for other grand public spectacles of sacrifice. These were the thrice-yearly mass pilgrimages, associated with the spring barley harvest festival of Pesah (Passover), the early summer wheat festival of Shavuot (Pentecost), and the autumnal harvest festival of Sukkot (Booths). On these Pilgrimage festivals, Jews from all of Palestine and many points in the Diaspora would stream toward Jerusalem.

The Bet Alpha Synagogue Mosaic

Source: E. L. Sukenik, *The Ancient Synagogue of Beth Alpha.* Jerusalem, 1932.

The Bet Alpha Synagogue Mosaic

Source: E. L. Sukenik, *The Ancient Synagogue of Beth Alpha.* Jerusalem, 1932.

The Dura-Europos Synagogue's Western Wall: Torah Niche Surrounded by Frescos

Source: Goodenough, E. R., *Jewish Symbols in the Greco-Roman Period*. Copyright 1988 by Princeton University Press. Reprinted/reproduced by permission of Princeton University Press.

The Dura-Europos Synagogue's Western Wall:
Pharaoh's Daughter Rescuing Moses

There, males in particular were obliged to show themselves in the temple with the Festival Presentation Offering (*hagigah*) required in the Torah of Moses (e.g., Exod 23:14–18). Only part of this offering was burned; the rest served as a festive meal that men would share with their households. Few Diaspora Jews could make frequent pilgrimages. Those who did, however, would return to their homes with vivid reports of the sights and sounds of the temple, an encouragement to others to undertake a similar journey.

Thus, the calendar of Pilgrimage Festivals enabled the temple to transform the entire Jewish Diaspora into a series of spokes emanating from the center of the temple. Along these spokes, Jews could move back and forth between the center of the world and its circumference. The rhythms of the sacrificial seasons transformed the temple into a kind of heart. Its beat circulated a stream of Jews throughout the body of Israel in a perpetual systolic-diastolic rhythm, geared to the cycles of the seasons.

THE TEMPLE RITUALS AND THE PALESTINIAN COUNTRYSIDE

For Jews who lived within the environs of Judea, the temple's presence was a more regular, if slightly less spectacular, part of experience. Apart from the official Sabbath and festival calendar, the random events of private life would also attract local Jews to the temple. Men and women were obliged to celebrate their purification from moral or physical pollution by bringing an appropriate sacrificial animal to the temple to be offered by priestly officiants. Communion offerings of cattle (*shelamim*) could be brought at various occasions as gestures of thanks for divine blessing. The poor participated for the relatively small price of a few pigeons or some grain meal.

The male Judean population was given an active role in the temple's life-giving rituals apart from their personal sacrificial offerings. According to reports from many ancient sources, priestly and levitical families throughout the country were organized into twenty-four divisions (Hebrew: *mishmarot*), each of which provided a bi-weekly rotation of sacrificial workers for the temple. After serving for its rotation, one division would be replaced by another throughout the year.[13]

Men of common origin were enlisted in these divisions as platoons of bystanders (Hebrew: *ma'amadot*). Some commoners would travel to Jerusalem with the priests and Levites of their towns, where they would officially witness the sacrifices as representatives of all Israel. Others would remain in their towns and villages. According to rabbinic tradition (M Taanit 4:2–3), they participated in the sacrifice by gathering at dawn and late afternoon, the times of the *tamid*-offering, to read aloud from the first chapter of the book of Genesis.

While the priests were sustaining creation through their sacrifices, villagers were intoning the story of the world's creation. In a real sense, then, through the bystanders, the ritual life of the priests extended beyond the temple into the lives of the Judean population. Non-priestly Jews could incorporate the temple, as the center of the world, into their own experience around the temple's actual borders.

Summary

For as long as the temple stood, the social rhythms associated with its ritual schedule constituted the hub of reality for the Jewish communities of the homeland and Diaspora alike. Few "natural" Jewish communities—the special cases of the Samaritans (see Chapter Four) and the Jews of Egyptian Leontopolis (Chapter One) come to mind—entirely rejected the temple's claim to be the unique meeting place of heaven and earth and the center of Jewish national unity in geographic dispersion. But that is not to say it enjoyed an absolute monopoly.

Far from it. Dissident "intentional" Jewish communities, such as the Qumran Yakhad, seem to have believed that the temple had fallen into the wrong priestly hands. It was, therefore, from their view, no longer legitimate as a ritual site. Accordingly, they began to construct their own ritual systems of worship that bypassed the temple.[14] Even those who revered the temple and routinely shared in its celebrations participated frequently in other centers of ritual life. These too could evoke with power other dimensions of diverse Judaic worlds. When the temple was destroyed, they began a steady rise to importance. Eventually the temple, as a heavenly reality without any physical expression in the material world, functioned as a metaphor for other spaces in which rather different rituals were enacted. One that became increasingly common from the first century CE onward was the synagogue.

The Synagogue as a Ritual Center

The earliest mention of Jews gathering for regular religious celebrations outside the sacrificial setting of a temple does not use the term "synagogue."[15] Archaeological remains from third-century BCE Egypt include Greek inscriptional references to an institution called the *proseuche* (prayer place), but there is little evidence that special buildings might have been set aside for this purpose.[16] The Greek word *synagoge* appears later. It is as likely to refer to a community of people (i.e., the Greek Orthodox Church) as to the place in which they meet. Thus, in Greek writings, the "synagogue of the Jews" often is a synonym for "the Jewish community."

Additionally, Greek-speaking Jews used many other terms to describe the nature of their communal gatherings and the places in which they were held (for example: *semneion* or "sanctuary"; *didaskaleion* or "place of instruction"; *sabbateion* or "Sabbath place"). In order to simplify our discussion, we shall use the term synagogue to designate all such public gatherings of Jews.[17]

It is only from the first century BCE and thereafter that archaeologists find remains of buildings in the Diaspora and Palestine that seem to have served as settings for the conduct of Jewish ritual activities. Most of the earliest of these buildings are from lands to the west of Palestine—in Egypt and Greece (Delos, from the first century BCE). This has led many to suggest that the synagogue as both a social institution and a physical gathering place originated in the western end of the Jewish Diaspora. An expression of what we have called "natural" Jewish communities, the synagogue enabled them to express a national identity and continue ancestral customs within the dominant non-Jewish environment.

In contrast to the Diaspora situation, synagogues seem to have been less prominent in Palestinian Jewish society prior to the third century CE. One inscription from the late first century BCE, to be discussed below, mentions a synagogue in Jerusalem. But only three buildings likely to be synagogues have been found prior to the late second century CE—those at Gamla, Masada, and Herodium. Jewish ethnic dominance within the Palestinian population and the influential presence of the Jerusalem temple may have hindered an essentially diasporic institution from making headway in the homeland until the temple was destroyed. In any event, by the third century the synagogue building was becoming as common in the areas of heavy Jewish settlement in northern Palestine, such as the Galilee and the Golan Heights, as it was in the Diaspora.

The Ritual Setting

Remains of synagogue buildings, most of which come from the second to sixth centuries, have been identified from Italy to Syria, with important examples in Asia Minor as well. Despite much stylistic diversity, many of these remains confirm reports from ancient writers that the synagogue was a multi-purpose gathering place. In addition to teaching and prayer activities, they hosted a variety of other events, including legal proceedings, and might even serve to house travelers. This diversity of synagogue functions perhaps explains why neither the Greco-Roman temple plans nor that of the Jerusalem temple provided any architectural models for synagogue builders.

Architectural Conventions. Rather, their architectural inspiration was the repertoire of ground plans and façades commonly found on all manner of public buildings in the ancient world. Usually there was an open central room with ample space for seating. Larger buildings had many adjoining rooms, presumably for a variety of functions. These aspects of its architectural design suggest that the synagogue was precisely what its Greek name implies: the hub of Jewish life in its town, a central gathering place of local Jews and others attracted to the community of Israel. Larger cities had more than one.

Despite its architectural inspiration, other aspects of the synagogue's design and decoration suggest that gatherings within it had more than a purely social meaning. In a variety of ways, the local scene of, for example, Sardis (Asia Minor) or Tiberias (Galilee) was routinely superimposed upon a more evocative one—that of Jerusalem. Consider the matter of spacial orientation. Although synagogues did not attempt to look like the temple, in most of them from the third century on the seating faced toward the city in which it had stood. Ruins from Italy, Greece, and Asia Minor direct the attention of audiences eastward toward Jerusalem, whereas those in Syria face west. In Galilee and the Golan Heights, to the north of Jerusalem, the synagogues commonly direct attention southward.

This spacial orientation discloses the synagogue's function beyond that of a simple meeting hall; quite literally, it was a place of reorientation. This particular hub of Jewish society was simultaneously a spoke in a much larger wheel, centered in Jerusalem. Jews gathered together in one space but were immediately reminded of their relation to another. Synagogue artisans often enhanced this reorientation, self-consciously evoking at every opportunity the sacred space of the temple.

Synagogues of Palestine

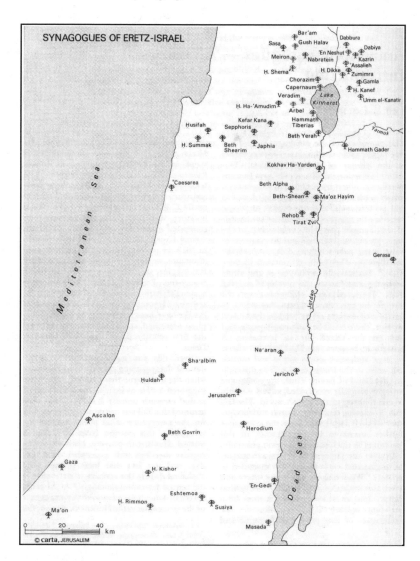

Range of Synagogue Remains, First to Sixth Centuries CE

As these maps demonstrate, there are dozens of archaeological sites that have been identified, with various degrees of certainty, as the remains of synagogues.

Source: Maps on this and facing page based on Lee I. Levine, *Ancient Synagogues Revealed* (Detroit: Wayne State University Press, 1982), pp. 2, 163.

Synagogues of the Diaspora

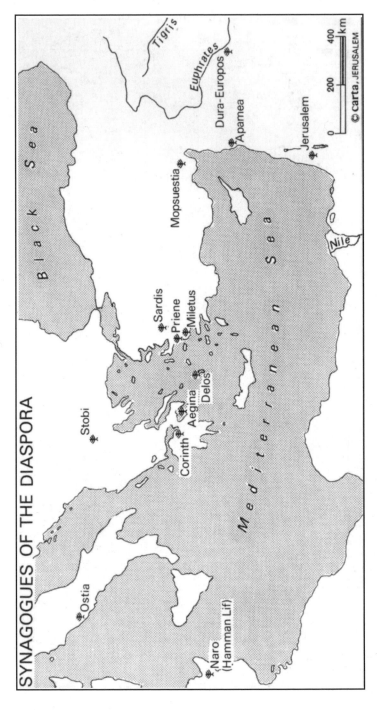

SYNAGOGUES OF THE DIASPORA

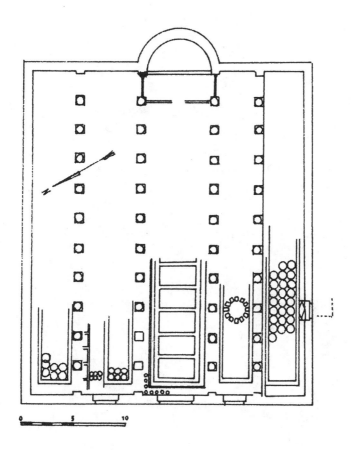

Typical Synagogue Floor Plans: The Basilica

The earliest synagogue finds employ the "basilica" ground plan, as shown above. In this ground plan, the focus of worship is at the narrow end of a rectangular building. Often an indentation or "apse" was built into that wall, presumably for the purpose of reading the Torah or other ritual activity. The inner space is divided by rows of columns. This example is from a fifth to seventh-century synagogue in Gaza.

Source: Israel Exploration Society, Jerusalem. Used with permission.

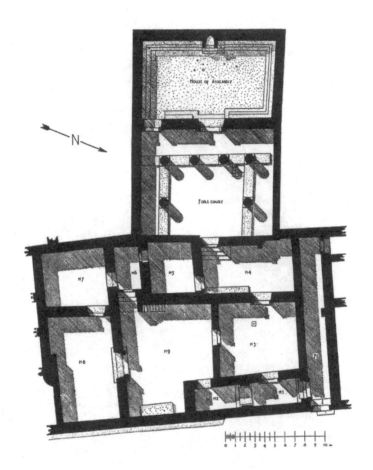

Typical Synagogue Floor Plans: The Broadhouse

This drawing shows the ground plan of the synagogue of Dura Europos, destroyed by a Persian invasion in 256 CE. It employs the "broadhouse" model. In this structure, the focus of worship is on the long wall, rather than the short wall. In the present example, at the very top, a niche is carved into the wall for the Torah scrolls. The actual worship space is at the top of the ground plan. Beneath it is a courtyard for gathering. At the bottom are various rooms for diverse social functions.

Source: C. Kraeling, *The Excavations at Dura Europos*, Vol. VIII: *The Synagogue* (New Haven: Yale University Press, 1956).

Temple Symbolism. Most synagogues of this period had impressively carved doorways or other masonry that incorporated temple ritual objects as symbols into the design. In addition to the *menorah* and *shofar*, symbols recognized as Jewish throughout the Greco-Roman world, artisans usually depicted the *lulav* (palm branch) and *etrog* (citron), both of which played a prominent role in the temple celebrations of the autumn festival of Sukkot. The intentions behind the selection of such objects are difficult to identify with certainty. Perhaps they mark off a particular building as belonging to the Jewish nation in Exile. But the persistent emphasis upon temple objects suggests that those who entered these synagogues wished to draw upon the temple's cosmic symbolism to exalt their own more humble setting.[18]

Synagogue Art at Beth Alpha. Indeed, the conception of the synagogue as a place for ritual, in addition to merely convivial or educational, activity is conveyed by other aspects of their interiors. Many synagogues were distin-

Symbols from the Synagogue in Ostia, Italy

An important synagogue from the fourth century CE is found in Ostia, the port of Rome. The carvings shown here are entirely typical of symbols found throughout synagogues of the Diaspora and the Land of Israel. The seven-branched *menorah* dominates the panel. From left to right are other objects used in the liturgies of various festivals—the *lulav* and *etrog* (Sukkot) and the *shofar* (Rosh Hashanah). The panel was placed in the niche used to store the Torah scroll.

Source: M. F. Squarciapino, *Archaeology* 16 (1963).

guished by artful mosaic tile floors. These can be particularly evocative of spaces and times far more enchanted than those of an urban street in Byzantine Diaspora. The floor mosaic of the Galilean synagogue of Beth Alpha (ca. fifth century) is a superb and well-known example.

The mosaic, which occupies a rectangular space of about 17 × 32 feet in the main room of the building, is a composition of three separate panels, leading from the doorway and extending to the opposite wall facing Jerusalem. Upon entry, the eye first falls upon an illustration of Abraham's near sacrifice of Isaac (Genesis 22). For those who used this building, it appears, passage from the outer foyer through the doorway of the main room was a passage from everyday time and place into the time of the ancestors and prophets of the scriptural past. This room's space offered a visual evocation of the past, complementing the actual scriptural readings in which that past was presented in holy words.

The next panel, occupying the center of the room, contains a representation of the sun as a chariot driver moving through the sky. The Sun Chariot and its horses are surrounded by zodiacal signs and symbols of the four seasons. Having reentered the Israelite past, the visitor was now asked to reflect upon the majestic cosmic setting presided over by the God of Israel. Thus the synagogue evoked more than the biblical past, when God spoke face to face to Israel's ancestors. It urged its visitors to contemplate the expanded spaces of the cosmic order, to reflect upon the larger setting of their lives beyond the intimately known world of the human city.

The final panel filled the rest of the floor, directing attention to the Jerusalem wall's semi-circular enclosure (apse) that probably held the Torah scroll. This panel depicts a parted curtain behind which lies a series of images of the temple's Holy of Holies, its menorahs, shofars and other ritual objects. Lions, representing the Davidic dynasty, flank an image of the Ark of the Covenant. Having passed, at least in imagination, from the Israelite past through the vast spaces of the heavenly world, the visitor's attention arrived finally at the heavenly temple—the eternal model of the building whose ruins alone were visible in Jerusalem.

What the high priest had seen with his own eyes once a year, the visitor to the synagogue could contemplate with the mind's eye at any time and anticipate as a reality in the messianic future. The Beth Alpha synagogue, in sum, evokes in its rather small space all that mattered in ancient Judaic worlds: the time of ancient Israel, the enormous spaces of God's universe, the timeless holy space of the temple, and the future restoration of Israel. All are simultaneously present, presided over by the room's sole sacred object, the scroll of the Torah.

Synagogue Art at Dura-Europos. In one remarkable case, the third-century synagogue unearthed in the Syrian town of Dura-Europos, illustrations were found not on the floors, but in a series of richly conceived wall paintings that surround an elaborate wall niche designed to hold the Torah scroll. Here, the biblical past and the eternal present represented by the temple are prominent. These paintings seem to have been intended as a pictorial commentary on various biblical stories, a kind of visual "scripture" anticipating the famous stained glass art of Latin Christianity and the iconography of Byzantine churches. Jews who frequented this synagogue could read in its walls' images the entire history of God's saving activities on behalf of Israel even as the words describing these events were proclaimed from the Torah and prophetic writings. Facing Jerusalem, they could contemplate a vivid depiction of the temple even as they sung Psalms that had once been performed there by levitical ancestors.[19]

The illustrations at Beth Alpha, Dura, and many other Byzantine synagogues are marvelous introductions to the imaginative life of the Jews who used them. They also raise important questions about the relationship of their communities to the rapidly growing rabbinic movement of the Roman and Byzantine period. Palestinian rabbinic literature of these centuries in particular generally disapproved of the representational images in synagogue decoration, such as Beth Alpha's Sun Chariot and astrological figures (cf. PT Av Zar 4:1, 43d; 3:3, 42d).[20] Surely, Dura's representation (just to the right of the Torah niche) of pharaoh's daughter bathing unclothed in a river would have been regarded as immodest in rabbinic circles—despite the painter's intention to celebrate the providential sparing of Moses from the Nile.[21]

Synagogue Communities and the Sages. One likely interpretation of the gap between rabbinic sensibilities and the reality of the Byzantine synagogue is that synagogues were not the centers of rabbinic authority that they would become in late medieval and modern times.[22] Indeed, as we shall see, the rabbinic sage had no official role in the synagogues' collective life. They were general community institutions representing the needs and tastes of local Jewish populations. Though sages served the patriarch and exilarch as public administrators, they did not build and decorate synagogues or preside over their activities.

These activities were initiated and overseen at the local level by whoever had the funds, the initiative, and the communal respect. Rabbinic authorities and their disciples surely visited and taught in such synagogues. From the third century onward, they seem also to have frequently prayed in them (and argued with other worshippers about how the service should be conducted). But, in the main, they appear to have accepted conditions they were temporarily unable to alter.

Many archaeologists have noted another striking discrepancy between rabbinic norms and the reality of the synagogue. Rabbinic law, especially by the end of our period, explicitly exempted women from the public performance of synagogue rites. Further, it required that men and women sit in separate areas of the synagogue divided by a partition (recall Philo's Therapeutae). The seating plans of surviving synagogues, however—where they can be reconstructed—show little indication of separate seating arrangements. Moreover, numerous inscriptions from throughout the Greek-speaking Jewish world testify that women were frequent visitors to synagogues, providing as well donations for their construction and decoration. Such evidence suggests that women were integrated with men in many synagogue environments beyond explicitly rabbinic communities.[23]

The question of their participation in its rituals is more difficult to answer. Even rabbinic sources acknowledge that women could be called to read from the Torah, although the sages discouraged the practice on a variety of grounds. Could women lead prayers? Here the evidence of Diaspora tomb inscriptions may yield a clue. These reveal that some Diaspora women

---

Rufina, the Head of the Synagogue (Archisynagogos)

This inscription, from second-century CE Smyrna in Turkey, is one of a number that suggest that wealthy women might serve as leaders of diaspora Jewish communities. Whether Rufina's title, "Head of the Synagogue," implies a purely civic function or one of greater involvement in religious leadership is not clear. The original inscription was carved on a marble plate that adorned a tomb.

> Rufina, a Jewess, head of the synagogue, built this tomb for her freed slaves and the slaves raised in her house. No one else has the right to bury anyone here. If someone should dare to do so, he or she will pay 1500 denars to the sacred treasury and 1000 denars to the Jewish people. A copy of this inscription has been placed in the archives.

Source: B. Brooten, *Women Leaders of the Ancient Synagogue* (Scholars Press, 1982), p. 5.

bore prestigious titles of office, such as *archisynogogus* (Head of the Synagogue) or *presbyteros* (Elder). Because the honor of leading prayers would be offered to a community officer, it is at least possible that women might indeed have served in this way in some Diaspora communities. But until firmer evidence emerges, we cannot clarify the question any further.

Despite disagreements between rabbinic sages and other Jews about propriety in synagogue decoration and seating plans, most Jews seem to have shared at least one common perception of the synagogue. Many remains of the Byzantine period contain inscriptions referring to the synagogue as a holy place (Greek: *hagios topos*; Aramaic: *atra qadisha*). Similarly, rabbinic sages, citing an obscure reference in the book of Ezekiel 11:16, commonly called the synagogue a *miqdash me'at*, a temple in miniature. Rabbinic and non-rabbinic Jews alike viewed the synagogue as a space that, wherever it was geographically, brought its congregants into a relationship with that center of the world represented by the temple. Within the ritual space of the synagogue, the heavenly temple continued to shape the way Jews experienced the subtle intersections of the mundane world and the heavenly order.

Ritual Activities

By the fourth century, there is little doubt that transitions between these two orders of reality were most often enacted through the rituals of public scriptural readings and communal prayer. The rabbinic literature of the Byzantine period takes for granted that Jews used the synagogue—the *bet haknesset* (meetingplace) in rabbinic terminology—for both the public declamation of the Torah and the celebration of communal prayer. Rabbinic *halakhah* neither justifies nor criticizes the practice. It simply organizes both activities in accord with rabbinic conceptions of order and propriety.[24]

Thus, on the one hand, the Mishnah provides lists of passages from the Torah, *Nevi'im*, and *Ketuvim* that should be read on various Sabbaths, weekdays, holidays, public fast days and so on (Meg 1:1, 3:4–6). On the other, it proposes ritual roles for prayer leaders and worshippers (Meg 4:1–10; Taanit 2:1–5) and establishes broad guidelines for the wording of the prayers themselves (Ber 4:1–5:5; T Ber 3:1–26). Most important, rabbinic traditions assume that the public reading of the scriptures was an act of worship itself, surrounded with its own benedictions, that could be integrated into the overall communal celebration.

An Early Rabbinic List of Scriptural Readings
for Festivals (Mishnah Megillah 4:5)

On Passover (*pesah*): the section concerning festivals as found in the
Guide for Priests (Lev 23:4ff.)

On the Feast of Pentecost (*atzeret*): the section "Seven Weeks"
(Deut 16:9ff.)

On the New Year (*rosh hashanah*): the section "On the Seventh
Month, on the First Day of the Month" (Lev 23:23ff.)

On the Day of Absolution (*yom hakippurim*): the section "After the
Death" (Lev 16:1ff.)

On the first festival day of Tabernacles (*hag*): the section concerning
festivals as found in the Guide for Priests (Lev 23:4ff.)

On the remaining days of Tabernacles: the section concerning the
sacrifices on the festival of Tabernacles (Num. 29:17ff.)

THE PUBLIC RECITATION OF SCRIPTURE

Despite rabbinic assumptions, there is good reason to doubt that prayer and
Torah study had always been linked into a single ritual performance. Most
probably, public scriptural readings and communal prayer emerged as independent rituals, originating in separate spheres of Jewish ritual life. The
oldest literary reports concerning public Jewish prayer, we have already
noted, associate it with a place known as a *proseuche* (prayer place). This may
or may not specifically associate it with the synagogues, which may simply
be a later coinage with the same essential meaning. But it is important to
recall that the earliest specific references to the synagogue describe it primarily as a setting for Torah study. Although it is not yet possible to trace with
certainty the independent histories of scriptural recitation and communal
prayer prior to their Byzantine synthesis, a few observations can be offered.

Public Torah recitation had surely played a role in at least some temple
celebrations during the Persian period. The depiction of Ezra's reading of
the Torah before the entire restored community of Yehud (Nehemiah 8–
9) assumes as much. But the practice of gathering outside the temple on
fixed days of the week and year to proclaim the Torah text in public gatherings is quite a different matter than occasional proclamations in the course
of temple celebrations. When the Torah was read in the course of the temple
service, it was a secondary element in a grander ritual spectacle, the sacrificial

avodah. The regular reading of the Torah and Nevi'im throughout the year in a specific communal setting, however, established the scripture-text as a unique center of attention, independently of the sacrificial order.

The impact of this development was profound. Removed from the overpowering setting of the temple, the Torah reading came into its own as an activity that could transform the place in which it was read. A common room or building, because of the texts it sheltered, became a center of holiness. Though independent of the sacrificial center, it was nevertheless a space in which different orders of reality could intersect. Its walls framed a repeated encounter with sacred utterances, the words given to Moses and other prophets, and offered unique access to the world from which those words originally had been imparted. The act of public declamation was more than the transmission of useful or interesting information. It was a setting for reestablishing the original moment of Israel's formation at Sinai, when the Torah was first heard "in public."

By the late first century CE, the Gospel writers could assume that the public recitation and exposition of sacred scriptures was the very essence of the synagogue's activity (e.g., Luke 4:16–22). Their contemporary, Josephus, shared this view, ascribing the practice to ancient Mosaic legislation (*Against Apion* 2:17). Similarly, a Greek inscription from first-century BCE Jerusalem records the proud declaration of one Theodotus, "priest and head of the synagogue," to have built a "synagogue for purposes of reciting the Torah (Greek: *nomos*, "law") and studying the commandments, and as a hotel with chambers and water installations to provide for the needs of itinerants from abroad."[25] Here, as elsewhere in the first century, prayer goes unmentioned among the list of services offered in the synagogue.

Yet we know that the synagogue ultimately became the preferred site for communal prayer as well. It became a place to address God as well as to hear him speak through the voices of those who read his words. Precisely how this happened, and from which areas of life public prayer emerged, is very difficult to say. Clearly enough, as Joshua ben Sira reported, the temple itself included among its rituals acts of public prayer in which those gathered prostrated themselves and uttered praises or petitions to God. These included the utterance of priestly benedictions over the community and communal responses. Scriptural texts, such as Psalms or the Ten Commandments, may have been publicly recited. But, as with the public Torah readings, such acts were adornments to the sacrificial offerings, not the substance of worship.

COMMUNAL PRAYER

Archaeological evidence for the existence of prayer as a communal activity outside the temple first emerges with the *proseuchai* of third century BCE Egypt. Historians, however, do not know what kinds of prayers were uttered in them. Nor are there many descriptions of associated ritual actions such as bowing, prostrations, or other common expressions of worshipful attitudes.

The Egyptian situation receives a bit more illumination from the second century BCE onward. The *Letter of Aristeas*, for example, assumes that "all Jews" wash their hands in a body of water as a prelude to prayers.[26] Philo, we saw, claims that communal prayer among the first century CE Egyptian Therapeutae involved the antiphonal singing of hymns on Sabbaths or holy days. He also describes daily prayers at dawn and sunset, but it is unclear whether this was a private devotion or a communal liturgy.[27] But we cannot project his description of a self-consciously intentional community onto the blank screen of larger Egyptian-Jewish society.

The earliest actual texts of Jewish communal prayers, outside the canonical boundaries of the book of Psalms, are Palestinian. These are the psalm-

---

A Sabbath Hymn from Qumran (4Q405)

The Book of Ezekiel's opening vision of the divine Throne-Chariot (*merkavah*) inspired much speculation in early Judaism. In liturgical texts from Qumran, it is clear that the worshipping community understood its prayers as corresponding to the heavenly adoration of God's celestial *merkavah* by cherubim, or angelic attendants. Below is a sample of such prayer from a collection commonly called "Songs for the Sabbath Sacrifice." The square brackets and ellipses represent the translator's effort to fill in or identify gaps in the preserved manuscript.

[Praise the God of...w]onder, and exalt him...of glory in the te[nt of the God of] knowledge. The [cheru]bim prostrate themselves before him and bless. As they rise, a whispered divine voice [is heard], and there is a roar of praise. When they drop their wings, there is a [whispere]d divine voice. The cherubim bless the image of the throne-chariot above the firmament, [and] they praise [the majes]ty of the luminous firmament beneath his seat of glory.

Source: G. Vermes, *The Dead Sea Scrolls in English*, 3rd ed. (Penguin, 1987), p. 228.

like hymns preserved primarily in the Thanksgiving Scroll and the Songs for the Sabbath Sacrifice discovered among the Qumran writings. These, stemming from the first century BCE, were probably sung in the worship groups of the Yakhad. The Songs for the Sabbath, in particular, offers rich evocations of the heavenly temple, with God's Throne surrounded by adoring angelic celebrants. They offer an important insight into the way the Yakhad understood its ritual space as a setting for invoking the heavenly order. The songs shed no particular light, however, on the rituals associated with the singing of the hymns.[28]

Another source of insight into kinds of prayers offered by Jews outside of rabbinic circles comes from a surprising source in fourth-century CE Syria. These are the daily, Sabbath, and festival prayers collected in a Christian liturgical document called the Apostolic Constitution. Among the many Christian prayers in this collection are at least seven that share a peculiar feature: scattered and ill-fitting references to Christian ideas. When these are deleted from the texts, the remaining prayers seem to reflect the sentiments of a Greek-speaking, highly philosophical, Judaism of the second and third centuries CE. Presumably, the prayers of a Jewish community had been carried, with appropriate editorial modifications, into the life

---

A Sabbath Prayer from the Apostolic Constitution (7.36)

The ease with which Jewish adoration of God might express Christian attitudes toward Christ is exemplified in the following Greek prayer text. In its present form, the prayer is clearly designed for Christian worship, yet much of it consists of passages that seem drawn from non-Christian Jewish sources. The latter are italicized in the present translation.

Lord, almighty, you created the world through Christ *and set apart the Sabbath to remember this—because on it you rested from (your) works* for meditation on your laws, *and you ordained feasts for the gladdening of our souls, so that we may be reminded of the Wisdom created by you*:

How he submitted to birth by a woman on account of us, he appeared in life manifesting himself in (his) baptism, how the one who appeared is God and man, by your consent he suffered on our behalf and died and arose by your power. Wherefore also we celebrate the resurrection festival on the Lord's Day and rejoice because of the one who not only conquered death but brought to light life and incorruption. For through him you brought the gentiles to yourself for a special people, the true Israel, the beloved of God, the one who sees God.

For you, Lord, led our fathers out of Egypt and saved (them) from the iron furnace and from the clay and the making of bricks. You redeemed them from the hands of Pharaoh and those under him, and you brought them through the sea as through dry land, and you endured their character in the wilderness with all sorts of good things.

You gave them the Law of ten oracles clearly expressed by your voice and written by your hand. You commanded (them) to keep the Sabbath, not giving a pretext for idleness but an opportunity for piety, *for the knowledge of your power, for prevention of evil. Therefore you confined (them) in the sacred precinct for the sake of teaching, for exultation in the number seven. On account of this (there are) one seven and seven sevens and a seventh month and a seventh year and according to this cycle the fiftieth year is for remission.*

(This is) so that men may have no excuse to plead ignorance. On account of this you entrusted (them) to keep every Sabbath that no one may desire to send forth a word from his mouth in anger on the day of the Sabbath. For the Sabbath is rest from creation, the complement of the world, the seeking of laws, thankful praise to God for (those things) which were given to men.

All of which the Lord's day surpasses, pointing to the Mediator himself, the Administrator, the Lawgiver, the Cause of resurrection, the Firstborn of all creation, God the Word and a man born of Mary, the only one begotten without a man, the one who lives a holy life; who was crucified under Pontius Pilate and died and rose from the dead. The Lord's day was commanded by you, Master, to offer thanks for all (these) things.

For your grace alone by its magnitude has obscured every (other) benefit.

Source: D. Fiensy, *Prayers Alleged to Be Jewish* (Providence, R.I.: Scholars Press for Brown Judaic Studies, 1985), pp. 75–79.

of a Syrian Christian community. Such texts show how profoundly Judaism's prayer traditions affected those of Byzantine Christianity. But here, as at Qumran, the ritual setting of the prayers in their original Jewish context is unclear.[29]

Communal prayer, therefore, developed independently of the rabbinic sages in a variety of different Jewish settings in Palestine and the Diaspora. Its presence in the synagogue was a given for the sages. Their own rules of communal worship, to a degree, depended upon these earlier developments even as they shaped them in the patterns distinctive to rabbinic tradition. But the sages' indisputable contribution was to make explicit the connections between the synagogue's communal prayers and the public recitation of the Torah and other scriptures. They did so by linking the Sinaitic memories stirred by the Torah reading to longings for the vanished temple service. Israel's great past and anticipated future were knotted together in the rabbinic worship service.

The Rabbinic Service. This service linked the community to heaven as well. As a dominant tradition of rabbinic masters conceived of it, communal prayers were a kind of sacrificial service that substituted for and, indeed, continued the ancient priestly sacrifices at the altar. The term commonly applied to prayer, *avodah* ("service"), is the very one used in scripture to describe the temple service. The point is explicitly drawn by a common interpretation of the custom of offering prayers in the early morning and late afternoon. Many sages argued that these times were selected in order to correspond to the biblical schedule for the *tamid*-offering. In this view, the cosmic effects of priestly sacrifices and public prayer recitations were the same. Just as the priestly offering of the *tamid* had brought the blessing of heaven into the world through the altar, so, too, the communal prayer of Jewish commoners turned the synagogue into a conduit for life-sustaining energies.

This conception of communal prayer ultimately governed the principles by which the Torah recitation was integrated into the worship setting. In the temple service the Torah reading served as a minor adjunct to the sacrificial service. In the rabbinic construction, the reading of scriptural passages on Sabbaths or other special occasions became a focal part of the sacrificial prayer service itself. Sinaitic pronouncements could blend with sacrificial offerings in a single "service of the lips" that opened the heavens to the petitions of Israel.

This conjunction of symbolic meanings can be seen from the daily prayer service assumed by the Mishnah and related early rabbinic texts. The service itself was relatively simple. In order to constitute a genuinely communal offering, it required the presence of ten adult males, who served as a deputation of the community of the town or village as a whole. The main sacrificial offering was a series of blessings, petitions, and praises of God collectively known as The Prayer (*hatefillah*), or The Eighteen Benedictions (*shmoneh esreh*). Recited in a posture of attention, they eventually came to be called the Standing Prayer (*amidah*). There was no official prayer book. Such written aids to memory emerged only in the eighth or ninth century CE. Rather, early rabbinic literature assumes that the texts of these benedictions were fluid. Sages of the third and fourth centuries concentrated on establishing the prevailing theme of each benediction and fixing the words with which each began and concluded. Within this structure, individual worshippers were free to amplify according to local custom.

Opening and Closing Benedictions of the Rabbinic Amidah

In rabbinic liturgical tradition, these six benedictions were recited three times daily every day of the year. The break between them was filled in with other benedictions depending on whether the prayer was offered on a weekday, a Sabbath, or a festival. The text below represents the version used by contemporary Jews who follow the medieval German tradition. No complete texts of these benedictions survive from premedieval times. The name "Adonai" is a euphemism used in rabbinic tradition to avoid pronouncing the actual letters of the Divine Name.

> Blessed are you, Adonai, our God and God of our fathers, God of Abraham, God of Isaac, God of Jacob. The great, mighty and awesome God, the Supernal God, who bestows profound kindness, creates all and recalls the righteous acts of the fathers, and shall bring a redeemer to their children's children in love, for the sake of His name—King, Helper, Redeemer and Shield. Blessed are you, Adonai, Shield of Abraham.
>
> You are eternally mighty, Adonai—reviving the dead. You redeem magnificently, sending round the winds and bringing down the rains. He sustains life with kindness, revives the dead in profound mercy, supports the fallen, heals the sick, frees the imprisoned and keeps his trust with those who sleep in the dust. Who is like you, Marvel Worker, and who is comparable to you?

A king who kills and gives life, who brings forth redemption—
you are certain to revive the dead. Blessed are you, Adonai, who
revives the dead.

You are holy and your name is holy, and the Holy Ones praise
you each day! Blessed are you, Adonai, the holy God.

★★★

Adonai our God, accept your people Israel and their prayer.
And restore the sacrificial service to the sanctuary of your house.
And accept with love their prayer, and may the service of Israel
your people be always acceptable to you. And may our eyes
witness your compassionate return to Zion. Blessed are you,
Adonai, who restores his presence to Zion.

We thank you! For you are Adonai—our God and the God
of our fathers for ever and ever. Foundation of our life, shield of
our salvation—this you are in all generations! We are grateful to
you and recount your praises for our lives, which are in your
hands, and for our souls, which are entrusted to you, and for your
miracles, which support us every day, and for your wonders, and
your kindnesses, which we receive each moment—evening,
morning, and noon. You are a source of goodness whose mercy
never fails, a source of mercy whose kindness is never exhausted.
Eternally do we place our hope in you. And for all this by your
name, our king, be blessed and exalted forever. And all life is
grateful to you and praises your name in truth—the God of our
salvation and our help. Blessed are you, Adonai—your name is
good and to you is all thanks due.

Grant peace, plenty, blessing, grace, kindness, and compassion
to us and all your people Israel. Bless all of us as one, our father,
with the presence of your face. For through the presence of your
face have you given us, Adonai our God, a Torah of life, and
loving mercy, and righteousness, and blessing, and compassion,
and life and peace. And you deem it good to bless your people
Israel at every moment and hour with your peace. Blessed are
you, Adonai, Blesser of his people Israel with peace.

In general, the opening series of benedictions praised God's loyalty to Israel's ancestors, his creative and redemptive power, and his absolute holiness. These opening benedictions introduced the central benedictions, the theme of which would change depending upon the occasion. On common weekdays, worshippers recited a series of benedictions that petitioned God for personal well-being and health, forgiveness of sins, as well as such collective Jewish concerns as the rebuilding of Jerusalem, the gathering of the exiles, and the restoration of the Davidic dynasty. On Sabbaths, festivals, and New Moons a single, longer benediction appropriate to the theme of the day replaced the central weekday petitions. On all days, the series of benedictions concluded with final benedictions of thanksgiving and a plea for God to establish peace in the heavenly and earthly realms.

On weekdays, Sabbaths, and festivals the manner of offering the Prayer was the same. Worshippers stood at attention, their faces toward Jerusalem. Before them stood a *hazzan* (supervisor), who took his place before the ark containing the Torah scroll, with his back toward the community. The leader would announce a call to prayer once uttered by priests in the temple:

The Rabbinic Kedushah

The *kedushah* is known in many versions within rabbinic liturgical tradition. The following translation represents the text used by contemporary Jews who follow the medieval German tradition. The paragraphs are recited antiphonally by the congregation and the prayer leader, in imitation of the angelic choir's song.

Let us sanctify your Name in the world, just as they sanctify it in the heights of heaven, as it is written by your prophet:
 "And they called each to the other, saying: Holy, holy, holy is Adonai of Hosts, his Glory fills all the world!"
Each opposite the other proclaims, "Blessed":
 "Blessed is the Glory of Adonai from his Place!"
And in your holy writings it is written, saying:
 "May Adonai reign for eternity, your God, O Zion, for all generations, halleluyah!"
In every generation we shall expound your greatness, and for all eternity we shall sanctify your holiness; and your praises, our God, shall never cease from our lips, for you are God, the great and holy King. Blessed are you, Adonai, the holy God.

"Bless now the Blessed LORD!" The community responded as the temple witnesses had once responded: "Blessed is the Blessed LORD, for all eternity!" Then the entire assembly would whisper its benedictions in unison from memory. The recitation was punctuated by prostrations at appropriate intervals, expressing submission to the kingship of God. Aside from these movements, the worshippers were not permitted even to shift their feet out of reverence for the divine king before whom they now stood.

At the conclusion of the collective act of prayer, the leader, repeated the blessings in a loud chant on behalf of those whose memorization or recitation of their own blessings had been defective. He acted as a messenger, gathering together the prayers of individuals into a single perfected, collective offering to Heaven. His recitation of the third benediction in particular, called the *kedushah* (sanctification), was the high point of the service. Composed of quotations from chapter six of the book of Isaiah, in which the prophet is overcome by a vision of God seated on his heavenly throne, the *kedushah* was offered in the form of a call and response by the leader and the community.

The rabbinic form of the benediction recalls the far richer hymns known from Qumran's Songs of the Sabbath Sacrifices. The Qumranian versions offer detailed descriptions of the angelic choir singing its praises to God in Heaven, as the human community offered its praises on Earth. It is likely that the rabbinic appropriation of this *kedushah* served a similar purpose. At the moment of its performance, the barrier between the world of the everyday and that of heaven was penetrated. The mortal worshippers became part of the immortal community of heaven.

On Sabbaths and festivals, as well as the market days of Monday and Thursday, rabbinic custom called for the public reading of the Torah as the capstone of the morning worship service. This was performed immediately following the Prayer, while the *kedushah*'s powerful evocation of heaven remained fresh. The procedure for this reading was carefully plotted to enable the assembly to stage for itself the original opening of heaven, when Israel first heard the Torah from God through the prophet Moses.

The Torah scroll was removed from its ornamental ark with great ceremony, carefully unwrapped from its decorative coverings, and unrolled on a reading table in the center of the synagogue. On Monday and Thursday, three members of the community—first a priest, then a Levite, and then a commoner—would be honored with an "ascent" (Hebrew: *aliyah*) to the Torah to read selected passages aloud. On Sabbaths there were seven such ascenders. These readers served as communal representatives. Through them, the entire people Israel ascended to Sinai to receive the Torah. Each would precede and conclude his reading with a benediction praising God for bestowing his gift of the Torah upon his special people Israel.

As each read, a specially designated interpreter (Aramaic: *meturgeman*) would render the Hebrew passage into Aramaic so that all would understand the holy utterance. In addition to the practical matter of helping Aramaic speakers grasp the Hebrew text, this procedure enhanced the ability of the audience to recapture the original revelatory moment. It duplicated the revelation process as understood in rabbinic tradition—God spoke and Moses interpreted. At the conclusion of the series of prescribed readings, the Torah scroll was rewrapped and returned to its ark. With the holy text returned to its place, the service was concluded, but for a summary recitation of hymns from the Psalms.

Summary

Let us now draw together some of our observations about prayer in the synagogues of the Byzantine period. While we cannot simply assume the universality of rabbinic descriptions of the Jewish worship, we can feel confident about certain basic assumptions. The first is that Torah recitation and communal prayer were seen by many Jews as natural elements of the larger worship offered in the synagogue. Secondly, the basic form of communal prayer was the utterance of benedictions of praise, petition, and thanksgiving that established a sense of genuine communication between the earthly community and the heavenly order. Human prayer in the synagogue was an earthly form of divine service that imitated an angelic celebration in the heavenly temple. Finally, while the imagery of the temple permeated the synagogue setting and the community's prayers, the synagogue ritual had a profound impact upon the ways in which Jews experienced the heavenly prototype of their own earthly community.

The priesthood, after all, was absent as officiants in the rabbinic prayer service in particular.[30] Priestly and levitical families of the Byzantine period (as today) maintained proud memories of their descent from those who served in the temple's celebrations. Many were treated with great social deference. But there seem to have been few official synagogue functions that they alone could perform. They might lead prayer services, if their recitation was fluent. But any male Jew with a pious heart, a good memory, and a pleasant voice might just as well call the community to its prayers as priests had once inaugurated the sacrificial service.

We recall that deference was given to priests and Levites in the order of calling men to read from the Torah scroll. But as the Mishnah put it, this was only a measure to protect the honor of a group deprived of its former lofty functions (Gittin 5:8). Whereas the high priest had once read the Torah to the people in the temple, now the people read it themselves without priestly supervision; the interpreter rendered its meaning and implications free of priestly guidance. Similarly, on regular occasions, priests were called before the community to confer upon it the ancient priestly blessings, as the high priest had done in the temple. But even here, their recitation of the blessing was directed not by a priest, but by a common leader who could be trusted to have memorized the blessings and its associated scriptural text.

So the world of the heavenly temple was persistently evoked in the synagogue's prayer service, but the earthly space of its evocation was utterly different from the Jerusalem temple. The cosmic symbolism of that temple survived, but in a transformed physical setting. Priesthood and sacrificial pageantry played no role in drawing heaven and earth together. Rather, a congregation of commoners led by one of their own number lifted up holy words to heaven in Torah recitations and communal chants. Most of the officiants of this new "sacrifice of the lips" could claim no holiness from priestly birth. They claimed only the holiness of their commitment to the Torah of Moses. Delivered to them in an ancient revelation, its physical embodiment in a leather scroll now sanctified the space of their common worship. Spoken to it and through it, their words continued the ancient sacrificial labor of linking God and Israel, heaven and earth.

The Home as a Ritual Center

The temple and synagogue did not exhaust opportunities for creating ritual openings to the heavenly realm in early Judaism. Even before the destruction of the temple and the emergence of the synagogue as a site of communal worship, the family home had provided the setting for numerous rituals. By the end of the first Judaic millennium, under the impact of rabbinic halakhic norms, it would become a prime ritual center in its own right. We shall describe some characteristic domestic rituals shortly. For the moment, however, we must understand the way in which the domestic space was marked out as an effective ritual setting.

The Ritual Space

The Doorpost Amulet. As in the synagogue, a piece of scriptural writing proved crucial. A common marker of a Jewish dwelling in antiquity was the *mezuzah,* an amulet of wood, leather, or metal containing a parchment on which were written certain verses from the Torah of Moses. Usually, such amulets were affixed to the right-hand entrance of the front door. In later

rabbinic custom, *mezuzot* (plural) adorned the doorway of every room
within the house (outhouses, bathhouses and other undignified places, were
not adorned with holy words).

The word mezuzah itself means "doorpost," as in the following passage
from Deuteronomy 6:9: "inscribe (these words) on the doorposts of your
house and upon your gates." The Bible itself is not clear as to which words
are to be posted in fulfillment of this commandment. This ambiguity is
reflected in the various passages that ancient Jews actually inscribed on the
mezuzah's scroll.

The mezuzah is already mentioned in the *Letter of Aristeas* (158–159).[31]
The earliest known examples of mezuzah scrolls, however, are included
among the other texts from Qumran. One of these, similar to Samaritan
mezuzot, contains the text of the Ten Commandments found in Exodus 20.
A commonly found passage is Deuteronomy 6:4–9, the core of a text that
rabbinic tradition knows as the *Shma*, after the first Hebrew word of the
passage. Some Qumran texts also include a second passage, Deuteronomy
11:13–21, which is mandated as well in rabbinic tradition.

Together, the two passages from Deuteronomy constitute a forceful
summary of the Torah's understanding of the covenant:

> Hear (*shma*), O Israel: The LORD is our God, the LORD alone. You shall
> love the LORD your God with all your heart, with all your soul, and with
> all your might. Keep these words that I am commanding you today in
> your heart. Recite them to your children and talk about them when you
> are at home and when you are away, when you lie down and when you
> rise. Bind them as a sign on your hand, fix them as an emblem on your
> forehead, and write them on the doorposts of your house and on your
> gates.
>
> If you will only heed his every commandment that I am commanding
> you today—loving the LORD your God, and serving him with all your
> heart and all your soul—then he will give the rain for your land in its
> season, the early rain and the later rain, and you will gather in your grain,
> your wine, and your oil; and he will give grass in your fields for your live-
> stock, and you will eat your fill. Take care, or you will be seduced into
> turning away, serving other gods and worshipping them, for then the
> anger of the LORD will be kindled against you and he will shut up the
> heavens, so that there will be no rain and the land will yield no fruit; then
> you will perish quickly off the good land that the LORD is giving you.
> You shall put these words of mine in your heart and soul, and you shall
> bind them as a sign on your hand, and fix them as an emblem on your
> forehead. Teach them to your children, talking about them when you are
> at home, and when you are away, when you lie down and when you rise.
> Write them on the doorposts of your house and on your gates, so that
> your days and the days of your children may be multiplied in the land that

the LORD swore to your ancestors to give them, as long as the heavens are above the earth.

The focus of the passages, quite clearly, is on a total, loving obedience to God as expressed in scrupulous regard for his commandments. But what explains their presence upon a parchment placed on doorposts?

The explanation comes from the passages themselves. You have probably noticed that each requires Israel to place "these words" on its doorposts and gates. But it is unclear precisely which of "these words" are to be inscribed. The archaeological evidence suggests that Jews made various choices within their understanding of the spirit of the commandment. The rabbinic understanding is only one among others. Whatever differences they had about the precise content of the mezuzah scroll, however, Jews agreed upon the theme of its text and the necessity of placing it at the entryway to the home.

Interpreting the Mezuzah. How did they understand the significance of this object that so clearly marked off their homes as Jewish dwellings? The biblical texts we have looked at suggest both an educational and a protective function. The words on the doorpost were to serve as a reminder of Israel's covenantal obligations to God. Those who took the reminder to heart would enjoy blessings, while those who did not would suffer other consequences. The theme of protection seems to have ultimately won out.

The first-century CE historian Josephus explained that the mezuzah was not a crude good-luck charm, but a sign of gratitude for all the benefits received from God (*Antiquities* 4:213).[32] That he had to make this point suggests that, in fact, many Jews did regard the mezuzah as a protective charm. The Palestinian Talmud, for its part, records a story about Rabbi Judah the Patriarch. In gratitude for the gift of a pearl, the compiler of the Mishnah sent a mezuzah. Rebuked that his gift was hardly equivalent in value to the precious pearl, Rabbi is said to have replied: "What you sent me I must guard, what I sent you will guard you!" (Pe'ah 1:1, 15d).

In Rabbi's view, "these words" of the Torah did not simply decorate a parchment. Rather, unread and wrapped in their case, they nevertheless conveyed the attention of God himself to the home. This perhaps helps to explain how the mezuzah helped to create a particular sort of ritual space. From their encasement in the doorpost amulet, the words of the Torah presided over a point of passage between two very different sorts of space. Beyond the door of the home lay "the world" at large, shared alike by Jew and non-Jew. It was a place of commonness, disorder, and impurity. But the domestic space, even though it served the commonest of needs, could be evocative of the heavenly world from which the Torah originally came.

What the presence of the Torah scroll did for the synagogue, transforming a mere meeting room into a place filled with the potential to host the divine Presence, the mezuzah did for the home. It marked off a space in which the name of God could be evoked in due regard for its holiness. Indeed, the mezuzah enabled the home to serve as a new hub of holiness. Sacred words from the Torah formed a barrier, keeping the common world outside the home were it belonged. At the same time, the mezuzah transformed the home into a space in which it was possible, as in the temple or synagogue, to communicate between the world of the everyday and that relatively inaccessible world of the heavens.

The Protective Incantation. It is clear, however, that many Jews of late antiquity, from Palestine to Babylonia, were of the opinion that the simple mezuzah was not alone sufficient to protect the home. Nor did it open communication with the entire range of beings who might populate the heavenly and earthly domains. Judaic worlds, you'll recall, included non-human personal beings—angels and demons—whose ability to affect the human order was no less real than that of God. Since the latter part of the nineteenth century and throughout the twentieth, archaeologists have discovered rich evidence of how Jews established (or avoided) relations with such visitors. This evidence is found in the remains of amulets and shards of pottery containing incantations designed to ward off demonic beings or, in many cases, to enlist their aid in enhancing the wealth, health, or romantic success of the amulet's owner.[33]

Here we can discuss only one form of "homeowner's insurance," that found in what archaeologists have called the Aramaic incantation or magic bowls. Many of these were discovered in 1913 in an archaeological site at the Iraqi city of Nippur, within the ancient Sasanian Empire. Dating from the sixth to eighth centuries CE, they reveal the degree to which the rabbinic concern with angelic and demonic powers, noted in Chapter Three, reflects a widespread concern of ancient Babylonians, Jews, and non-Jews alike. It appears that bowls were inscribed with various prayers. After the utterance of the prayer, the text was built into the foundations of homes or placed in other appropriate places, such as thresholds. These had the effect of protecting the household and its members from the demonic visitors who might otherwise meddle in the family's affairs.

Note how the following example interweaves the text of the *Shma*, found on the mezuzah, with other scriptural passages as a kind of introduction to its real concern—to protect the writer of the incantation and his wife from the curses of the demoness Lilith:

Hear, O Israel, the LORD is our God, the LORD alone (Deut 6:4). According to the command of the LORD they would encamp, and according to the command of the LORD they would travel. The observance of the Mighty One they kept according to the Command of the LORD through Moses (Num 9:23). And the LORD said to Satan: May the LORD rebuke you, Satan, may the LORD who chose Jerusalem rebuke you. Is not this a fire-brand snatched from the fire? (Zech 3:2).

Again, bound and seized are you, evil spirit and powerful Lilith, so that you may not appear to Brikhyah Beyah bar Mami and this Ispandarmed bat Hotedora either during the day or during the night, during any evening or morning, during any hour, during any time. But depart from their presence and take your divorce and your separation and your letter of dismissal. I have written against you as demons write divorces for their wives and furthermore, they do not return to them.[34]

As the text's conclusion makes clear, it was viewed by its owner as a symbolic divorce document. Demons themselves honored the institution of divorce, and so Lilith could be adjured to honor a human's desire to end all further relations with them.

The combined evidence of the mezuzah and the magical bowls shows the degree to which Jews of antiquity sought to transform the home into a refuge from dangers lurking beyond the threshold of the domestic space. People ate, slept, worked, raised children and, routinely died in this space. The home was no less common than the street and, therefore, just as subject to the incursion of worldly and otherworldly forces. Accordingly, the home required protection, on the one hand, and a positive source of blessing, on the other. The bowl built into the foundation warded off otherworldly dangers, but the mezuzah made the home permeable to the world of holiness and blessing. The words of the Torah, formerly intoned by priests in the temple and regularly read by synagogue readers on Sabbaths and festivals, functioned even silently and unread to draw divine blessing upon those who held fast to them.

Ritual Activities

The guardianship of texts enabled the home, like the synagogue, to serve as a center of ritual performance. But we should not assume that rituals performed in the home were defined as "private," in distinction from the public ceremony performed in the synagogue.[35] In view of the home's frequent importance as a site of work and other economically important activities, it was in many ways no less a public space than the synagogue. Especially after the destruction of the temple, the home gradually became the preferred site for the celebration of feasts that had formerly been part of the temple's festival calendar. Meals eaten at the domestic table became occasions for ritual invocations of the temple and its powerful spaces.

The transformation of the Passover sacrificial meal from a temple rite to a domestic celebration called the Seder ("Liturgical Order") is a well-documented example.[36] But even common meals in unexceptional times were surrounded by ritual activities. These recognized eating itself as a public event involving a communal invocation of divine blessing and attention to the proceedings. This is particularly obvious in the prescriptions for mealtime rituals preserved in rabbinic halakhic traditions in the Mishnah and the Talmuds. For this reason, we focus immediately upon two ceremonial acts associated with meals in the rabbinic tradition. The first is directly connected to eating itself: the recitation of benedictions that transform the necessary act of nourishment into a social experience of dining. The second, which links the consumption of wine and food to a larger celebration, is the ritual of infant circumcision, the prelude to what rabbinic sages called a *se'udat mitzvah,* "an obligatory feast."

THE RITUAL TRANSFORMATION OF BREAD

With the exception of rituals concerning marriage and purification in preparation for marital relations, most rabbinic ritual activity is the responsibility of males and assumes the primacy of male actors. The centrality of women to the domestic setting, however, made them crucial participants in a ritual act that most vividly evoked the temple's exclusively male priestly activities. This is because the center piece of the meal was a loaf of bread, and women, in their role as housewives, were assumed to be the principal bakers of bread (M Ketubot 5:5).[37] We can best appreciate the priestly resonances of the act of eating by following the trail of that loaf, from the time the dough was formed in the kneading trough until its consumption at the table.

The transformation of bread into a ritual object began with the kneading of the dough. In the halakhic form of the ritual, the kneader (whether the housewife or a professional baker) was required to remove a measure of dough, called *hallah,* from each batch and set it aside before the baking of the bread. The removal of this lump of dough was accompanied by a benediction linking the act to a divine commandment: "Blessed are you, LORD our God, King of the Universe, who sanctified us by his commandments and commanded us to remove the *hallah.*"

The rabbinic ritual is based upon a scriptural injunction: "When you enter the land to which I am taking you and you eat of the bread of the land, you shall set some aside as a gift to the LORD: as the first yield of your kneading you shall set aside a loaf *(hallah)* as a gift" (Num 15:17–20). The sense

---

The Third Benediction of the Birkat Hamazon

The third of four benedictions recited after every meal in which bread is eaten, this benediction draws special attention to Jerusalem and the temple.

Have compassion, Adonai our God, upon Israel your people, and upon Jerusalem your city, and upon Zion the dwelling place of your Glory, and upon the dynasty of David your Messiah, and upon the great and holy House over which your Name is invoked. Our God, our Father, our Shepherd, our Provider, our Rescuer—rescue us, Adonai our God, speedily from all our troubles. Do not make us needful, Adonai our God, of human gifts or loans. Rather, may we depend only upon your generous, open, holy and broad hand, that we may never be shamed or humiliated. And build Jerusalem your holy city speedily in our days. Blessed are you, Adonai, who builds Jerusalem in compassion, Amen.

---

of the passage suggests the offering of baked loaves rather than dough. Indeed, non-rabbinic authorities, such as Josephus and Philo, speak matter-of-factly of bread routinely offered to priests in fulfillment of scriptural rules.[38]

It is unclear exactly when and why the removal of raw dough came to substitute for baked loaves. The substitution is probably associated with the destruction of the temple and the dissolution of the priesthood as a functioning institution. In light of the new situation, rabbinic *halakhah* transformed a customary tax of bread for the priests into a ritual of temple commemoration. The *hallah*-offering ceased to feed priestly families in the temple compound. Instead, because there was no temple in which priests might eat the sanctified bread, a symbolic portion of dough was burned in the oven until black and inedible. All the remaining bread made from that batch of dough became permissible as food through the surrender of the *hallah*. Centuries after the temple's destruction, each loaf of bread baked in a rabbinic household was an occasion for recalling the temple of the past and anticipating the future time when priests would once again be fed from the land's bounty.

The capacity of bread to invoke the symbolic presence of the temple did not cease with its preparation and baking. Indeed, as we saw in Chapter

Two, rabbinic tradition had inherited from Pharisaism a tendency to see the domestic table as more than a place to take a meal. If rabbinic sages came to view the synagogue as a "temple in miniature," they viewed the domestic table as a substitute for the temple's altar. All who dined at that table could, in principle, transform their act of nourishment into one that nourished the world with the blessings of the divine Presence.

This was accomplished by surrounding the eating of bread with actions that called to mind priestly activities in the temple. Here, Jewish men and women alike took upon themselves priestly roles. Just as priests had washed their hands from a laver prior to their conduct of the sacrificial service, rabbinic custom required common men and women to rinse their hands prior to eating bread. Just as priestly sacrifices had been accompanied with offerings of salt, so too rabbinic custom required bread to be eaten with salt. After the utterance of a benediction praising God "who brings forth bread from the earth," the loaf was broken, dipped in salt, and distributed to the diners.

In breaking and consuming their bread, then, diners enacted at the domestic table a small commemoration of the temple's sacrificial service. Only after partaking of the sacrificial bread could they then begin to eat the other foods that had been prepared for the meal. Moreover, having blessed the bread, diners were released from the obligation to recite benedictions over the other foods served in the meal. The benediction over the bread served to consecrate the entire meal as an act that ensured that God's plentiful blessings would continue.

As the meal began with a benediction, so was it concluded. Neither men nor women could take leave of the table-altar without first formally acknowledging the Presence, which had graced the gathering. The common rabbinic ritual of leave-taking, the "benediction over food" (Hebrew: *birkat hamazon*), mandated a series of blessings of praise and thanksgiving. The theme of these benedictions is instructive. They focus on God's graciousness in providing food to the world, praise him for giving Israel a holy land rich in agricultural produce, and petition him to rebuild Jerusalem, the heart of the land.

The meal, then, began with acts that recalled the temple ritual and concluded with reminders of the centrality of Jerusalem in God's restorative plan for Israel. As we have seen throughout our discussion of ancient Judaism's ritual life, whatever came under the control of ritual was made to point to a rather limited framework of meanings. In the rabbinic world these are simple: the vanished-but-still-present temple, the eternal Torah, and the Land of Israel, awaiting the return of its exiled people.

THE RITUAL TRANSFORMATION OF A MALE INTO A JEW

The domestic table's transformation into a ritually evocative site analogous to the temple altar brought into the home a variety of celebratory rituals. We have already seen that various aspects of the temple's festival calendar were transferred to the home as feasts, especially within the emerging rabbinic communities of the late Roman and early Byzantine periods. We may close our discussion of the ritual life within the rabbinic domestic space with one final example. It was among the most notorious aspects of Jewish religious behavior in the ancient world: the custom of removing the male foreskin shortly after birth.

We saw in the previous chapter that the Jewish practice of infant circumcision is grounded by the Hebrew Bible in the precedent of the patriarch, Abraham. According to Gen 17:23–27, Abraham circumcised himself, his son Ishmael, and his entire male household as a visible covenant sign for all generations. The nature of this covenant and its implications are clearly stated in the text. Speaking to Abraham, God says:

> I make you the father of a multitude of nations. I will make you exceedingly fertile, and make nations of you....I will maintain my covenant between me and you, and your offspring to come, as an everlasting covenant throughout the ages....I assign the land you sojourn on to you and to your offspring to come, all the land of Canaan....You shall circumcise the flesh of your foreskin, and that shall be the sign of the covenant between me and you. And throughout the generations, every male among you shall be circumcised at the age of eight days....Thus shall my covenant be marked in your flesh as an everlasting pact (Gen 17:5–12).

Clearly, the covenant of circumcision offers this-worldly rewards: the promise of many offspring who will, ultimately, possess and dwell upon the land promised to Abraham.

But this and the many other scriptural texts that mention circumcision as a covenant sign leave important questions unanswered. Namely, why is this covenant sign incised into the penis of an infant on his eighth day of life? Moreover, if the covenant of circumcision represents a visible sign of God's relationship to the entire people, Israel, why is there no corresponding covenantal sign prescribed for Israelite girls? Finally, and most importantly, why does this covenant sign require the shedding of an infant's blood? The answers to these questions are an important foundation for interpreting the meaning of the circumcision ritual eventually developed within rabbinic Judaism.

Recent interpreters of the Hebrew Bible's texts on circumcision have suggested that the practice originated in Israelite priestly groups, prior to the destruction of Yehudah, as a celebration of male priestly lineage and a guarantee of the fertility of the male patriarchal lines of those inheriting the priesthood.[39] The practice was universalized to include all Jewish males during the priestly reconstruction of Persian Yehud. This period, from about 515–450 BCE, saw the restoration of the temple, the rise of Zadokite priestly families to communal leadership, and the prominence of the Torah of Moses as an authoritative Judean text. The descendants of returning priestly Judeans, apparently, established circumcision as a marker distinguishing "genuine" Judeans from others living in Yehud.[40] Linking together the covenant promise to Abraham and the priestly concern for proper lineage, the returnees sought to ensure a populous community of pure lineage, beginning with Abraham and extending into the distant future, capable of propagating itself on the ancient land of the covenant promise.

This hypothesis concerning the priestly origins of Jewish circumcision and its eventual transformation into a commandment imposed upon all Jewish males helps answer some of the questions raised above. Why does the surgical alteration of a boy's genitals constitute a testimony to the covenant between God and Israel? As Howard Eilberg-Schwartz, a pioneering interpreter of circumcision, has pointed out:[41]

> As a ceremony of birth, Israelite circumcision did not incorporate themes of virility and social maturity [as is common in other circumcising societies: MJ]. But it did symbolize the initiate's fertility. As the priests saw it, a boy's procreative powers were granted by God as a privilege for having been born into Abraham's line. They were granted in fulfillment of the divine promise that Abraham and his descendants would be fruitful, multiply, and inherit the land. A male's ability to reproduce was not simply the outcome of his maturation, but also a privilege of having a certain genealogy. Circumcision was thus a rite that simultaneously conferred and confirmed one's pedigree.

The excision of the foreskin is a kind of preparation of the infant sexual organ for the task of fecundity it will assume in the boy's adult life. Removal of the foreskin is performed in infancy, rather than, for example, at puberty, as a way of stressing that the boy's identity as an Israelite is genealogical rather than freely chosen. Established long ago by God's choice of Abraham as the covenantal patriarch, circumcision merely confirms and affirms an inherited identity.

The circumcision must be performed on the eighth day of life. Why not before? Why not much later, at puberty? The answer is probably grounded in a priestly law preserved in Lev 12:2–3. This text states that, in the case of a son, the mother's birthing blood renders her unclean for seven days. On the eighth day, she may undertake her purification. The text then immediately stipulates that the male child must be circumcised upon the eighth day. Presumably, the boy, too, is purified on the eighth day from his mother's blood. His circumcision draws forth his own blood as a kind of covenantal purification, thus incorporating him into Israelite covenantal identity.[42] Since this identity is a birthright, rather than an act of choice, the circumcision that represents it is performed at the earliest possible moment in the boy's life.

Finally, why is there no corresponding covenant celebration for girls in the scriptural tradition and early Judaism? The answer lies in the very origins of Israelite circumcision in the exclusively male priesthood. As Eilberg-Schwartz explains:[43]

> God had promised to make Abraham fertile and provide him with successful progeny. As we have seen, the removal of the foreskin symbolizes the fertility of the organ. But the cut also suggests that the lineage, represented by the penis, is set apart from all others. In this way circumcision symbolizes and helps create intergenerational continuity between men. It graphically represents patrilineal descent [that is, descent through the father's family: MJ] by giving men of this line a distinctive mark that binds them together. Since circumcision binds together men within and across generations, it also establishes an opposition between men and women. Women cannot bear the symbol of the covenant. Only the bodies of men can commemorate the promise of God to Abraham.

Just as females were excluded from the priesthood, so, too, were they excluded from the covenant ceremony that transmitted priestly holiness to another generation. When the realities of Second Temple times required rethinking and extension of priestly identity beyond the inherited priesthood, circumcision was extended to all males, distinguishing them as a "priestly nation." Women were, obviously, part of Israel. But, as women, their participation in the covenant community came by virtue of their relationship to their fathers or husbands. The key ritual expressions of covenantal identity were reserved for men.

Thus far, we have accounted for the purpose of circumcision in the earliest centuries of the formation of Israelite national identity. In view of its ideological centrality and universal spread among Jews all over the Greco-Roman world, we should imagine that circumcision was an important ritual among Jews. But, as it happens, there is no biblical or extra-biblical evidence, until well into the Common Era, for the existence of a standard liturgy associated with this act of surgery. The earliest evidence of liturgical rites for circumcision is found in the Mishnah (Shab 19:1–6) and Tosefta

(Ber 6:12–13, Shab 15:9–10), which discuss the procedure and associated blessings. The Mishnah, assumes, moreover, that the preparations for this ritual include those appropriate for a meal (Shab 19:2). By the third century, rabbinic stories assume that the meal following a circumcision rite is also an occasion for drinking wine, feasting, and the sharing of Torah study (e.g., PT Hag. 2:2. 77b–c).[44] This all suggests that by the later centuries of our period, rabbinic circumcision was fully domesticated as a home ritual associated with the table as a feasting site, replete with the appropriate recollections of the temple.

The key figures in the rabbinic ritual are the surgeon (*mohel:* ideally, the father of the boy, but necessarily someone with surgical skills!), the one who holds the boy during the rite (*sandek*), and the child himself. We can assume the presence of other celebrants—the mother, relations, and friends—who are the audience of the ritual and who will participate in the feast to follow. The core ritual has two basic acts. Each act is punctuated by benedictions and brief prayers associated with the ritual actions.[45]

In the first act, the child is placed on the lap of the *sandek* and the surgery is begun by the *mohel*, who makes an incision in the foreskin. Prior to making the incision, the *mohel* intones a benediction proclaiming that the approaching act is performed in conscious fulfillment of the command of God: "Blessed are You, Lord our God, King of the Universe, who sanctified us by His commandments and commanded us concerning circumcision." Immediately after the incision, he intones a second benediction: "Blessed are You, Lord our God, King of the Universe, who sanctified us by His commandments, and commanded us to admit [this child] to the covenant of Father Abraham." Upon hearing this benediction, the onlookers reply: "As he has entered the covenant, so may he enter [study of] Torah, marriage, and good deeds."

The second act completes the surgical procedure and introduces the child to the covenant community by conferring upon him his name. After the incised foreskin is peeled away and the blood flowing from the wound is staunched, the *mohel* takes a cup of wine and recites the following benediction: "Blessed are You, Lord our God, King of the Universe, Who creates the fruit of the vine." This benediction, intoned as well at the feast that inaugurates the Sabbath and all other rabbinic festivals, concludes the circumcision surgery. Immediately, the *mohel* adds two further formulas, the first a benediction praising God for his covenantal love, and the second a kind of petition that simultaneously names the child and invokes divine blessing upon him.

The benediction, beginning with the standard formula, "Blessed are You...," addresses God as the one:

who sanctified the beloved one [i.e., Abraham] from the womb, and set a statute in his flesh, and stamped his descendants with the sign of the holy covenant. Therefore, as a reward for this, O Living God, our Portion and our Rock, command that the beloved of our flesh shall be delivered from the pit, for the sake of his covenant that He set in our flesh. Blessed...who makes a covenant.

The public naming and petition now follow:

Our God and God of our fathers, sustain this child to his father and to his mother, and let his name in Israel be (so-and-so, son of so-and-so, his father). Let the father rejoice in what has come forth from his loins, and let the mother be happy with the fruit of her womb, as it is written: "Let your father and mother rejoice, and let her that bore you be happy" (Prov 23:25). And it is said, "I passed by you and saw you wallowing in your blood, and I said to you: in your blood, live; I said to you: in your blood, live" (Ezek 16:6).

Thus the rabbinic form of the ritual concludes, and the celebratory meal, complete with its own version of the *birkat hamazon,* begins.

What, then, is the circumcision ritual about? What has it achieved? Clearly the introduction of the boy into the covenant community of Israel is conceived as a kind of initiation into Jewish life. As the audience exclaims at the end of act one, circumcision into the covenant is the first of many entries: into Torah, marriage, and good deeds. But more is going on here. Recall our question, in the introduction to this discussion, regarding the reason for inflicting a bodily wound on the infant. In addition to the real blood shed by the baby in circumcision, there are other references to blood made by the *mohel,* as well as a blessing over wine, long associated in ancient religions with blood.

As Lawrence Hoffman has argued, the circumcision ritual sheds the blood of an infant in order to recall to the participants the redemptive blood that was shed, first in Egypt, by the slaughter of the Passover (or paschal) lamb on the night of the Exodus, and, year upon year thereafter, in the wilderness Tabernacle and in the first and second temples during the priestly sacrificial service. The primacy of real blood and references to it function, according to Hoffman, as an *anamnesis,* a reminder, both to God and the audience, of the redemptive moment that begins with the shedding of innocent blood, and that is recreated here and now in the circumcision rite. Here, according to Hoffman, is how it works:[46]

Wine thus recollects the covenant. In that capacity it is also a symbol for blood,…not just the blood of the paschal lamb, but that other blood of the covenant associated with deliverance, the blood drawn from every Jewish male on the eighth day of his life…. The Rabbis replaced the fertility symbolism of the Bible with blood as a symbol of salvation. In this blood symbolism, they merged the two biblical concepts of covenant—sacrifice …and circumcision…. Blood now became the dominant symbol of covenant, both sacrificially…and through circumcision. One form of blood recalls the other; the blood of the paschal lamb and the blood of circumcision become merged because both are items given by God specifically to effect salvation.

From this perspective, the blood of circumcision reestablishes the covenantal bond between God and Israel. As we have seen in other ritual constructions of rabbinic Judaism—communal prayer and mealtime benedictions—the meaning of the here and now is constantly reconstructed in light of the paradigms of divine service preserved in memories of the temple *avodah*. Although the temple of Jerusalem vanished from Jewish life forever in 70 CE, its priestly perspectives and institutions continued to shape Jewish ritual life for the rest of the first Judaic millennium and beyond.

Conclusion

We have seen that the ritual spaces of ancient Judaism can be understood metaphorically as a series of wheels—hubs and spokes. The synagogue and the home derived their power as centers of holiness from the central hub of the earthly (and heavenly) temple. As such they were spokes emanating from the temple as the center. But they also served as hubs in their own right, sacred centers or privileged spaces in which ritual evocations of the most sublime dimensions of reality could routinely take place.

Indeed, as the temple receded into the past and became a purely heavenly reality, the synagogue and home seem to have come into their own as ritual spaces. But within them the presence of the temple was powerfully evoked, even as the time of its destruction continued to move more deeply into the past. This development coincided, we have suggested, with the increasing dominance of the Torah scroll as a source of holiness in the ritual space and as a symbol of connection between heaven and earth, God and Israel. In the absence of the temple, both synagogue and home were marked off as ritual spaces by the sacred words of the Torah—the entire scroll or a selection of texts that summarized its essential covenantal focus. Within these spaces a variety of ritual activities—prayer, eating, birth rites—were constructed. For those engaging in them, the priestly vision of Israel as a covenant nation, so crucial to the origins of Judaism in Persian Yehud, was restated and represented to a community for whom actual liturgical sacrifice was a matter of literary memory, rather than daily experience.

Notes

1. For a survey of sacrificial cults in the ancient world, see Wolfram von Soden, *The Ancient Orient: An Introduction to the Study of the Ancient Near East* (Grand Rapids, Mich.: Eerdmans Publishing, 1985), pp. 188–198.

2. In fact, the first edition of this book offered one. It is found on pp. 164–165.

3. Catherine Bell. A scholar thoroughly trained in classical theories of ritual illustrates some of the newer approaches in Catherine Bell, "Performance," in Mark C. Taylor, ed., *Critical Terms for Religious Studies* (Chicago and London: University of Chicago, 1998), pp. 205–224.

4. The English word "liturgy" stems from the Greek *leitourgia*, which refers to the public service of the gods. It is a direct semantic parallel to the Hebrew *avodah*, routinely used in the Hebrew Bible to describe the sacrificial service in the Tent of Meeting.

5. Feminist scholars of religion have developed a variety of critical perspectives that help to correct for the androcentrism of both classical religious texts and the modern scholarship that interprets them. An excellent introduction is Rita M. Gross, *Feminism and Religion: An Introduction* (Boston: Beacon Press, 1996), esp. her discussion of androcentrism, pp. 18–20. In her view, androcentrism in the academic study of religion expresses itself in three primary and complementary traits: (1) "the male norm and the human norm are collapsed and seen as identical"; (2) "research about religion deals mainly with the lives and thinking of males"; (3) "females are presented only in relation to the males being studied, only as they appear to the males being studied."

6. The works of Ross Kraemer, referred to frequently in these pages, are foundational for any further work on the religious lives of women in antiquity. Some of the most interesting attempts to get "behind" Jewish writings to reconstruct the religious experience of women or, at least, to retrieve "women's voices" submerged in male literary texts are offered by Daniel Boyarin, *Carnal Israel: Reading Sex in Talmudic Culture* (Berkeley, et al.: University of California, 1993); Tal Ilan, *Mine & Yours Are Hers: Retrieving Women's History from Rabbinic Literature* (Leiden, et al.: E.J. Brill, 1997); Miriam B. Peskowitz, *Spinning Fantasies: Rabbis, Gender, and History* (Berkeley, et al.: University of California Press, 1997); Charlotte Elisheva Fonrobert, *Menstrual Purity: Rabbinic and Christian Reconstructions of Biblical Gender* (Stanford: Stanford University Press, 2000).

7. Recall from Chapter One that a competing Jewish temple existed in Leontopolis in Egypt, from about 160 BCE until 73 CE. But not enough is known of its origins and ritual system to assess its role in Egyptian-Jewish life or its impact beyond Egypt. See Emil Schuerer, revised and edited by G. Vermes, F. Millar, and M. Goodman, *The History of the Jewish People in the Age of Jesus*

Christ, Volume III.1 (Edinburgh: T & T Clark, 1986), pp. 47–49, 145–147.

8. See Carol Meyers, "Temple, Jerusalem," in David Noel Freedman, ed., *The Anchor Bible Dictionary, Volume VI* (New York: Doubleday, 1992), pp. 364–365; and, more expansively, E.P. Sanders, *Judaism: Practice & Belief, 63 BCE–66 CE* (London and Philadelphia: SCM Press and Trinity Press International, 1992), pp. 47–76. Archaeologists tend to present their measurements in biblical cubits or in metric language. I have done my best to approximate these measurements in terms of feet and yards (1 cubit = ca. 18 inches).

9. See his discussions in H. St. J. Thackeray, trans., *Josephus: The Jewish War, Books IV–VII* (Cambridge, Mass. and London: Harvard University Press, 1928), pp. 265–267. Josephus' estimate of the temple as a symbol of the cosmos is anticipated by the mid-second century BCE Letter of Aristeas and echoed in his own time, by the famous first-century Jewish writer, Philo of Alexandria. See the anthology of sources cited in C.T.R. Hayward, ed., *The Jewish Temple: A Non-Biblical Sourcebook* (London and New York: Routledge, 1996), pp. 26–37, 108–118.

10. See Sanders, *Judaism*, p. 61.

11. The Torah, primarily in Leviticus 12–16, prescribes a number of sources of bodily pollution—blood, sexual discharges, and skin eruptions—that prevent men and women suffering them from entering the camp or Tent of Meeting. These were all regarded as applicable to the temple as well. By the end of the Second Temple period, these various types of uncleanness had begun also to serve as metaphors for moral conditions. See Jonathan Klawans, *Impurity and Sin in Ancient Judaism* (Oxford and New York: Oxford University Press, 2000).

12. See Sanders, *Judaism*, pp. 103–118 for an overview of the sacrificial offerings.

13. Reports about this institution are found in later biblical works, the Dead Sea scrolls, Josephus, rabbinic traditions, and in inscriptional remains discovered by archaeologists. For an attempt to cover all the various types of evidence, see E. Schuerer, *The History of the Jewish People in the Age of Jesus Christ*, Volume II. Rev. and edited by G. Vermes, F. Millar, and M. Black (Edinburgh: T&T Clark, 1979), pp. 245–250.

14. For a brief overview, see Lawrence H. Schiffman, *Reclaiming the Dead Sea Scrolls* (Philadelphia: Jewish Publication Society, 1994), pp. 290–305.

15. I owe my colleague, Prof. Steven Fine of the University of Cincinnati, a great debt of gratitude for reading and commenting upon this section of the book. His comments have been taken quite seriously and have engendered a number of changes from the text of the first edition.

16. Here I follow the view of Stevan Reif, *Judaism and Hebrew Prayer: New Perspectives on Jewish Liturgical History* (Cambridge: Cambridge University Press, 1993), p. 73.

17. The most important resource for the study of the synagogue in early Judaism is Lee I. Levine, *The Ancient Synagogue: The First Thousand Years* (New Haven and London: Yale University Press, 1999). See also Steven Fine, *This Holy*

Place: On the Sanctity of the Synagogue during the Greco-Roman Period (Notre Dame: University of Notre Dame Press, 1997).

18. On the difficulties in interpreting the symbols in ancient synagogues, see Levine, *The Ancient Synagogue*, pp. 571–579; and Seth Schwartz, *Imperialism and Jewish Society, 200 BCE to 640 CE* (Princeton, N.J.: Princeton University Press, 2001), pp. 243–263.

19. Spectacular reproductions of the Dura paintings are available in the color plates at the back of Carl H. Kraeling, Augmented edition, *The Synagogue: The Excavations at Dura-Europos* (New York: KTAV, 1979). For an excellent interpretation of their religious meaning, see the recent essay of Jonathan A. Goldstein, "The Judaism of the Synagogues (Focusing on the Synagogue of Dura-Europos)," in Jacob Neusner, ed., *Judaism in Late Antiquity. Part 2: Historical Syntheses* (Leiden: E.J. Brill, 1995), pp. 109–155.

20. A full discussion of the relation of existing synagogues to rabbinic communities is available in Levine, *The Ancient Synagogue*, pp. 440–470.

21. A remarkable reflection upon the meaning of nudity in the Dura paintings has recently been offered by Warren G. Moon, "Nudity and Narrative: Observations on the Frescoes from the Dura Synagogue," *Journal of the American Academy of Religion* 60 (1992), pp. 587–658. Prof. Steven Fine, in a personal communication of July 28, 2004, cautions that it is dangerous to assume, on the basis of rabbinic literature, a general rabbinic reticence about pictorial nudity. As he points out, early printings of the Talmud and other Jewish writings in the sixteenth century often had frontispieces richly decorated with nudes, this in a time of great emphasis in contemporary rabbinic preaching upon avoiding sexual arousal.

22. See, most recently, Seth Schwartz, *Imperialism and Jewish Society*, pp. 215–263. But this view is now coming under increasing challenge. See the nuanced discussion of Stuart S. Miller, "'Epigraphical' Rabbis, Helios, and Psalm 19: Were the Synagogues of Archaeology and the Synagogues of the Sages One and the Same?" *Jewish Quarterly Review* 94 (2004), pp. 27–76.

23. On the subject of women in ancient synagogues, see Levine, *The Ancient Synagogue*, pp. 471–490. Among earlier studies, see Hannah Safrai, "Women and the Ancient Synagogue," in Susan Grossman and Rivka Haut, eds., *Daughters of the King: Women and the Synagogue* (Philadelphia: Jewish Publication Society, 1992), pp. 39–49 and the pioneering scholarly study in this field, Bernadette J. Brooten, *Women Leaders in the Ancient Synagogue* (Chico, Calif.: Scholars Press, 1982).

24. There are two essential works on the development of prayer in Judaism. The first is by Ismar Elbogen, *Jewish Liturgy: A Comprehensive History*, trans. Raymond P. Scheindlin (New York: Jewish Theological Seminary and Philadelphia: Jewish Publication Society, 1993). This is an encyclopedic discussion of all aspects of the worship that became normative in Judaism from rabbinic antiquity into the early twentieth century. The second, to which I've referred in a previous note in this chapter, is Stefan C. Reif, *Judaism and Hebrew Prayer*. It provides a marvelous synthesis of all the textual and archaeological

evidence relevant to the development of Judaic prayer traditions from the temple period through modern times. Also of great value for the rabbinic development of the synagogue liturgy are Levine, *The Ancient Synagogue*, pp. 501–560 and S. Schwartz, *Imperialism and Jewish Society*, pp. 263–274. Schwartz offers an excellent discussion of synagogue liturgical poetry (*piyyut*) in particular.

25. Cited in Eric M. Meyers, *Anchor Bible Dictionary*, VI, p. 252.

26. See R.J.H. Shutt's translation in James H. Charlesworth, ed., *The Old Testament Pseudepigrapha*, II (Garden City, N.Y.: Doubleday & Company, 1983), p. 33.

27. See his *Contemplative Life*, 27, translated by F.H. Colson, *Philo IX* (Cambridge: Harvard University Press and London: Heinemann, 1967), pp. 127–129.

28. For detailed studies, see Daniel K. Falk, *Daily, Sabbath, and Festival Prayers in the Dead Sea Scrolls* (Leiden: E.J. Brill, 1997).

29. These prayers may be consulted in D.R. Darnell's translation in J. Charlesworth, *The Old Testament Pseudepigrapha*, II, pp. 677–697. D.A. Fiensy's introduction to the translation (pp. 671–676) helps to explain how to distinguish the Christian from the Jewish elements of the prayers.

30. On the priestly role, see Levine, *The Ancient Synagogue*, pp. 496–500.

31. See the translation of Shutt, p. 23. For further details of ancient *mezuzot*, see "Mezuzah," *Encyclopaedia Judaica* (1972), 11, 1474–1477 and L. Schiffman, *Reclaiming the Dead Sea Scrolls*, pp. 305–312.

32. See H. St. J. Thackeray, *Josephus: Jewish Antiquities, Books I–IV* (Cambridge: Harvard University Press and London: Heinemann, 1930), p. 577.

33. Many of these can be consulted in English translation in Charles D. Isbell, *Corpus of the Aramaic Incantation Bowls* (Missoula, Mont.: Scholars Press, 1975); Joseph Naveh and Shaul Shaked, *Amulets and Magic Bowls: Aramaic Incantations of Late Antiquity* (Leiden: E.J. Brill and Jerusalem: Magnes Press, 1985); and Lawrence H. Schiffman and Michael D. Swartz, *Hebrew and Aramaic Incantation Texts from the Cairo Genizah* (Sheffield: JSOT Press, 1992).

34. Isbell, *Corpus*, pp. 89–90.

35. An interesting example of a private, home-centered, rite that migrated to the public realm of the synagogue is the recitation of the *Shma*. The first edition of this book has a discussion of the ritual dimensions of this recitation, pp. 204–207. I have omitted it from the new edition in order to focus upon the importance of the rite of circumcision.

36. This transformation is documented in Baruch Bokser, *The Origins of the Seder: The Passover Rite and Early Rabbinic Judaism* (Berkeley, et al.: University of California Press, 1984).

37. See the broad discussion of "women's work" in rabbinic literature by M. Peskowitz, *Spinning Fantasies*, pp. 96ff.

38. See Philo, *The Special Laws* I:132 (Colson, p. 175) and Josephus, *Antiquities*

IV: 4 (Thackeray, p. 511).

39. The now classic essay of Howard Eilberg-Schwartz, "The Fruitful Cut: Circumcision and Israel's Symbolic Language of Fertility, Descent, and Gender," is a fundamental source of this interpretation. See H. Eilberg-Schwartz, *The Savage in Judaism: An Anthropology of Israelite Religion and Ancient Judaism* (Bloomington and Indianapolis: Indiana University Press, 1990), pp. 141–176.

40. The complexity of this process, and especially its political implications, is explored in Shaye J.D. Cohen, *The Beginnings of Jewishness: Boundaries, Varieties, Uncertainties* (Berkeley, et al.: University of California Press, 1999), pp. 209–225.

41. H. Eilberg-Schwartz, *The Savage in Judaism*, pp. 175–176.

42. H. Eilberg-Schwartz, *The Savage in Judaism*, p. 174.

43. H. Eilberg-Schwartz, *The Savage in Judaism*, p. 171.

44. The close connection between the ritual and the feast recalls ways in which Greco-Roman voluntary associations served both as dining clubs and ritual communities (see Chapter Four). This has led a pioneering scholar of Jewish liturgy, Lawrence Hoffman, to argue that the ritual of circumcision as described in rabbinic texts may have its origins as a ritual in the first century CE Khavurah. See Lawrence A. Hoffman, *Covenant of Blood: Circumcision and Gender in Rabbinic Judaism* (Chicago and London: University of Chicago Press, 1996), pp. 60–63.

45. My description and interpretation of the classical rabbinic form of the ritual, shorn of later medieval additions, is adapted from Hoffman, *Covenant of Blood*, pp. 70–72.

46. Hoffman, *Covenant of Blood*, p. 109.

CHAPTER 6

Initiation into Transformative Knowledge

THE JUDAIC WORLDS OF ANTIQUITY all assumed that common humans, after appropriate preparation, had the capacity to penetrate worlds beyond that of ordinary experience. The Jerusalem temple, the synagogue, and the home all served as settings for traversing, at least for a moment, the boundary between this world of mortality and the eternal world of God and his angels. In worlds so permeable to the heavenly order and its awesome beings, it should not surprise us to find specialists who cultivated otherworldly knowledge, teachers who could guide efforts to experience the wonders that lay at the boundaries of the ordinary. We shall look at some of these efforts presently.

The Jews, of course, were hardly alone among Hellenistic peoples in their preservation of otherworldly knowledge. Rather, knowledge of a heavenly "mystery" (Greek: *mysterion*) was a common feature of many Hellenistic religious worlds. People knew about such mysteries, just as many of us know about (but hardly understand) certain concepts of nuclear physics. But only the few truly claimed to possess such knowledge (Greek: *gnosis*). To have it was a sign of inclusion in an elect spiritual fellowship. Its collective knowledge was withheld from outsiders who had not undergone some initiatory induction into the group.

Such esoteric or hidden knowledge flowed through various channels. From ancient Greece, Hellenistic culture inherited and further developed many secret societies devoted to experiential knowledge. Some of these societies transmitted the teachings of sublime teachers, such as Pythagoras, or claimed to preserve knowledge granted to ancient Egyptian or Babylonian priesthoods. Others imparted their knowledge in the initiatory mysteries of various gods (Dionysius, Mithras) and goddesses (Isis, Cybele). Yet other groups, often referred to derisively by early Christian polemicists as Gnostics ("Knowers"), claimed knowledge revealed by a god greater than the one known to Jewish tradition as the Creator of the World.[1]

Possession of these traditions of knowledge was more than an intellectual achievement. To truly know was, in a sense, to become a transformed person or, commonly, to be translated into a different sort of being altogether. This experiential dimension of knowledge was, indeed, the essential value of these traditions. Knowledge of the immortal world—experienced in one's psychological depths rather than simply as a subject for learned discourse—ushered a person into the companionship of the immortals. As a quasi-celestial being, one might enjoy the fruits of that companionship even during one's transitional period of embodied, earthly life.

In this chapter we will examine some particularly Judaic versions of transformative knowledge. We saw in Chapter Four how intentional Judaic communities could provide a context for the pursuit of special experiences. In the last century of the temple's existence, the Therapeutae, the Yakhad and, most probably, the earliest Jewish followers of Messiah Jesus all cultivated forms of transformative knowledge. They associated such knowledge with conversion to a new communal life. Now, however, we will focus on groups emerging after the temple's destruction, apparently in at least loose association with the emerging rabbinic communities of the second through seventh centuries.

We begin with some observations about the nature of rabbinic knowledge itself. In early rabbinic communities, the very process of becoming a disciple was an initiation into a body of transformative knowledge. We will have to ask, however, whether such knowledge was indeed "esoteric" in the rabbinic setting. The question is important in light of the remainder of our chapter, which explores knowledge that was certainly restricted to small groups. Though such knowledge was usually quite compatible with rabbinic conceptions of the world, it was also seen—by those possessing it, at least—to be more profound.

The Transformative Knowledge of the Rabbinic Sage

In the first century CE Pharisaic teachers had claimed to possess ancestral traditions that were fundamental to the proper maintenance of Israel's covenantal obligations. Second-century rabbinic sages made similar claims, going so far as to designate some of their customs "*halakhah* stemming from Moses on Sinai" (e.g., Mishnah Yadayim 4:3). By the third century, discipleship to rabbinic sages involved the complete transformation of behavior in accordance with the master's conception of this traditional Torah. The Torah sage, it was believed, had himself been transformed by his own master's Torah, and his master before him, in a chain of transformative relationships that had begun with Moses' relationship to God: "Moses was sanctified in the Cloud so as to receive Torah from Sinai" (Avot d'Rabbi Nathan A, 1:1).

The Communal Setting of Knowledge. Scrupulous behavior in accordance with the norms of the sage's Torah was, of course, the outer sign of a disciple's transformation into a sage. To be a sage was not a professional choice. Rather, it was to enjoy a certain status. Many sages seem to have come from landed families and some inherited wealth; others earned their livings as farmers, artisans, or merchants, as did other Jews. But the sage transformed these tasks into forms of divine service by virtue of his particular absorption of revelation. Whatever he did could be interpreted by his disciples as an embodiment of Torah in human form. Moreover, the sage made it clear to all disciples that his behavior was a reflection of knowledge that he had mastered in a most particular way. His personal transformation into a model of Torah had been made possible by his diligent memorization of words of Torah, both those written in Israel's national scripture and those preserved in the oral teachings of earlier sages. In rabbinic culture, the training of a disciple's memory was the key to his moral transformation as a person worthy of covenant partnership with God.

The rabbinic learning community (*bet midrash*, "House of Study") was the social setting of this transformation of memory and character.[2] Like the *schola* (Latin: "school") of Greco-Roman philosophers and other teachers of redemptive truths, the rabbinic schools were organized as communities of disciples supervised by a sage, who was both a teacher of traditional knowledge and a role model of wisdom. These were not endowed institutions like our contemporary universities, but much more like extended families embarking in common on a distinctive way of life. Within them the traditions of the sage were mastered and elaborated, as disciples and their immediate households undertook to live in accordance with norms embodied by their teachers.[3]

In rabbinic culture, accordingly, the bet midrash was the central religious institution, of greater importance than the synagogue itself. Prayer was important, and the synagogue as the house of prayer was respected. But, as we saw earlier, the synagogue was a public institution that the sages could try to influence but not always control. Their power there would depend upon the degree to which those attending the synagogue knew or respected rabbinic traditions of piety. What the sages could control, however, was the disciple circle, where their own traditions reigned supreme and they themselves constituted the unquestioned authorities. It was the community of the bet midrash that forged the characters of those who would fan out into

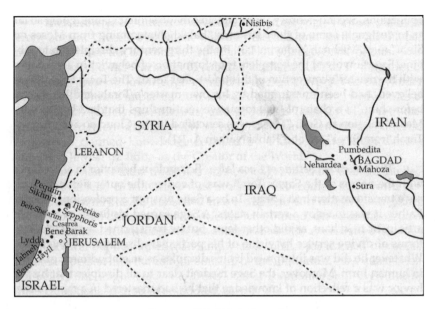

Centers of Rabbinic Learning

A bet midrash existed wherever disciples gathered around a rabbinic sage to absorb the traditions of Oral Torah. Rabbinic literature mentions as well the existence of a number of major centers of learning (Hebrew: *yeshivot*) that attracted large numbers of disciples. This map locates those that loom largest in later rabbinic memory. The Palestinian academy of Sepphoris is usually regarded as the site at which Rabbi presided over the editing of the Mishnah. The Babylonian academies of Sura and Pumbedita served as the setting for the compilation of much of the Babylonian Talmud.

Source: *Based on Encyclopedia Judaica*, Vol. 2. (Jerusalem: Keter Publishing House), pp. 203–204.

the larger Jewish community to make the rabbinic tradition the common tradition of Israel.

The Innovation of Rabbi's Mishnah. From the third century on, the Mishnah of Rabbi Judah the Patriarch became the primary focus of study in the bet midrash, the most prestigious representation of rabbinic Torah. Prior to Rabbi's work, it is likely that learned traditions were organized for transmission (if they were organized at all) as lists of teachings under the names of a particular sage. These were cultivated and preserved within the bet midrash of that sage and, perhaps, shared with the disciples of other sages. But until the ascension of Rabbi to the patriarchate in the late second century, no one sage had commanded enough authority throughout rabbinic communities to transform the diverse traditions of the rabbis into a single shared curriculum.

This was the primary achievement of Rabbi's editorial efforts in his Mishnah. He supervised the reshaping of the received traditions of various masters into coherent tractates or weavings *(masekhtot;* sing., *masekhet)* on specific legal topics. Eventually, sixty-two such tractates came to be included in the mishnaic canon. They were organized into six divisions of thematically related tractates. These divisions or orders *(sedarim)* covered agricultural practices (Seeds = *zera'im),* the celebration of festivals (Times = *mo'ed),* various elements of family law pertaining to women in particular (Women = *nashim),* civil and criminal law (Damages = *neziqin),* the conduct of the sacrificial system in the temple (Sanctified Things = *qedoshim)* and, finally, forms of pollution and modes of purification from them (Purities = *tohorot).* The result was a comprehensive compendium of legal tradition on all topics relevant to rabbinic communities.[4]

The main innovation of these tractates was in the way they presented the teachings of past sages. Students were discouraged from learning lists of statements by their own masters alone. With only a few exceptions, tractates were organized thematically rather than in terms of the names of specific teachers. Where a teacher's name appeared, it was invariably attached to a specific opinion on a given question, and normally was juxtaposed with the position of another sage on the same matter. It was now possible to determine each sage's place in the development of a coherent body of halakhic principles and cases.

This synthesis of the teachings of diverse first- and second-century masters into a coherent system was more than a teaching innovation. It also clarified the role of the sage in the larger stream of halakhic tradition. As Rabbi conceived it, sages were bearers of universal principles of Torah. Their authority was rooted in the mastery of those principles and the ability to apply them. Students of Rabbi's Mishnah, accordingly, were encouraged to see themselves as heirs to a tradition in which their own masters were contributors to an ancient knowledge that transcended the opinions of any one of them. Moreover, the topical organization of tractates highlighted the rational, logical character of the tradition. It helped students to see how apparently unrelated principles intersected, yielding contradictions or resolutions. Mastering the principles through the cases, students were then in a position to discern how the opinions of diverse masters drew upon and employed them.[5]

Perhaps a brief look at a very famous mishnaic text will help to illustrate the economy of Rabbi's method. Here is the very first paragraph of the

Mishnah, the beginning of Tractate Beraḵhot (Blessings) in the Order of Seeds. Recall that rabbinic law obliges men to perform every morning and evening a ritual recitation of the collection of biblical verses known as the *Shma*.[6] The Mishnah assumes that everyone knows this and offers no explanation as to why the *Shma* must be recited. The problem, rather, is to define the moment in the evening at which a man becomes obliged to recite it.

We have divided the paragraph into four sections so that the flow of its topics is more clear:

> 1. From when do they recite the *Shma* in the evenings?
> From the time the priests enter to eat their priestly offerings.
> > Until the end of the first watch—the words of Rabbi Eliezer.
> > But sages say—until midnight.
> > Rabban Gamaliel says—Until the morning star rises.
> 2. A case: His sons once came from a wedding feast.
> They said to him—we haven't recited the *Shma*. He said to them—
> if the morning star hasn't risen, you are obliged to recite.
> > 3. And not only this: But whenever sages said a commandment should be filled by midnight, its obligatory deadline is the rise of the morning star.
> > The burning of sacrificial fat and limbs—its obligatory deadline is the rise of the morning star.
> > And every sacrifice that must be eaten within a single day—its obligatory deadline is the rise of the morning star.
> 4. If so, why did sages say until midnight?
> To remove a person from transgression.

This compact paragraph begins in a simple question, but the answer engulfs the student in a mire of unexpected details. Let's move through each of the four units to see exactly how the Mishnah involves its student in its own distinctive picture of the world.

The Mishnah's answer to the question of when to recite the evening *Shma* has, first of all, to be decoded. It assumes you know that, when the temple stood, priests would eat their holy offerings shortly after sundown, after they had bathed in purification pools that removed whatever sources of uncleanness might prevent them from touching sanctified food. The evening *Shma*, we now learn, is recited so as to coincide with a moment in the temple's rhythm of purification.

But, in fact, the Mishnah is not really interested in the answer to its question. Other traditions not included in the Mishnah inform us that the rule of thumb is to recite the evening *Shma* after three bright stars have appeared in the evening sky (Tos Ber 1:1; PT Ber 1:1, 2a; BT Ber 2b). What really concerns the Mishnah is not the *earliest* moment the *Shma* may be recited, but the *last* moment. The allusion to the temple is carried forward in the three opinions that round out unit 1. Rabbi Eliezer, the majority of sages, and Rabban Gamaliel are all assigned opinions regarding the latest moment it is possible to fulfill one's obligation to recite the *Shma* in the evening. When does "evening" end? Briefly, Rabbi Eliezer's opinion would correspond to "bedtime," the sages' to the middle of the night, and Rabban Gamaliel's to shortly before dawn. What they are disputing, of course, is whether "evening" ends when people go to sleep or, to the contrary, when some celestial event occurs.

We might put it this way: Is evening determined by social conventions or by natural occurrences? Practically speaking, if you followed Rabbi Eliezer's society-oriented view, you'd have to recite the *Shma* by the conventional bedtime of your community, even if you stayed up later. sages, who want to divide the night into two equal halves between sunset and sunrise, give you a bit more latitude. You can go to bed, get up before the night is half over, and still satisfy your obligation to recite the evening *Shma*. But Rabban Gamaliel insists that you have the entire period of darkness until the dawn of a new day. The case at unit 2 illustrates Rabban Gamaliel's view and, by implication, suggests that his is the one to be followed. You can party all night, or rise before dawn, and still satisfy your obligation.

The truly interesting contribution, however, comes at unit 3. It shows, first of all, that the opinions of sages and Rabban Gamaliel amount to the same thing. Those parts of the sacrificial service that had to be completed by midnight could, in fact, be delayed until dawn without spoiling the procedure. These last illustrations, of course, reinforce unit 1's view that the recitation of the *Shma* continues in some sense the liturgical life of the temple, for the principles that govern the temple's sacrificial rites govern those of the *Shma*'s performance as well.

Unit 4 asks the natural question: If the sages agreed with Rabban Gamaliel in principle, why didn't they say so? The answer is to the point: sages didn't want people to get lax in meeting their duties. So they stipulated an earlier time for the performance of certain commandments even though, technically speaking, they could be satisfied many hours later.

You will appreciate how the Mishnah orients its student to the outlines of a specific world. At one level, this world is evoked through the very terms used by the Mishnah. It doesn't speak simply of "twilight," for example, but does so only indirectly by reference to an obscure moment in the priestly regimen. Moreover, when individual teachers offer opinions, their grounds are taken for granted rather than explained. You are expected to infer for yourself that underlying their dispute is an issue of whether social convention or celestial realities govern the time for the *Shma*'s performance. Similarly, you are expected to understand that the sages' choice of terms allude to the details of sacrificial procedures last performed by priests well over a century before the Mishnah's compilation. Finally, you are shown how two opinions in particular—those of sages and Rabban Gamaliel—agree in substance despite the apparently dramatic difference in their language.

The compact language of Rabbi's Mishnah, then, communicates a subtle intellectual exercise in a kind of technical code. Mastery of the Mishnah entails more than memorizing its terse diction. What is required, rather, is a prior knowledge of the code its language supposes. But whereas the Mishnah speaks in the code, it nowhere supplies the student with a decoding key. It assumes that the key to the code will be supplied by the oral teaching of the sage. In this way knowledge of the Mishnah's mere text is not knowledge of the Mishnah at all. Textual knowledge can only become personal knowledge when the words are enlivened in the face-to-face relationship with a rabbinic master. Only on that basis, presumably, will the disciple be able to apply his knowledge to his own circumstances, based upon the entire body of traditions that he absorbed in his studies, as well as through his observations of how his own teacher had applied the principles.

Rabbi's Mishnah, then, established the centrality of the sage as a transmitter of Torah even as it provided a body of knowledge that transcended the teaching of any particular sage. As with most major innovations in education, Rabbi's edition of Repeated Teaching may have met some initial resistance. Nevertheless, within a century the Mishnah became the universal text of rabbinic discipleship training. It inspired at least one supplementary compilation of traditions, the Tosefta, and ultimately became the basis of the Talmuds of Palestine and Babylonia. Wherever rabbinic communities spread, they brought Rabbi's Mishnah with them and used it as the foundation of their efforts to teach Jews to think like sages. Mastering their knowledge was the first step on a journey that would transform a disciple into the kind of person the sage was—an embodiment of Torah.

The Orality of Oral Torah. The transformative project represented by disciplined study of the Mishnah is best understood by pointing to the way the Mishnah was taught. According to the evidence of the rabbinic literature, it is clear that the Mishnah was memorized by students who listened to teachers repeating it as a kind of song or chant; and they analyzed the Mishnah in the process of their own recitations before teachers. While there is good reason to believe that the compilation of the Mishnah required the tool of writing, its life in the setting of rabbinic instruction was almost entirely oral.[7]

The manner of this oral teaching, as well as its larger meaning in the religious world of the sages, is described in a famous passage from the Babylonian Talmud (Eruvin 54b):

> Our rabbis taught: How was oral teaching conducted?
>
> Moses learned from the mouth of the Almighty. Then Aaron entered and Moses repeated his portion for him. Aaron stepped aside and sat at the left of Moses. Aaron's sons entered and Moses repeated their portion for them. They stepped aside, Elazar sitting to the right of Moses and Itamar to the left of Aaron.... The elders entered, and Moses repeated their portion for them. They stepped aside. All the people entered, and Moses repeated their portion for them.
>
> Thus Aaron heard it four times, his sons three times, the elders twice, and all the people once.
>
> Then Moses stepped aside and Aaron repeated his portion with them. Then Aaron stepped aside and his sons repeated their portion with them. Then his sons stepped aside and the elders repeated their portion with them. It turns out, then, that everyone heard it a total of four times.
>
> On this basis said Rabbi Eliezer: A man is obliged to repeat for his disciples four times....
>
> Rabbi Aqiva says: How do we know that a man is obliged to repeat for his disciples until he teaches them? For it is said in Scripture: "Teach it to the children of Israel" (Deut 31:19).
>
> And how do we know that he does so until it is mastered orally? For it is said in Scripture: "Place it in their mouths (Deut 31:19)."

The passage links rabbinic methods of instruction to the original imparting of Torah to Moses by God. The relation of sage and disciple imitates that of God to Moses and of Moses to his original associates. Clearly, as the comments of Rabbis Eliezer and Aqiva make clear, interest in Moses' teaching method was generated by the need to explain the origins of the pedagogical techniques developed by the sages themselves.

The method of teaching rabbinic tradition reinforced the conviction that, with the Mishnah and its associated halakhic traditions, the disciple was absorbing more than mere knowledge; he was absorbing the oral tradition of Mosaic revelation, the Oral Torah. Indeed, by the third and fourth centuries, many sages formally prohibited study of Oral Torah from a written manuscript. The only way to gain knowledge of this Torah was to learn it from a sage as a disciple. This requirement helps us to appreciate the degree to which the authority of the sages and that of the Oral Torah was mutually intertwined.

In the first place, preservation of mishnaic studies in oral form preserved the sages as the authoritative interpreters of the tradition. Masters of a text committed to memory, they alone could transmit it. Sole mediators of the text imparted to their students, they were able to control and direct its range of interpretation. As the passage of tractate Berakhot has shown, Oral Torah wasn't the kind of thing that could be readily grasped without the help of an expert. Someone who could only read a copy of the Mishnah would remain in the dark about its meaning without the sage's oral instruction.

Secondly, oral transmission of the Mishnah ensured that the text would be mastered only as part of a personal relationship between master and disciple. In this way, the student learned not only the code of the text and its intellectual substance, but a way of being human in imitation of the sage. The sage was the trustee of Oral Torah until all Israel could be taught its ways, until all of Israel could be transformed into a bet midrash humming with the recitation of Oral Torah.

The Mishnah as Mystery. Clearly, knowledge of Oral Torah was treasured in rabbinic communities as knowledge that truly changed the knower. Possession of the knowledge in one's memory, as demonstrated in one's oral performance of the Mishnah, made one a different sort of Jew than one had been before, and continued to distinguish the knower from other Jews. Moreover, the content of this knowledge was difficult and required devoted efforts of understanding. Was such knowledge, then, esoteric in the sense we discussed at the beginning of this chapter?

At least one passage in the classical rabbinic midrashic literature, with a clear anti-Christian bias, might yield that impression (Midrash Tanhuma Ki-Tissa 34):

> Said Rabbi Judah ben Rabbi Shalom: Moses wanted the Repeated Tradition (*mishnah*) to be written. But the Blessed Holy One foresaw that the other nations would translate the Torah and read it in Greek. And they would say: "The Jews are not Israel (for we have the Torah as well)!"
> Said the Blessed Holy One to Moses: O Moses! The other nations will say: "We are Israel! We are the sons of the All Present!" And Israel, too, will say: "We are the sons of the All Present!"
> Said the Blessed Holy One to the other nations: You claim to be my sons, but I recognize him alone who holds my mystery (*mistoryn*) in his hands. He alone is my son!
> They said: What is this mystery of yours?
> He said to them: It is the Repeated Tradition!

The passage clearly identifies rabbinic Oral Torah as a "mystery" of God, employing a Hebraized form of the very Greek term *mysterion*, which others used to denote heavenly secrets. Does this passage, then, suggest that we should consider the Mishnah and its related traditions part of an ancient rabbinic gnosis?

Probably not. The polemical nature of the passage makes its meaning clear: at issue is whether Jews or Christians are the true people of God. Just as Christian theologians routinely accused Jews of misunderstanding their own scripture's hidden references to Christ's redemptive power, rabbinic sages repaid the complement, arguing that the true meaning of Scripture lay well beyond the comprehension of Christians. Only one who knew the Oral Torah knew what God truly wanted of his covenant partner. And here is the point. The Mishnah is not the possession of the rabbis alone, but of all Israel. All Jews, not simply sages and their disciples, are God's covenant partners.

Surely, knowledge of Oral Torah did, indeed, distinguish its possessors as a special social group, and the knowledge was, in itself, arcane. Although it was carefully preserved within the sages' communities of memory, it was guarded in order to be spread. Oral Torah had been given by God to Moses on behalf of all Israel. It came from heaven but was now on earth, the possession of humans who developed and expanded that knowledge through their own intellectual labors. Moses' descendants, the sages, were only the trustees of the knowledge and its preservers. The entire point was to transform all Israel as the sages' disciples had been transformed. The discipleship was rigorous, but it was a discipleship open to all Jewish men and, through them, to their wives and children. As the sages' vigorous missionary activity among Jews demonstrated, they hoped their tradition could transform Israel into what it had originally committed itself to becoming—loyal covenant partners of God.

The Transformative Visions of God's Glory

For all its obscure language and arduous process of memorization, then, knowledge of the Mishnah and its associated traditions was public knowledge open to all who would accept rabbinic discipline. But this body of knowledge hardly exhausted the range of knowledge cultivated by rabbinic sages or other Jews who shared many aspects of the sages' religious world. At least some Jews both within and beyond the communities of the bet midrash cultivated types of knowledge that were reserved for a small, select group.

The major texts of rabbinic tradition, beginning with the Mishnah itself (Hagigah 2:2) alluded to it indirectly as knowledge of the Heavenly Throne-Chariot (*merkavah*) of God. sages believed that this Throne-Chariot, and the divine beings surrounding it, had been seen in its totality in ancient times by the prophet Ezekiel, who described such a vision in the first chapter of his scriptural book. The Mishnah itself counsels caution in expounding this chapter of prophetic teaching in public. Many Jews—and at least some sages were certainly among them—believed that even now a person with proper preparation and guidance could still make the journey.[8]

The Puzzle of the Hekhalot Literature

Rabbinic tradition alludes episodically to those who travel to the Merkavah, the most explicit discussion of this transformative journey comes from outside the officially transmitted rabbinic literature of antiquity. It is found in a collection of obscure, loosely edited texts called the literature of the *hekhalot* (Heavenly Halls). Most of these texts are early medieval compilations of prayers, instructions, and narratives. Most historians, however, believe them to have been transmitted as a kind of esoteric knowledge for many centuries prior to their compilation into specific literary documents. Thus, their traditions were formulated during the time of rabbinic Judaism's spread throughout Byzantine Palestine and Sasanian Babylonia, even thought the current shape of the material stems from the ninth century and later.[9]

The identities of those who transmitted the original traditions, as well as the later editors, remain unknown. Certain famous mishnaic sages, however, such as Rabbi Akiva and Rabbi Ishmael, figure prominently in the hekhalot texts. Those who transmitted these traditions, then, seem to have been in some communication with the major rabbinic schools. At the very least, they assumed that rabbinic heroes were important enough to be depicted as transmitters of this most hidden of knowledge. Nevertheless, few historians believe that the traditions recorded in these texts stem from the same groups responsible for the widely studied literature gathered into the Talmuds. These texts remind us that, beyond the tight circles of the sages, elements of rabbinic culture spread in diverse forms, often beyond the control of established rabbinic masters.

What is clear is that some of the knowledge offered in the hekhalot literature had circulated among Jews since the early centuries BCE. In Chapter Three we read Palestinian texts from the Hasmonean period and earlier that described the heavenly visions of ancient prophets like Enoch and Ezra. We know that speculation about the angelic beings surrounding God's throne in the heavenly temple attracted the attention of the Yakhad as well, and figured prominently in their Sabbath hymns. The hekhalot texts drew deeply upon these earlier traditions of esoteric knowledge.

They differed, however, in a number of crucial respects. The earlier apocalyptic literature described the experiences of ancient biblical heroes and seemed to serve readers as food for intellectual nourishment or inspi-

The Mystery of Ezekiel's Vision
of the Divine Throne-Chariot

The rabbinic traditions recorded in the Mishnah and its major talmudic interpretations are highly suspicious of those who cultivate speculations on the experience described in Ezekiel 1:1–28 (cf. 10:1-22). The Mishnah's tractate Hagigah (2:1) summarizes such speculation under the title "Dynamics of the Throne-Chariot" (Hebrew: *ma'aseh merkavah*). It limits instruction in the matter to a single disciple, under the condition that "he already understands it on his own." The Babylonian Talmud (Hagigah 13a) expresses its reservations with the following story about one who came too close to grasping Ezekiel's mysterious reference to *hashmal* (Ezra 1:27), a gleaming substance that conceals a humanlike figure sitting on a Throne.

> *Our Masters transmitted an oral tradition: There was the case of a child who was reading from the book of Ezekiel in his Teacher's house and penetrated the mystery of the hashmal. Immediately a tongue of fire spat forth from the hashmal and consumed him. Accordingly, the sages sought to suppress public access to the book of Ezekiel.*

ration to hold on a little longer for the ultimate redemption of Israel. The Qumran hymns were primarily concerned with descriptions of the angelic adoration of God. The newer traditions, by contrast, placed such descriptions in the mouths of rabbinic figures of the mishnaic generation. More important, the texts containing these traditions seem designed to serve as a kind of guidebook for one who would experience what sages had seen. In further contrast to the apocalyptic literature, the messianic end is not a fundamental focus. Rather, the immediate goal is to confront the fullness of the divine Presence here and now, in one's own personal experience.

Some of these texts insist that preparation for a journey to the Merkavah involved complete self-purgation. Note the disqualifying character traits, for example, named in Hekhalot Rabbati (Chapters of the Heavenly Halls, 15:2 [par. 199]):[10]

> What is it like to have the ability to descend to the Merkavah? It is like having a ladder in one's house. Any person who would descend to the Merkavah must be purged and cleansed of idolatry, sexual excess, blood-

shed, slander, vain oaths, profanation of the Name of God, haughtiness, and arbitrary hatred. And he must observe every positive and negative commandment.

These vices are commonly criticized in rabbinic writings, and the division of the Torah into positive and negative commandments is unique to rabbinic legal thought. This text seems to assume, therefore, that only a person who already embodies rabbinic Torah is suitable for the ultimate transformation awaiting those who have a heavenly ladder in their homes.

This insistence upon complete immersion in rabbinic halakhic norms is characteristic of only some of these texts. In most, however, the would-be traveler was at least expected to engage in extended prayer and fasting prior to the journey. Indeed, the journey itself was often portrayed as being the culminating point of prayer. We saw in the last chapter how the public recitation of the *kedushah* in the later rabbinic synagogue liturgy explicitly sought to make the earthly worship service an opportunity to share in the angelic adoration of God in heaven. In some hekhalot texts, the *kedushah* seems to serve as the immediate setting for the worshipper's actual journey to the Merkavah. Others, however, offer private prayers as meditative hymns that either aid the traveler's efforts to penetrate the divine realm or serve as exultant signs of his safe arrival.

The Realm of the Merkavah

Common to most of the texts is the detailed description of seven stages of heavenly journey. There are a series of ascents through the seven hekhalot or heavenly halls, culminating in a final descent to the actual chamber of the Merkavah itself.[11] Each stage of ascent and descent has its own character, which the traveling teacher describes to his disciples. The following example is from *Ma'asei Merkavah* (The Dynamics of the Merkavah, par. 556), which depicts angelic recitations of the *kedushah* and other portions of the rabbinic liturgy. In this translation, the letters YH, YHWH, and YY represent the unpronounced name of God:[12]

> Rabbi Akiva said: Who can contemplate the seven Hekhalot, and gaze at the highest heavens, and see the inner chambers, and say, "I have seen the chambers of YH?...In the first Hekhal, Merkavot of fire say, "Holy, holy, holy is YHWH of Hosts, the whole earth is full of His Glory" (Isa 6:3) and their flames spread out and gather together to the second Hekhal, and say, "Holy, holy, holy." In the second Hekhal, Merkavot of fire say, "Holy, holy, holy"; and their flames gather together and spread out to the third Hekhal and say, "Holy, holy, holy." In the third Hekhal, Merkavot of fire say: "Blessed is the name of His Majesty's Glory forever and ever from

the place of His Presence"; and their flames gather together and spread out to the fourth Hekhal and say, "Blessed is the name of His Majesty's Glory for ever and ever." In the fourth Hekhal, Merkavot of fire say, "Blessed is YY, living and enduring forever and ever, magnificent over all the Merkavah"; and their flames gather together and spread out to the fifth Hekhal and say, "Blessed is YHWH, living and enduring forever and ever." In the fifth Hekhal, Merkavot of fire say, "Blessed is the Holiness of His Majesty from the place of His Presence"; and their flames gather together and spread out to the sixth Hekhal and say, "Blessed is the Holiness of His Majesty from the place of His Presence." In the sixth Hekhal, Merkavot of fire say, "Blessed is YHWH, Lord of all power, Who creates power, and Ruler over all the Merkavah"; and their flames gather together and spread out to the seventh Hekhal and say, "Blessed is YHWH, Lord of all might, and Ruler over all the Merkavah. In the seventh Hekhal, Merkavot of fire say: "Blessed be the King of Kings, YY, Lord of all power. Who is like God, great and enduring? His praise is in the heavens' heaven, the holiness of His majesty is in the highest chambers...."

In other accounts, the basic knowledge required of the traveller is mastery of specific incantations or bits of hidden wisdom. At each of the seven stages of the journey, these can be recited in order to appease the various angelic beings, with unpronounceable names, who seek to protect heaven from invasions by mortals. The following example, from Hekhalot Rabbati 21:3–22:1 [par. 233–235], reveals its rabbinic milieu as the traveller enters the sixth hall. The capital letters indicate elements of secret divine names:

At the gate to the sixth hall, Dumiel the Prince, who guards the threshold of the gate to the right of the sixth hall, sits on a bench of pure ivory that radiates heavenly luminescence as at the Creation of the world. 'RST'N W'RZ' 'RST'R WBNPYNN SMNSH 'RGH YHWH, Lord of Israel, and Dumiel the prince receive him with gladness and set him on a bench of pure ivory and sit beside him to his right.

Dumiel says to the traveller: Of two things must I testify and warn before you: No one descends to the Merkavah unless he possesses the following two virtues. He must be able to study the Torah, the Prophets and the Writings, and he must have mastered Repeated Tradition, halakhic and aggadic interpretation, and the resolution of legal decisions regarding the permissible and forbidden. Also, he must have fulfilled all that is written in the Torah in its entirety, observing all the warnings, the statutes, the judgments, and the teachings that were given to Moses on Sinai.

And if he says to Dumiel the Prince, "I have one of these virtues," immediately Dumiel the Prince takes counsel with Gabriel the Scribe, who writes on parchment with permanent ink on behalf of that man, saying,

"This is the Torah learning of this particular person and those are his deeds, and he requests to enter before the Throne of Glory."

The recommendation of Dumiel and Gabriel, however, is not entirely sufficient to safeguard the traveller. First he must pass two final tests (HR 26:1–2 [par. 258–259]):

"I saw one like the lightning" (Ezek 1:27) who would interrogate the descender to determine if he was worthy to descend to the Merkavah or not. If one was worthy to descend to the Merkavah, when they say to him "Enter," he does not enter. They repeat to him, "Enter," and he enters immediately…. But if he was not worthy to descend to the Merkavah, when they say to him, "Do not enter," he enters immediately. They then throw thousands of iron bars on him.

Then the guards of the gate of the sixth palace throw upon him a million waves of water, but there is not any water there, not even a drop. And if he says: "What kind of water is this?" they immediately pursue him for stoning. They say: "Numbskull! Perhaps you are the offspring of those who kissed the Golden Calf! You are not worthy to see the King and his Throne of Glory." They do not move from there until they throw a million bars of iron on him.

One wonders about the consequence of failure. What is the experiential equivalent of being buried under thousands of iron bars? Are millions of them a harsher punishment?

At any rate, the text is more concerned with success. One who overcomes the deceptions of the angelic protectors of the Throne is ushered into the goal of his journeys at last (HR, 22:2 [par. 236]), attaining his personal experience of the vision of Ezekiel:

They then present him before the Throne of Glory, parading before him all types of music and song, and they proceed to sing until they raise him and seat him near the Cherubim, near the Ofanim, and near the holy Creatures (cf. Ezek 1:10–21). He sees wonders and powers, majesty and greatness, holiness and purity, terror and humility and righteousness at the same time.

Having experienced this vision, the traveller returns to earth. His experience has forever distinguished him among the earthbound, enabling him to have a ladder in his house that he can ascend at his pleasure. Other Jews may imagine the heavenly world in prayer; he has visited it, matched wits with heavenly beings, and penetrated their gates to gaze upon the unseeable and the indescribable. For most people, one supposes, this would be sufficient.

Enoch's Transformation

At least one text, however, usually known as the Third Book of Enoch, reports that the first heavenly traveller, the biblical Enoch, had himself been transformed into a heavenly being. He had become none other than Metatron, the angelic Prince of the Divine Presence (*sar hapanim*). The question remains whether the account of Enoch's heavenly transformation is to dissuade others from seeking such angelic transformation or to encourage them to hope for it. In any event, the account, as reported in the name of Rabbi Ishmael, is remarkable (III Enoch 9):[13]

> Rabbi Ishmael said: Metatron, Prince of the Divine Presence, said to me: In addition to all these qualities, the Blessed Holy One laid his hand on me and blessed me with 1,365,000 blessings. I was enlarged and increased in size till I matched the world in length and breadth. He made to grow on me 72 wings, 36 on one side and 36 on the other, and each single wing covered the entire world. He fixed in me 365,000 eyes and each eye was like the Great Light. There was no splendor, brilliance, brightness, or beauty in the luminaries of the world that he failed to fix in me.

The transformation of Enoch-Metatron's body beyond all human proportions prepares him to be placed by God on a special throne (in Greek, Metatron means "behind the throne") signifying his rulership of the entire heavenly domain beneath God. At that point, his physical transformation completed, he receives at last the transformative knowledge that distinguishes the immortal celestial beings from their mortal, earthbound inferiors (III Enoch 11):[14]

> The Blessed Holy One revealed to me from that time onward all the mysteries of wisdom, all the depths of the perfect Torah, and all the thoughts of men's hearts. All the mysteries of the world and all the orders of nature stand revealed before me as they stand revealed before the Creator. From that time onward I looked and beheld deep secrets and wonderful mysteries. Before a man thinks in secret, I see his thought; before he acts, I see his act. There is nothing in heaven above or deep within the earth concealed from me.

Such a transformed being, of course, need never leave heaven for earth. His home is now with God and the angels.

The Merkavah and Rabbinic Knowledge. Clearly, those who journeyed to the Merkavah sought an esoteric, experiential knowledge that had little to do with rabbinic halakhic interest in the precise performance of divine commandments. For this reason, as we have seen, recent scholars have argued that the Merkavah literature originated in groups at the edges of the rabbinic culture of the bet midrash. This may indeed be so. But by the early Middle Ages, descriptions of Merkavah journeys came to be copied and studied within rabbinic communities. Viewed as part of ancient esoteric lore, they were deemed compatible with the public knowledge transmitted in rabbinic schools.

From the perspective of our study of Judaic worlds, it appears that the tradition of the bet midrash and that of the hekhalot literature offer complementary, not opposed, bodies of knowledge. Knowledge of Oral Torah transformed a man into a proper Jew, the kind of human being God had created him to be. But knowledge of the Merkavah made him into a kind of angel. It helped him to exceed the possibilities inherent in his creation.

This, of course, had been the aspiration of the first human couple as well, leading to their eating from the forbidden tree of knowledge. But thanks to the new knowledge of the Merkavah, some men could become like heavenly beings without violating the divine will. Indeed, they would be helped along by heavenly associates. Even a rabbinic sage might be tempted to overcome the constraints of mortality with divine help.

Preparing to Meet the Prince of the Torah

Not all Jewish seekers sought transformative experience in a journey to heaven. Some portions of the hekhalot literature seem to describe attempts to evoke the presence on earth of an angel known as the Prince of the Torah (*sar hatorah*). As his name suggests, he was conceived as the angelic guardian of all knowledge of the Torah. When properly appealed to, he could disclose in a flash the esoteric knowledge that others traveled to heaven to discover.

Some texts suggest, moreover, that his aid was particularly useful for enhancing the mental faculty of greatest use to rabbinic disciples—the memory. The angelic Prince could enhance their ability to memorize the traditions of Oral Torah and help strengthen the memory against forgetfulness. We shall see, however, that we cannot be overly hasty in locating these traditions firmly within the central schools of the rabbinic movement.

Invoking the Sar HaTorah. Attempts to achieve an earthly audience with the Prince of the Torah seem to have drawn on techniques quite similar to those used by the navigators of the heavenly halls. Both heavenly travellers and invokers of the Prince felt it important to know the unpronounceable names of countless heavenly beings and the spells that pacify them. Both seekers of transformative experience, similarly, made extensive use of prayer and ritual to trigger the desired transformation or as a sign of having attained it.

An interesting example of the Prince of the Torah invocation is found in a document we examined a moment ago, the *Ma'asei Merkavah*. In the midst of its descriptions of the heavenly journeys of Rabbis Akiva and Ishmael, the text breaks off to report upon a quite different exercise (*Ma'asei Merkavah* II, 560):[15]

> Rabbi Ishmael said: I was thirteen years old and my mind was occupied every day I was engaged in fasting. When Rabbi Nehuniah ben HaQannah revealed to me the Prince of the Torah, Suriel, the Prince of the Presence was revealed to me. He said to me: The name of the Prince of the Torah is Yofiel, and every one who seeks him...must sit for forty days in fast, eat his bread with salt, and must not eat any kind of defilement; he must perform twenty-four immersions, and not look at any kind of colored garments; his eyes must be cast to the ground. And he must pray with all his strength, direct his heart to his prayer, and seal himself with his own seal, and pronounce twelve utterances.

The text describes a sustained period of bodily self-affliction and purification as a preparation for a visionary experience of the Prince. This is similar, of course, to the practices used by Merkavah travellers. But the goal is different. Now the idea is to bring the Prince, with the aid of the Prince of the Presence, down to the seeker of Torah.

In order to do so, the initiate must make himself as much as physically possible into an inhabitant of the heavenly realm. The first step is to utter a series of prayers that surround his body with diverse divine names. The various unpronounceable names in these prayers (signified below in capital letters) serve as "seals." Their purpose seems to be to attract like to like— by surrounding the human with divine names, they encourage the descent of the angelic figure from the divine world. Thus (*Ma'asei Merkavah* II, 562):[16]

> In purity I pronounce Your name, You Who are One over all creatures. SBR DR'Y 'DYR DRY'S WHPS DRSYN, a seal for his body...., 'P M'WPP' YHW, holy and blessed be His name; a seal above my head; secrets, secret above all secrets: HGGBWB YH YHW, may You be blessed; in Your name: may evil demons be silent in fear of the majesty of Your Dignity; let there be a seal on my limbs.... I have pronounced the name of SQDHWZYH Your servant so that there may be miracles, wonders, many marvels, signs and many great and wondrous portents for me, in the chambers of wisdom and the orders of understanding....

A later portion of the text suggests, in fact, that the "seals" of the seeker's body were physical objects as well as verbal utterances (II, 566):[17]

By the seven seals that Rabbi Ishmael sealed on his heart: 'WRYS SSTYY on my feet; 'BG BGG on my heart; 'RYM TYP' on my right arm; 'WRYS TSY Y'H on my left arm; 'BYT TL BG 'R YYW DYW'L on my neck...

And so on. The text seems to describe amulets that were bound upon various limbs, a kind of esoteric version of the phylacteries that Jewish males would have worn while reciting the *Shma*. Here, they serve to garb the seeker in a "camouflage suit," enabling him to inhabit the same space as an angelic presence.

His body surrounded by such seals, the seeker is then prepared for the actual act of invocation (II, 562):[18]

> He must raise his eyes to heaven so that he does not die; he must stand and recite a name and give praise so that the name be engraved on all his limbs and wisdom and the search for understanding be in his heart; and he should call upon His name, and he should pray in His name. He should make a circle for himself and stand in it, so that the demons will not come and liken him to the angels and kill him.

Before us is a rather clear description of the ritual used to prepare for the way for an audience with the Prince of the Torah. The seeker is psychologically prepared through fasting and prayerful meditation, which alter normal consciousness. His body, deprived through fasting of material sources of strength, is adorned by a new source of power, the utterances and amulets containing sacred words. Finally, the space surrounding the seeker is itself marked off as a pure space into which demons may not enter. Here is the ritual arena within which a human being prepares for his confrontation with a being from the world of heaven.

Our text, unfortunately, is reticent about describing the actual encounter with the Prince of the Torah. Nor do others describe details about the "interview" with the Prince. But we may surmise from other texts of this type the results of the meeting. The final chapter of *Hekhalot Rabbati* (par. 300–303) describes a ritual similar in its basic outlines to the one we have just discussed. After a period of fasting, purification and self-isolation, the seeker of an audience with the Prince is advised to "recite the *midrash* (i.e., invocation) of the Prince of the Torah regularly in his prayer three times every day after the Prayer (i.e., the *Amidah*)" for a period of twelve days.

The expected results are made clear in this text. "At the end of twelve days, he [i.e., the disciple] may proceed to any aspect of Torah he requests: whether to Scripture, to Repeated Tradition (*mishnah*), to dialectic argument *(talmud)*, or gazing at the Merkavah." In other words, whatever body of knowledge a disciple would master—from Written Torah, to the genres of Oral Torah, to the hidden mysteries of the heaven—all can be acquired in a flash and retained perfectly in the memory.[19]

Who Met the Sar Ha Torah? It would seem that in a community of disciples competing with each other for mastery of Torah and the approval of their masters, the Prince of the Torah offers the "competitive edge." This is, however, only one possible way of imagining the communal setting of such writings. It is frequently observed, for example, that aspects of the purification practices described in these texts are not wholly compatible with the legal traditions found in the canonical rabbinical traditions. The continuation of the text we have just examined, moreover, is difficult to imagine in a rabbinic setting: "For we have in hand a teaching, a decree of the forebears and a tradition of the ancients, who wrote it down and left it for the generations, so that the humble could make use of it. Whoever is worthy is answered by them."

This is one of many allusions in the hekhalot literature and elsewhere to secret writings known to only a few. Why would the chief proponents of Oral Torah claim to preserve a written tradition beyond Scripture that itself enables one to master Oral Torah? We cannot solve the puzzle of the social origins of the hekhalot and Prince of the Torah traditions here. Obviously, the transmitters of these texts had at least a superficial knowledge of rabbinic learning and viewed rabbinic sages as models of authoritative teaching. But, just as obviously, they cultivated types of written traditions that would seem to be foreign to the rabbinic schools that, in the wake of the seventh-century Islamic conquests, would gather together what would become the mainstream traditions of rabbinic literature in the Babylonian Talmud and its cognate sources.

Perhaps, as some scholars have suggested, the "humble" referred to in this passage were Jews excluded from formal rabbinic studies, yet who nevertheless aspired to the social prestige increasingly accorded to rabbinic disciples. Among such Jews it became possible to enlist heavenly aid in learning all that the sages knew, and more.[20]

Sharing the Power of Divine Speech

The traditions of heavenly travel and of the Prince of the Torah both imagined personal transformation to involve an absorption of mysterious information. But there were Jews in the last centuries of antiquity with yet other perspectives. In addition to viewing the Torah as a body of information awaiting their understanding, many Jews had for centuries conceived it as a creative cosmic power. The Israelite wisdom tradition, as reflected in

Proverbs 8, had long ago identified Wisdom as a primordial creation of God. In the Hellenistic era, many Jews—from Joshua ben Sira to Philo—viewed the Torah itself as this cosmically creative Wisdom. Rabbinic midrashists, we have noticed earlier, inherited and elaborated this view, describing the Torah as an architectural plan for the structure of the cosmos.

As the first Judaic millennium drew to a close, however, a new development of this tradition was about to unfold. It bore obvious similarities with theories, stemming from Hellenistic Pythagorean philosophy, about the creative role of number as a structuring principle of the cosmos.[21] Whereas non-Jews might speculate about the role of triads (groups of three), septads (groups of seven), and decads (groups of ten) in ordering worlds visible and invisible, the Judaic form of this theorizing took a distinctive and predictable twist. Among some Jews, the basic elements of the Torah—the letters in which the record of divine wisdom was recorded—were themselves ascribed creative powers. The principle of number, in this view, was itself an expression of these more basic cosmic forces.

Thus, again, an aspect of an encompassing non-Judaic conception of reality was absorbed into a distinctively Judaic world-picture. In light of the covenantal images of Judaic worlds, we should not be surprised that Jews absorbed numerological thinking in a way that placed them at the center of the cosmic process. The forces represented in the Hebrew letters could be mastered only by those humans who were, in all creation, closest to the Creator—the Jews. Some Jews sought to use the letters of the Hebrew alphabet as God was said to have done—as a Creator of worlds. They attempted, so to speak, an exercise in self-transformation that would allow them to share directly in the most distinctive of divine prerogatives.

The Origins of Sefer Yetzirah

The most explicit theory of how the power of creation could be harnessed in the Hebrew alphabet was offered in a text called *Sefer Yetzirah*, the Book of Formation. As with the hekhalot literature discussed earlier, it is difficult to identify the originators of Sefer Yetzirah's traditions, those who compiled them into a literary composition, or even the precise time or place in which they did their work.[22] Historians have suggested dates from 300–900 CE as plausible settings for its composition. Is this a product of a specifically rabbinic esoteric tradition? If so, it fails to employ one of the most common elements of rabbinic literary style. That is, Sefer Yetzirah ascribes none of its teachings to any rabbinic sages.[23]

The Sage as a Creator

Rabbinic traditions recorded in the Babylonian Talmud and elsewhere assert that at least some sages had the ability to create living beings. The techniques under their control are not specified, but the following passage alludes to a control of the Hebrew alphabet such as we find in Sefer Yetzirah. The introduction modifies the magical elements of the two stories by linking the sages' powers to their righteousness. The passage is from tractate Sanhedrin of the Babylonian Talmud 65b:

> *Said Rava: If they so desired, the righteous could create the world, for it is said: "Nothing but your sins distinguish you from your God" (Isa 59:2) Rabbah once created a man. He sent him to serve before Rabbi Zeira. The latter tried to speak to him, but he hadn't the ability to reply. Rabbi Zeira said to him: You must have come from my colleagues! Return to your dust!*
>
> *Ray Hanina and Ray Oshayah spent an entire Sabbath Eve immersed in Sefer Yetzirah. They created a three-year-old calf and ate it.*

On the contrary, it follows a literary convention common in non-rabbinic Jewish circles but largely ignored by the editors of rabbinic traditions. It appeals for its authority to an ancient biblical hero. Some versions of the text identify Abraham, the first Jew, as the source of its knowledge. The description of Abraham's achievement is worth reporting (SY 6:4):[24]

When Father Abraham came, he gazed, saw, delved, grasped, engraved, carved out, and succeeded at Creation. The Lord of All was revealed to him, and He placed him at His bosom, and He kissed him upon his head, and He called him His beloved, and made him His son, and He cut a covenant with him and with his offspring forever, "And Abraham believed in the LORD and it was accounted as his righteousness" (Gen 15:6)..., and He cut a covenant with him between the ten toes of his feet, and that is the flesh of the circumcision, and between the ten fingers of his hands, and that is the tongue, and He tied the twenty-two letters upon his tongue, and the Holy One revealed to him a secret.

The mysterious powers of creation given to Abraham are covenantal gifts, a reward for Abraham's devotion to God. By implication they are accessible as well to later members of the covenant community, true disciples of Abraham, his "offspring forever." Men are prepared for this knowledge by the covenant sealed in their bodies by circumcision. Their initiation into the covenantal knowledge is expressed in their mouths through creative mastery of the letter powers of the Torah. With the secrets of Abraham in his possession, any worthy Jew could be transformed from a creature of God into a co-creator, a former of worlds.

While Sefer Yetzirah alludes to the methods for such creative efforts, it is impossible to fully reconstruct what was involved. The book's second chapter prescribes a contemplative exercise in which the mind is trained to focus upon and then manipulate various combinations of letters. Since each letter is both a graphic image and a creative force in its own right, the visual combination of the letters achieves results that are at once both psychological and external to the mind. A "word" created in the mind is translated into a creative event, a "thing" in the world.

Sefer Yetzirah's real interest is theoretical rather than practical. That is, you would be disappointed if you opened its pages looking for just that combination of letters that might create a freezer full of steaks or a suitcase filled with dollars. Rather, its brief chapters offer an exposition of how disparate dimensions of existence—primarily space, time, and the moral order—are woven into a single web of reality through the creative and formative forces sealed in the letters of the Hebrew alphabet. Here is how it works.

The Letter Powers and Cosmic Structures

The twenty-two letters of the Hebrew alphabet are divided into three basic categories. First are the Three Mothers: the letters *aleph* (which has no sound), *mem* (sounded "mmmm"), and *shin* (sounded "shhhhhh"). They are seen as the basic linguistic sounds and, therefore, correspond to basic cosmic forces. "Their foundation is the scale of merit and the scale of guilt, but the tongue decisively tips the balance between them.... *Mem* stands still, *Shin* hisses, *Aleph* is Air that tips the balance between them" (SY 2:1). At the foundation of existence stand moral categories, actualized in reality through speech.

Sefer Yetzirah is interested in how this delicate linguistic balance of sounds is connected to the balance of cosmic forces (SY 3:3–4):

> There are Three Mothers—Aleph, Mem, Shin—in the universe: Air, Water, and Fire. The heavens were created first from Fire, and earth was created from Water, and the ether was created from Air, and tips the balance between them.
>
> There are three Mothers—Aleph, Mem, Shin—in the year: Air, Water, and Fire. Heat was created from Fire, Cold was created from Water, and Moderation was created from Air, and tips the balance between them.

Sefer Yetzirah's Alphabetic System

	NAME	SYMBOL	LATIN SIGN	SOUND
I. Three Mothers	Aleph	א	$'$	(silent)
	Mem	מ	M	Mmmm
	Shin	שׁ	Š	Shhh
II. Seven Doubles	Bet	ב	B	Ba, Bha
	Gimel	ג	G	Ga, Gha
	Dalet	ד	D	Da, Dha
	Kaf	כ	K	Ka, Kha
	Peh	פ	P	Pa, Pha
	Resh	ר	R	Ra, Rha
	Tav	ת	T	Ta, Tha
III. Twelve Simple	Heh	ה	H	Ha
	Vav	ו	V	Va
	Zayin	ז	Z	Za
	Khet	ח	Ḥ	Kha
	Tet	ט	Ṭ	Ta
	Yod	י	Y	Ya
	Lamed	ל	L	La
	Nun	נ	N	Na
	Samekh	ס	S	Sa
	Ayin	ע	c	(silent)
	Tzadi	צ	Ṣ	Tza
	Qof	ק	Q	Qa

There are three Mothers—Aleph, Mem, Shin—in the body. The head was created from Fire, the belly was created from Water, and the torso was created from Air, and tips the balance between them.

Here cosmic space, seasonal patterns, and the bodily sites associated with human thought and passion are viewed as various transformations of three elemental powers—Air, Water, and Fire as represented in the Three Mothers. These divine speech elements are the basic stuff from which all things are compounded. Existing things are modifications of these elements held in an essential balance. Specially directed speech governs all the creative modifications.

This theory is expanded by discussion of the second category of creative letters. These are the seven letters of the Hebrew alphabet that, in Sefer

Yetzirah's view, have a dual pronunciation. For example, the letter Bet can be pronounced as a hard *b* (*beged,* clothing) or as a soft *v* (*kavod,* glory). At the simplest level, each of these letters corresponds to a certain kind of destiny that can be "hard" or "soft." Thus (SY 4:1):

> Seven Double Letters: Bet, Gimel, Dalet, Kaf, Peh, Resh, and Tav. Their foundations are: Life, Peace, Wisdom, Wealth, Fertility, Beauty, and Dominion. And they are activated through two sounds that are transformations of dualities: Bet/Vet, Gimel/Ghimel, Dalet/Dhalet, Kaf/Khaf, Peh/Feh, Resh/Rhesh, Tav/Thav—corresponding to hard and soft, modelled upon power and weakness. And these are their transformations: the transformation of Life is Death, that of Peace is Evil, that of Wisdom is Foolishness, that of Wealth is Poverty, that of Fertility is Devastation, that of Beauty is Ugliness, that of Dominion is Subjugation.

On this scheme, the vagaries of human experience—long life versus early death, comfort or misery—are not normally subject to human planning. Rather, destiny is a product of lawful processes governed by elemental structures of reality. Knowing this, of course, one can control these forces, the Seven Doubles, rather than be manipulated by them.

The Seven Doubles are primarily viewed as extending the structuring powers of the Three Mothers. This structuring role is described in two complementary ways. On the one hand, they structure the extremities of space—the four compass points, the two directions above and below. Linking these six directional points into a unified structure of cosmic space is "the Holy Temple [which] is set in the middle and supports them all" (SY 4:2). Here, the ancient priestly motif of the Heavenly Temple as the center of the cosmos receives yet another expression. As an expression of the letter Tav, the temple itself is conceived as a function of a primordial letter of the Torah.

But Sefer Yetzirah gives most of its attention to another formulation of the structural role of the Seven Doubles. At the moment of Creation, God (SY 4:3–4 + 5:5–6):

> …engraved them, carved them out, combined them, weighed them, established their transformations, and formed through them: Stars in the cosmos, Days in the year, Gates in the body—seven of each…
>
> And these are the seven Stars in the cosmos: Sun, Venus, Mercury, Moon, Saturn, Jupiter, Mars. And these are the seven Days in the year: the seven Days of Creation. And these are the seven Gates in the body: two eyes, two ears, the two nostrils and the mouth…
>
> He first established the reign of Bet and bound it for his Crown, and combined them each with the other, and formed from this Saturn in the cosmos, the Sabbath in the year, and the mouth in the body.

> He next established the reign of Gimel and bound it for his Crown, and combined them with each other, and formed from this Jupiter in the cosmos, Sunday in the year, and the right eye in the body.

The text goes on to describe how the remaining Seven Doubles were fused in various combinations. Each such combination enabled a single letter to govern dual possibilities of experience for all the elements of the cosmos, the year and the head created under its dominion.

The completion of the cosmic system is assigned to the remaining twelve letters of the alphabet. These are the Simple Letters: Heh, Vav, Zayin, Khet, Tet, Yod, Lamed, Nun, Samekh, Ayin, Tzadi, and Quf. They are simple because each represents only a single sound. As powers they correspond to the various states of being characteristic of the senses and the physical and emotional life: "Their foundation is sight, hearing, smell, speech, taste, sexuality, work, process, anger, laughter, thought, sleep" (SY 5:1).

While the Seven Doubles correspond to six spatial dimensions and the dynamic power that holds them in stable relationship, the Twelve Simples expand the borders of space diagonally in twelve directions (SY 5:1). But, as with the Doubles, this spatial function is secondary to their penetration of various aspects of the cosmos, time, and the human body: the twelve constellations of the heavens, the twelve months of the year, and twelve bodily organs (SY 5:2 + 6:4):

> These are the twelve Constellations in the heavens: the Ram (Aries), the Bull (Taurus), the Twins (Gemini), the Crab (Cancer), the Lion (Leo), the Virgin (Virgo), the Scales (Libra), the Scorpion (Scorpio), the Archer (Sagittarius), the Goat (Capricorn), the Waterer (Aquarius), and the Fish (Pisces).
>
> These are the twelve Months in the year: Nisan (March-April), Iyar (April-May), Sivan (May-June), Tammuz (June-July), Av (July-August), Elul (August-September), Tishrei (September-October), Kheshvan (October-November), Kislev (November-December), Tevet (December-January), Shevat (January-February), Adar (February-March).
>
> These are the twelve Organs in the body: two hands, two feet, two kidneys, liver, gall, spleen, large intestines, small intestines, and stomach,...
>
> He first established the reign of Heh and bound it for His crown, and combined them with each other, and formed from this the Ram in the cosmos, Nisan in the year, and the liver in the body.

The Simples complement the creative powers of the Seven Doubles. Where the latter govern the moving planets, the former govern the fixed constellations; where the latter govern the rhythms of the seven weekly circuits of the sun, the former govern the cycle of months, established in Judaic reckoning by the moon. Finally, where the Doubles govern the apertures of the head, the Twelve Simples govern organs distributed throughout the body.

Who is "The Creator"?

As interesting as these speculations might be, we must at this point wonder how these descriptions of what God did to create the world count as transformative knowledge? Why do we not simply regard Sefer Yetzirah as an example of abstruse philosophical speculation? Note the description of Abraham that concludes Sefer Yetzirah. It claims that God transmitted his world-creating knowledge to Abraham as a kind of covenantal gift. Just as this gift enabled Abraham to "grasp, explore, engrave, carve out and succeed at Creation," so, too, are such powers available to Abraham's descendants.

The very first chapter of Sefer Yetzirah, in fact, explains how this is so and what the consequences are. This chapter introduces Sefer Yetzirah with the claim that in addition to the twenty-two letters of the alphabet God used ten creative forces called *sefirot* to form the world. In Sefer Yetzirah, *sefirot* probably should be rendered as "defining powers." Together with the twenty-two letters, the *sefirot* constitute "thirty-two wonderful paths of wisdom" by which God "engraved" the world (SY 1:1).

Much of the chapter offers various metaphors by which the creative powers of the *sefirot*, in particular, may be understood. The chapter settles on no single metaphor as the right one; rather, it presents each model on its own terms. One is particularly important for our discussion (SY 1:3–4):

> Ten Intangible *Sefirot*: the number of ten fingers, five opposite five. And in the center is set the covenant of the Only One, with the circumcision of the tongue and mouth, and with the circumcision of the sexual organ.
>
> Ten Intangible *Sefirot*: ten and not nine, ten and not eleven. Understand with wisdom, and be wise with understanding. Test them and explore them. Know, count, and form. Give it a firm foundation and restore the Creator upon His place. Their attributes are ten and infinite.

The striking thing about the first paragraph is that the *sefirot* are imagined as two sets of hands emanating from a covenantal being. This is precisely the image ascribed earlier to Abraham. This being's covenantal powers are located in his power of speech and his sexual organ—the centers of intellectual and biological expression and creativity.

Apparently, the divine creative powers are here imagined as having penetrated the Jew who would employ them. Emanating from a body sealed in covenantal signs, his hands "form" reality in a way comparable to God's own sefirotic fingers. The second paragraph complements this picture. The wielder of this creative power is now advised to thoroughly explore and test his powers. He will find, if he reaches the utter extremities of his knowledge, that his powers are none other than God's. He "restores the Creator upon his place."

But which Creator and which place? The language is ambiguous. We might think that the man utilizing the tools of creation discovers his indebtedness to God for these powers. On this interpretation, our text conforms rather neatly to general Judaic conceptions of the absolute difference between humans and God. By restoring the Creator to his place, the man underscores his inferiority to God and recognizes himself only as a borrower of divine powers.

It is possible, however, to interpret the phrase rather differently. Why, after all, should God be restored to his place? Can he have left it? Perhaps, then, it is the man using the sefirotic tools who is now restored to his proper place as Creator? If so, Sefer Yetzirah constitutes a radical claim indeed: humans can acquire a power appropriate only to God! If Enoch, a descendant of Noah, became the angel Metatron, might not a Jew born of Abraham anticipate an even more remarkable transformation? The possibility is a tantalizing one, but Sefer Yetzirah does not enable us to give a decisive interpretation.

CONCLUSIONS

Our survey of transformative knowledge in the closing centuries of the first Judaic millennium forces a question upon us: Do these journeys move through distinctly different Judaic worlds or do they describe alternate paths through a single world? Do rabbinic disciples, merkavah travellers, seekers of the Prince, and manipulators of letter powers share one comprehensive view of reality, or must we view these various pursuits as evidence of many different worlds of Judaism? On balance, it seems that we have traveled through the same world, seeing it from a variety of vantage points.

Surely, all the texts we have examined recognized a similar organization of cosmic and terrestrial space—angelic figures attending the divine Throne populated the heaven of Mishnah memorizers just as surely as they confronted those who struggled for a glimpse of the Merkavah. What differs is a judgment about the relevance of the angels to one's transformative goals.

Moreover, as we have seen, the focus on Torah in all these texts reveals broadly shared conceptions of Israel's covenantal responsibility and uniqueness within the larger human community. Torah, in all the texts we have examined, is the absolute value, a unique gift of God to his special community of Israel. Where the texts differ is in their estimate of the inner nature of Torah and the implications of possessing knowledge of that inner nature.

The editors of the rabbinic literature were disciples of masters of Repeated Tradition. Accordingly, they found in the sage's embodiment of Oral Torah a unique transformative project that they sought to emulate. Matters of heavenly transport seemed of lesser moment than the ability, through the master's teaching, to experience the ancient Sinaitic revelation in their own study circles on a routine basis. *Their transformative quest, in other words, was focused upon efforts to reinhabit in the present a specific moment in the distant past—the perfect submission to covenantal laws manifested by Israel at Sinai.* They wanted to reexperience Moses' sanctification in the Cloud again and again as they mastered in ever greater detail the traditions of learning that constituted a living link to God's original self-disclosure to Israel.

Merkavah explorers and those calling upon the Prince of the Torah, by contrast, sought transformative revelation in a different direction. For them, the transformative possibilities of mastering rabbinic tradition were genuine. Yet surer, more immediate, and more profound opportunities made possible by the assimilation of heavenly secrets. *The task was not to bridge the gap between the sacred past and the mundane present, but that equally yawning gulf between the heights of heaven and the depths of earth.* The cloud of historical Sinai was not the goal; it was a far more distant site beyond the seventh heavenly hall. There, in the seventh hall itself or in an appropriate ritual recreation of it on earth, one might master in a flash all the Torah disclosed at Sinai as well as matters never heard by earthbound ears.

The transformative possibilities of Torah are, of course, at the very heart of the tradition represented by Sefer Yetzirah. But the gap that must be bridged is not between past and present or heaven and earth. Rather, *it is the gap between human createdness itself and the cosmic source of creation.* For Sefer Yetzirah, therefore, the transformative value of Torah is not in any specific message. It is in the very syllables that convey the message, for these are the tools of God's work of creation. One needn't travel to heaven, therefore, to learn a mystery from an angel or apprentice oneself for years to a master of Oral Torah. Better to master the discipline employed by the Creator at the moment he formed the world. One might "restore the Creator upon his place" and, thereby, become his earthly associate and colleague. A master of God's own creative power was surely the equal of any created angel and the superior of any sage.

Notes

1. For an overview of such currents in the Hellenistic world, I recommend Luther H. Martin, *Hellenistic Religions* (Oxford: Oxford University, 1987), pp. 58–155. Marvin W. Meyer, ed., *The Ancient Mysteries: A Sourcebook* (San Francisco: Harper & Row, 1987) offers a fine selection of translated original sources. These should be supplemented by the works of Ross Kraemer on women's religious experience in the Greco-Roman world: *Her Share of the Blessings: Women's Religions among Pagans, Jews, and Christians in the Greco-Roman World* (New York and Oxford: Oxford University Press, 1992) and *Women's Religions in the Greco-Roman World: A Sourcebook,* 2nd ed., (Oxford: Oxford University Press, 2004).

2. Other terms commonly used as synonyms are: *bay midrasha* (Aramaic), *yeshivah* ("session:" Hebrew), and *metivta* ("session:" Aramaic).

3. For the situation among Palestinian sages in our period, see Catherine Hezser, *The Social Structure of the Rabbinic Movement in Palestine* (Tübingen: Mohr Siebeck, 1997). This should be supplemented by Stuart S. Miller, *Sages and Commoners in Late Antique Erez Israel: A Philological Inquiry into Local Traditions in the Talmud Yerushalmi* (Tübingen: Mohr-Siebeck, 2004). Jeffrey Rubenstein, *Talmudic Culture* (Baltimore: Johns Hopkins University Press, 2004) offers the richest description of life in Babylonian rabbinic academies toward the very end of our period, as rabbinic disciple circles were undergoing a transformation from informal study communities to organized, institutionalized, and bureaucratized educational institutions. The earlier period in Babylonia is brilliantly illumined by David Goodblatt, *Rabbinic Instruction in Sasanian Babylonia* (Leiden: E.J. Brill, 1975).

4. The circumstances of the editing of the Mishnah and the operative principles that shaped the editors' work remain a controversial matter among scholars. The best survey of the discussion is offered in Guenther Stemberger, *Introduction to the Talmud and Midrash,* 2nd edition, trans. M. Boeckmuehl (Edinburgh: T & T Clark, 1995), pp. 130–140.

5. For an account of the intersection of literary style and pedagogical method in the Mishnah, see Jacob Neusner, *The Mishnah: An Introduction* (Northvale, N.J.: Jason Aronson, Inc., 1989).

6. The ritual of reciting the *Shma* is discussed in the first edition of this volume, pp. 204–206.

7. See Martin S. Jaffee, *Torah in the Mouth: Oral and Written Tradition in Palestinian Judaism, 200 BCE–400 CE* (New York and Oxford: Oxford University Press, 2001), pp. 126–152.

8. The pioneering discussion of the relation of the Merkavah traditions to those of early rabbinic Judaism is that of Gershom Scholem, *Major Trends in Jewish Mysticism* (New York: Schocken Books, 1961), pp. 40–79. A comprehensive recent study of what rabbinic sages and disciples knew and did not know about the journey to the Merkavah is that of David J. Halperin, *The Merkabah in Rabbinic Literature* (New Haven: The American Oriental Society, 1980).

His is the most careful account of the main rabbinic sources on the Merka-vah: Tosefta Hagigah 2:1–7, Palestinian Talmud Hagigah 77a–d, and Babylonian Talmud Hagigah 11b–16a.

9. For an up-to-date account of the various hekhalot texts and their major ideas, see Peter Schaefer, *The Hidden and Manifest God: Some Major Themes in Early Jewish Mysticism*, trans. A. Pomerance (Albany, N.Y.: SUNY Press, 1992).

10. My own translations are based upon the texts presented in Peter Schaefer, ed., *Synopse zur Hekhalot-Literatur* (Tübingen: J.C.B. Mohr [Paul Siebeck], 1981). For convenience of citation, I use both the traditional chapter numbers (e.g., 15:2) and the paragraph numbers of Schaefer's edition (e.g., par. 199).

11. For an explanation of the relationship of "ascent" to "descent," see Elliot R. Wolfson, *Through a Speculum that Shines: Vision and Imagination in Medieval Jewish Imagination* (Princeton, N.J.: Princeton University Press, 1994), pp. 82–85.

12. All translations of *Ma'asei Merkavah* are based upon the translation found in Michael D. Swartz, *Mystical Prayer in Ancient Judaism: An Analysis of Ma'aseh Merkavah* (Tübingen: J.C.B. Mohr [Paul Siebeck], 1992), pp. 224–251.

13. The translation follows that of P. Alexander, in James H. Charlesworth, ed., *The Old Testament Pseudepigrapha*, I (Garden City, N.Y.: Doubleday & Company, 1983), p. 263.

14. Charlesworth, *The Old Testament Pseudepigrapha*, I, p. 264.

15. Translated following Swartz, *Mystical Prayer*, p. 235.

16. Swartz, *Mystical Prayer*, p. 236.

17. Swartz, *Mystical Prayer*, p. 238.

18. Swartz, *Mystical Prayer*, p. 236.

19. My interpretation of this ritual is dependent upon that of Michael D. Swartz, "Like the Ministering Angels: Ritual and Purity in Early Jewish Mysticism and Magic," *AJS Review* 19 (1994), pp. 135–168. Swartz discusses this and other rituals of the Merkavah tradition in great detail in *Scholastic Magic: Ritual and Revelation in Early Jewish Mysticism* (Princeton, N.J.: Princeton University Press, 1995).

20. David M. Halpern, *The Faces of the Chariot: Early Jewish Responses to Ezekiel's Vision* (Tübingen: J.C.B. Mohr [Paul Siebeck], 1988) offers the fullest argument that most of this literature stems from Jews relatively ignorant of rabbinic tradition who felt at a disadvantage in relation to the powerful sages. His view remains a minority one among specialists in this field.

21. A wonderful introduction to the numerological systems of world religions is that of Annemarie Schimmel, *The Mystery of Numbers* (Oxford: Oxford University Press, 1993). Her discussion of Pythagoreanism is on pp. 11–16.

22. The editors of the Mishnah already knew of an esoteric tradition regarding the creation of the world, which they called *Ma'aseh Bereshit* (Mishnah Ha-

gigah 2:2). Similarly, the Talmud recalls a book entitled Sefer Yetzirah that enabled two sages to create a calf for their Shabbat dinner. But the relationship between these ideas and the book known since the tenth century as Sefer Yetzirah is by no means clear.

23. Gershom Scholem, the great pioneer of the study of Jewish mysticism included Sefer Yetzirah in his discussion of the Merkavah tradition, even though he acknowledged its uniqueness. See his *Major Trends in Jewish Mysticism*, pp. 73–78. More recently, scholars have argued that the book in its present form is more likely to have been composed after the advent of Islam and reflects either Gnostic or rationalistic tendencies. See Steven M. Wasserstrom, "Sefer Yesira and Early Islam: A Reappraisal," *Journal of Jewish Thought and Philosophy* 3 (1993), pp. 1–30 and Joseph Dan, "Three Phases of the History of Sefer Yezira," in *Frankfurter Judäistische Beiträge* 21 [1994] 7–29). As with the hekhalot literature, however, it is likely that much of the tradition behind the text originated in the latter centuries of the first Judaic millennium. The Babylonian Talmud, for example, assumes that a "Sefer Yetzirah" contains secrets regarding creation. For an attempt by a great scholar to locate Sefer Yetzirah's basic worldview within the setting of Roman late antiquity, see Moshe Idel, *Golem: Jewish Magical and Mystical Traditions on the Artificial Anthropoid* (Albany, N.Y.: SUNY Press, 1990), pp. 9–26.

24. This translation follows the text published by Ithamar Gruenwald, "A Preliminary Critical Edition of Sefer Yezira," in *Israel Oriental Studies* 1 (Tel Aviv: Tel Aviv University, 1971). A useful translation of all Sefer Yetzirah, which I have also consulted, is that of Blumenthal, *Understanding Jewish Mysticism*, pp. 15–44. My enumeration of chapters and verses follows Gruenwald's text. A new edition of this text is now available: A. Peter Hayman, *Sefer Yesirah. Edition, Translation and Text Critical Commentary* (Tübingen, Mohr-Sieback, 2004).

Afterword

WE HAVE NOW CONCLUDED our survey of the religious worlds of the first Judaic millennium. If you find, at this point, your picture of Judaism from 450 BCE to 640 CE to be a barely intelligible pattern of many dots connected by a few sketchy lines and pocked by large islands of blank space, fear not. This is what the picture ought to look like at this point. The disciplines of historical-literary criticism, archaeology, and the comparative study of religion can help us to construct more or less plausible pictures of various aspects of the Judaic past; but we should not hope in the near future to have a single, coherent, master narrative of early Judaism that ties all the "facts" into a tidy package of "history."

Early Judaism, after all, is an invention of historical scholarship, not an identity embraced by any human soul during the period we have studied. Its distinctions from "Israelite Religion," on one end of the time-line, and "Medieval Judaism," on the other, are conventional imaginative tools that help us to sort information into patterns that answer our own questions. As our questions change and grow more precise, we begin to see some parts of the field of facts more clearly, others shift in their significance, and still other cease to appear as facts at all. They become redescribed as failed hypotheses! My own conception of Early Judaism has shifted considerably since completing the first edition of this book, and these shifts are reflected in the second. All the more so will treatments by different scholars produce reconstructions of Early Judaism that may have very little similarity to the one I have offered here.

This lack of conclusion in knowledge is the sad fate of the academic disciplines; science, under any description, does not bring us to certainty for very long. It brings us, rather, to puzzles, and, more importantly, to reconsider whatever is established as settled and proven. To stay solely within the range of the human sciences—e.g., history, sociology, anthropology, and the comparative study of religion that shamelessly poaches in all these domains—no "last word" can ever be stated. It is unlikely, for example, that the field of religious studies will ever arrive at a definition of religion useful for every single kind of research problem. For this very reason, studies of specific religions, like Judaism, are unlikely ever to entirely agree about the limits of the phenomenon they explore. The model of "religion" that I bring to my study of Judaism will have to shape my conception of what Judaism is as a religion. The problem is not only that there are many Judaisms out there in history; the problem is also that there are many Judaisms in the minds of historians. And not many of the latter are so obviously in error that we may ignore them entirely when trying to make sense of the civilizations produced by Jews.

What, then, can a book like this hope to contribute? Standing at the end of our historical-interpretive exercise in the study of Early Judaism, I believe it my responsibility to offer some preliminary answers to that question. There is very little in this book which is new in the sense of fresh research findings, or unanticipated conceptions. Rather, if I have sought an inno- vation it lies in the decision to tell a story that is structured by the research agendas of the comparative study of religion, rather than the more common principles of political, social, and intellectual history. One consequence of this decision is that, in a certain sense, the narrative flow of the book reflects the present state of theoretical approaches to the study of religion—there are many subtopics that do not combine to create a larger single topic. Thus the story of Early Judaism is told here without a single narrative time-line that begins at the beginning, ends at the end, and demarcates clear steps at all points in between. Instead of telling a single story about Early Judaism, I have attempted to tell multiple stories that intersect at various points. I leave it to my readers—the teachers who may assign this book and the students who are asked to read it—to discern not only the intersections I have stressed, but to seek out their own. For it is the intuiting of hidden connections and the attempt to demonstrate them that is the real learning process in historical-interpretive scholarship. That is where facts, theories, and interpretations rub shoulders and produce in their friction knowledge.

What are the multiple stories told in this book? Only one of them— Chapter One's survey of the social and institutional history of the Jews from the Persian restoration till the Islamic invasions—even makes a pretense of offering a conventional narrative history of the Jews and their main political, social, and religious institutions. It provides some landmarks that we revisit time and time again in our attempt to tell other stories. I have not yet figured out how to tell a story about Early Judaism without referring to such tradi- tional players as dominant non-Jewish empires (Persian, Greek, etc.), dispersed Jewries (in the Land of Israel and beyond), inner-Judaic political and cultural conflicts (the ascendancy of Babylonian Jews in Persian Yehud, the Hasmonean rebellion, the emergence of Christianity), and the emerging political leadership of late Roman and Sasanian Jewries. I have tried to tell this story as competently and economically as possible. But ultimately it is not the story that most interests me as a student of religion.

The stories of real interest to me, of course, are told in the subsequent chapters. Each of these chapters presents a theoretical approach to the study of religion in narrative form. I try to tell a story that draws lines between dots of the same magnitude. Thus, in my view, religions of literate peoples virtually all share a common problem: they harbor prestigious writings that are in perpetual danger of being forgotten, ignored, misappropriated, or corrupted. Their solutions to this common problem are the processes of canon-formation and the development of interpretive canons. Chapter Two, therefore, attempts to distill from the record of Early Judaism dots that represent key moments in the Jews' diverse struggles to achieve canonical clarity and interpretive consensus about the content of Jewish tradition. It is a comparative historian of religion's way of mediating such otherwise deadly material as the names and divisions of the scriptural books, the principles of redaction criticism, or the genres of rabbinic literature. I hope I've managed to enliven these topics by enabling them to serve as illustrations, from the history of Judaism, of universal cultural processes.

As a teacher of comparative religions, I have been drawn to that part of the field concerned with portraying religions as maps of cosmic and transcosmic realities condensed into an historically evolving repertoire of symbols and governing ideas. This basic conception governs Chapter Three's unwieldy attempt to wedge our available knowledge of Early Judaism's "religious world" into some core elements of an imagined "symbolic vocabulary." I am willing to grant that the fit between my proposed model of the Judaic symbolic vocabulary and the actual texts of Early Judaism may not always be exact. But I also claim that an attempt to test the parameters with a narrative about the diverse relations between vertical and horizontal symbolic axes yields more order and sense than confusion and gibberish. Let the reader decide!

In my own view, the most innovative chapter is Chapter Four's discussion of Judaic societies and Judaic worlds. This chapter is my attempt to reconfigure standard historical discussions of a grab-bag of sociological and theological topics such as the distinctions between diaspora and Palestinian Judaism, the nature of Second Temple Jewish sectarianism, and the emergence of Christianity and rabbinic Judaism. The chapter's narrative illustrates the idea that the self-definition of human societies is grounded in attempts to distinguish each one from various "Others" in its immediate environment. Religion is clearly one the most powerful and abiding ways of drawing such distinctions in absolute, cosmological terms. That is why this chapter is so preoccupied with how Jews and non-Jews constructed images of each other, and especially with why diverse Jewish societies persisted in seeing other Jews both as fellows and also as Others. The most fascinating part of this story, in my own opinion, is how this perception of Otherness among Jews yielded a host of religious societies that viewed conversion from one way of life to another as the proper model for their specific forms of self-differentiation.

The final two chapters, Five and Six, are experiments in telling cogent narratives that illumine the ritual performances of Early Judaism. The demand for cogency and limitations of space, required that I confine my theoretical interests to basically a single theory of the nature and function, the idea that ritual spaces and ritual performances combine to re-present and evoke the lines of connection between societies and their conceptions of the cosmos. Chapter Five describes a ritual tradition of public ceremonies that originated in the Second Temple and was reiterated after its loss in such disparate substitutes as public buildings and private homes. It offers as well an opportunity to trace the profound ways in which the priestly ritual sensibilities expressed in the privileging of maleness shaped most later forms of Judaic public ritual. In this way, the description of the temple sacrificial service can serve as the narrative thread that leads, at the end of the chapter, to a discussion of the priestly elements in the rabbinic ritual for circumcision.

Chapter Six focuses on a different type of ritual activity, involving initiation into hidden knowledge. It thus poaches on the territory often marked out by comparative religionists as mysticism. But the chapter itself discusses the mainstream rabbinic movement as well as the various traditions associated with heavenly travel and creative cosmology. By telling a story about transformative knowledge rather than mysticism, the chapter is able to collapse mysticism back into religion, illustrating how the search for extraordinary personal experience is itself connected to the quite public traditions of the temple and synagogue discussed in Chapter Five.

To sum up: If this book contributes anything to the study of Early Judaism, that contribution lies in its ability to suggest new ways of constructing the material of Early Judaism into historical narratives that illustrate what is specifically "religious" in Early Judaism. It is a study of Judaism shaped by the intellectual agenda of the comparative study of religion. As such, I hope it will facilitate the comparative study of Early Judaism in relationship to other religious traditions of Mediterranean antiquity.

Index

Glossary of Foreign Terms

(only first appearance cited)

Aggadah (Heb.: non-legal rabbinic tradition) 82

Amidah (Heb.: rabbinic prayer rite) 206

Am/mei ha-aretz (Heb.: non-rabbinic Jew/s) 159

Angelos (Gr.: heavenly messengers, angelic beings) 15

Archisynogogos (Gr.: Head of the Synagogue) 199

Atzeret (Heb.: Feast of Pentecost) 200

Avodah (Heb.: work, divine service) 181

Avot (Heb.: "Fathers," mishnaic tractate) 79

Bet Midrash (Heb.: rabbinic House of Study) 232

Birkat hamazon (Heb.: rabbinic grace after meals) 217

Bnei yisrael (Heb.: sons/children of Israel) 20

Christos (Gr.: Anointed One, viz., Messiah) 152

Codex (Lat.: bound book) 51

Diaspora (Gr.: dispersion, viz., Jewish communities outside Land of Israel), 10

Doresh hatorah (Heb.: Yakhad's Interpreter of the Torah) 146

Ekklesia (Gr.: community, viz. Church) 155

Eretz yisrael (Heb.: Land of Israel) 20

Eruv (Heb.: mixture, viz. of private and public domains) 161

Etrog (Heb.: citron) 195

Euangelion (Gr.: good news, viz., gospel) 155

Eucharist (Gr.: Christian ritual meal of communion) 153

Eusebeia (Gr.: piety) 10

Galut (Heb.: exile) 25

Hakham/im (Heb.: sage/s 39

Halakhah (Heb.: procedure, rabbinic legal tradition) 82

Hallah (Heb.: loaf, rabbinic dough-offering) 216–17

Hatefillah (Heb.: the prayer, viz. Eighteen Benedictions) 206

Haver/im (Heb.: associate/s, viz., member of early rabbinic community) 159

Havurah (Heb association, viz., early rabbinic community) 159

Hazzan (Heb.: prayer leader) 208

Hekhal/ot (Heb.: hall/s, viz., heavenly realm) 241

Hellenismos (Gr.: Hellenism) 28

Hokhmah (Heb.: wisdom) 95

Iesou (Gr.: Jesus) 152

Ioudaios/oi (Gr.: Judean/s, viz., Jew/s) 9

Ioudaismos (Gr.: Judaism) 9

Kavod (Heb.: divine glory) 22

Kedushah (Heb.: liturgical sanctification) 209

Ketuvim (Heb.: writings, viz., third canon of Hebrew Bible) 58

Kiddush (Heb.: rabbinic blessing over wine at Sabbath or Festival meal) 77

Logos (Gr.: word, principle) 99

Lulav (Heb.: palm frond) 195

Ma'amad/ot (Heb.: bystander, viz., lay
      witness[es] to priestly
      liturgy) 187
Ma'asei Merkavah (Heb.: dynamics of the
      heavenly Throne/Chariot)
      242
Malakh (Heb.: messenger, angel) 99
Masekhet (Heb.: tractate of Mishnah) 234
Mashiakh (Heb.: Anointed One, viz.,
      Messiah) 92
Matnyta (Aram.: repeated oral teaching)
      82
Menorah (Heb.: lamp, viz., in Jerusalem
      Temple) 179
Merkavah (Heb.: chariot, viz., heavenly
      Throne) 240
Mezuzah (Heb.: doorpost amulet) 211–
      14
Midrash (Heb.: biblical interpretation) 84
Mishmar/ot (Heb.: division/s of priests)
      187
Mishnah (Heb.: repeated oral teaching)
      42
Mohel (Heb.: circumcisor) 222
Moreh Tzedek (Heb.: Yakhad's Teacher
      of Righteousness) 146
Mysterion (Gr.: mystery) 230

Nevi'im (Heb.: prophets, viz., second
      canon of Hebrew Bible) 58
Nomos (Gr.:, law, structure) 99

Palaestina (Lat.: Philistia, viz. land of the
      Philistines, Palestine) 36
Parthenos/oi (Gr.: virgin/s, unmarried,
      widowed) 151
Perushim (Heb.: separatists, viz.,
      Pharisees) 75
Pesah (Heb.: Passover) 182
Pharisaioi (Gr.: Pharisees) 75
Philosophos (Gr.: lover of wisdom, viz.,
      philosopher) 96
Presbyteros (Gr.: elder, viz., leader of
      Christian worship, priest)
      199
Proseuche (Gr.: place of prayer) 189

Resh galuta (Aram.: head of the exile,
      Exilarch) 43
Rosh Hashanah (Heb.: New Year
      Festival) 200

Sar hatorah (Heb.: Prince of the Torah)
      247
Sefirah/ot (Heb.: sphere/s, viz., of divine
      creativity) 257
Se'udat mitzvah (Heb.: a celebratory
      meal, e.g., at a circum-
      cision) 216
Shabbat (Heb.: Sabbath) 127
Shavei Yisrael (Heb.: converts of Israel,
      viz., the Yakhad) 144
Shavuot (Heb.: Festival of Pentecost) 182
Shekhinah (Heb.: presence of God) 179
Shma (Heb.: hear, viz., ritual recitation of
      scriptural verses) 212
Shmoneh Esreh (Heb.: eighteen, viz. daily
      18 Benedictions) 206
*Shofar (Heb.: instrument made from ram's
      horn)* 195
Shomron (Heb.: territory in central area of
      Land of Israel) 136
Sukkot (Heb.: Festival of Tabernacles)
      182

Talmid/ei hakhamim (Heb.: disciple/s of
      rabbinic sages) 60
Tamid (Heb.: perpetual, viz., daily
      Temple sacrifice) 180
Tanakh (Heb.: acronym for canon of
      Hebrew Bible) 50
Theosebeis (Gr.: God Fearers) 131–32
Tzadukim (Heb.: Zadokites) 139

Yakhad (Heb.: community, viz., at
      Qumran) 139
Yehud (Aram.: Persian province in
      former Yehudah) 19
Yehudah (Heb.: territory in southern
      Land of Israel) 9
Yehudi/m (Heb.: Judean/s, viz., Jew/s) 9
Yeshivah/ot (Heb.: session/s, e.g. of
      rabbinic study) 44
Yeshivah shel ma'alah (Heb.: Heavenly
      Torah Academy) 115

Yeshua (Heb.: Jesus) 152

Yisrael (Heb.: territory in northern Land of Israel) 22

Yom Hakippurim (Heb.: Day of Absolution) 179

Zaqen (Heb.: elder, viz., teacher of wisdom, sage) 96